THE PROMISED LAND

Daniel Harris is a writer and a journalist, in shorter form and about sport, mainly for the *Guardian*. At the 2012 British Sports Book Awards, he was shortlisted for best new writer for his book *On The Road: A Journey Through a Season*, which follows United away from home during 2009–10.

He can be found on Twitter @DanielHarris.

First published in Great Britain in 2013 by Arena Sport,
an imprint of Birlinn Ltd.
Birlinn Ltd
West Newington House
10 Newington Road
Edinburgh
EH9 1QS
www.arenasportbooks.co.uk

ISBN: 978-1-90971-505-9
eBook ISBN: 978-0-85790-640-3

British Library Cataloguing-in-Publication Data
A catalogue record for this book is available on request from the
British Library.

Typeset by FMG using Atomik ePublisher from Easypress
Printed and bound by Clays Ltd, St Ives plc

CONTENTS

Acknowledgements

Thanks to Belinda for everything, thanks to Mum and Dad, thanks to Rob for plenty, thanks to Jeremy who I should have thanked last time, thanks to Paul, thanks to Stan, thanks to Pete and Neville at Arena Sport; and thanks for reading.

There's something very weird about peeling yourself off a pile-on and realising that, at 20 years old and from that second onwards, things can only get worse. But if it's a pile-on beneath the Nou Camp seats, at 22.33:31 on 26 May 1999, then it's an incontrovertible fact; there resides the intersection of ecstasy and despair. Nothing and no one can ever trump that moment.

And yet, to call the moment a moment is to bypass the absurdities that preceded it – nine whole months' worth of unprecedented, inexplicable, compelling Manchester United moments..

Here's the greatest season in the history of football.

AUGUST

A happy, smart Arsène Wenger; imagine! But that was the sight in the Wembley tunnel as United and Arsenal lined up before the 1998 Charity Shield, Wenger positively gushing equilibrium and resplendent in blazer with embroidered cannon, rather than the cartoon car badge that superseded it. And the players looked bang-on too, both jerseys genuine classics: United's the brightest possible red, magnifying the round, hard head of an incredibly taut Roy Keane, bristling with unresolved violence; Arsenal in smart yellow and blue, matching Tony Adams highlights. And all of them, with the exception of Martin Keown, were in black boots, and generally without haircuts and tattoos.

With the enmity between the managers at its delightful, sustained peak, there was not the merest hint of a handshake, Alex Ferguson forcing as relaxed a look as possible for a man exothermic with residual rage. Their rivalry and enmity had been building since Wenger's arrival, just after the start of the 1996–97 season, but at that point, though top of the league, Arsenal weren't considered a threat. Nor were they the following year, until suddenly snatching the title with a murderously poetic, post-January charge that surprised everyone, Fergie in particular, to cement the rivalry that dominated a generation.

The day was properly hot, kick-off brought forward to give United more time to prepare for their Champions League qualifier against LKS Lodz in midweek. As the players emerged, in the commentary box Martin Tyler and Trevor Francis noted their domestic backgrounds; only eight foreigners amongst the 22 starters, 11 of them English. Shortly afterwards began the compulsory discussion of David Beckham and his World Cup slip, Keane laughing as he "introduced" him to the various "dignitaries", while Richard Keys felt authorised to "wish him well on behalf of English football".

With Gary Pallister back at Middlesbrough, Jaap Stam made his debut alongside Ronny Johnsen, and also gone, at very long last, were Karel Poborsky and Brian McClair. In midfield, Nicky Butt partnered Keane, with Paul Scholes pushed further forward to support lone striker Andy Cole – who had played for Arsenal in the 1991 fixture. This was an area in which United were hoping to strengthen, but earlier in the week, Patrick Kluivert – wanted because it was felt that the squad had become too lightweight – had not only rejected a move to the club, but volunteered to sign for Arsenal, who had no interest. He would eventually leave Milan for Barcelona.

Amongst those on the bench was Teddy Sheringham, punished for a first season of missed penalties and misplaced conceit. He'd also managed to fall out with the well-liked Cole, accusing him of playing for personal glory rather than the team, hypocrisy significantly more spectacular than anything he'd accomplished on the pitch. None of this was much appreciated.

"Knowing United are to play Tottenham in the first game of the season, he goes and gives interviews to anyone who'll listen," had thundered *Red Issue* the previous spring, "slagging off his former club ensuring that a majority rather than a minority will be awaiting his imminent return. A severe shortage of class that one might expect of someone who has spent such a long time in North London but not of Manchester United players. Hopelessly unaware of the enigma that he was effectively replacing, a person who was never one for flaunting his good fortune and always conducted himself with utmost style, our Teddy proceeded to ponce about Deansgate as though he owned the place impressing no one, especially not those who actually recognised him."

But Gary Neville saw things differently. Though few among the support had ever coveted him, he recalled Sheringham as "obviously always interested in moving here", asking about United at England gatherings, and also that "Teddy was one of the toughest players I'd ever played against." Accordingly, he blamed injuries and surrounding incompetence for the state of his first season, but by any standard, it was a risible failure.

While United made do, Arsenal fielded their settled first XI, though a substitutes' bench comprising Bould, Vivas, Wreh, Grimandi and Boa Morte appeared an oversight even then. But the nature and manner of their double win and Wenger's role in it, had already worked the shamanic magic that would last a generation, the *Arseweb* site noting in its season preview that "a sizeable proportion of fans retain an almost blind faith in the Frenchman's ability to bring on the younger players".

Almost straight from the kick-off, a bristling Nicolas Anelka worried Stam down the inside-right channel, a threat he just about handled, but with the minimum of fun. Then, before two minutes had elapsed, Keane announced his return from injury by charging in late on Marc Overmars, downed again seconds later by Gary Neville, who was subsequently booked. Keane registered his protest with characteristic chopping arm, the signifier of middling fury, and to illustrate it further, allocated a whack to Patrick Vieira shortly afterwards.

But otherwise United started the livelier, the sumptuously curled Ryan Giggs the main prompt and the darting interplay between Scholes and Cole looking promising. Surprisingly, it took a full ten minutes for the Arsenal end to get after Sheringham with a taunt of "Oh Teddy, Teddy, went to Man United and he won fuck-all."

While the baiting continued, Anelka eased away in pursuit of another long ball, without contravening the purity of the Wenger philosophy – in those days about beauty not intricacy. Johnsen, like Stam, was able to keep up, and when he won possession United broke, Emmanuel Petit motoring into a brilliant, saving challenge on Butt just inside the left corner of the box after good work from Giggs.

Oddly, given the relationship between the teams and early aggression, it took until the 22nd minute for the next bad tackle to arrive, Keown's red boots sending Scholes flying. Not before he'd turned a pass around the corner for Cole, but a trigger-happy Graham Poll had already stopped play.

Next, Overmars isolated Stam on the left-wing, who stood up as long as possible before diving in when it appeared his man had vanished, winning the ball cleanly with a perfectly-timed challenge. And though it took him a while to settle at Old Trafford, the man Dick Advocaat declared to be "the defender of the future" showed plenty by way of explanation, even in the early weeks; obviously shy of his best, he still clearly knew his business.

The longer the half wore on, the longer it became evident that United were playing more on the fly than off the cuff, while Arsenal, a settled, confident side, knew exactly what they were doing, far more threatening despite enjoying less possession. Or in other words, they were a team, not just a collection of like-minded individuals.

But United still hinted menace. After Denis Irwin was booked for a late slide on Dennis Bergkamp, Giggs appeared on the right, weaving away to find Scholes who was wrongly given offside. But the pass, one that eliminated Keown and Lee Dixon, was another sign of the late-developer's brain that became his principal asset in middle age. The potential to turn a weakness into a strength, a rarity in any context, had first suggested itself against Middlesbrough in October 1995 when he moved into midfield after Keane was sent off, and then again against Porto in March 1997, but was still at least half a decade from maturity.

During the teams' previous meeting, Gary Neville had managed to hide at centre-back whilst Overmars deconstructed John Curtis, but now, back on the right, he escaped for only 27 minutes. Eventually, Overmars sought him out, enticing him in before skipping and turning away, and though Keane was on hand to limit the embarrassment, that would not be the end of it. "I can't wait for this to fucking end," he told Beckham sometime between roastings.

Quiet hitherto, Bergkamp then announced himself, creating a yard of space and firing a low shot that forced Schmeichel into the game's first serious save, low to his right, before, a minute later, Arsenal went ahead. Pausing from filling and emptying his cheeks, Nigel Winterburn hit a crossfield pass for Ray Parlour, who turned inside and found Vieira. Given time and space, he lifted a ball over the top and deep into the United box on its right-hand side, to where Bergkamp and Anelka were gathered, the former back-heeling into the stride of the latter from close to the by-line, Stam caught behind him and rendered useless. But Johnsen, left standing initially, recovered well before slipping into a clearance that clipped the persevering Anelka – how curious those words now seem – and the ball rolled towards Overmars on the other side of the box. Retreating a little, he sprung into a thumping shot that scorched high past Schmeichel to his left.

At the break, Bergkamp was replaced by Christopher Wreh, the previous season's fiddler of crucial goals. News of the change was communicated by way of manual board, with no adverse consequences.

The second half started fairly slowly, Giggs sent infield before Solskjær came on for Butt and he returned to the left. Then, Overmars, his mere presence reducing Gary Neville to a quivering, convulsing melt, picked up possession well inside his own half and zoomed 40 yards along the left touchline, Neville backing off yet still unable to keep up, slipping as he dipped inside onto his right foot. Sliding the ball square in the same step, the benefit of a feetballer as opposed to just a footballer, Overmars also lost Stam, over to assist, and found Anelka who, on the turn, immediately transferred to Wreh, suddenly through on goal. Though Schmeichel got down to his first effort, he had no chance with the second. 2–0, and the difference was clear: Arsenal knew what they were doing and had improved simply by virtue of knowing that they knew it; even when being out passed, they could rely on their defence to keep the opposition out and their attackers to produce the relevant moments that got the job done.

United still struggled along, the closest they came to a goal being Johnsen's near-post header from Beckham's corner that almost went in off Keown. Otherwise, Arsenal enjoyed their superiority, knocking the ball around as their support crowed "same old Arsenal, taking the piss", 112 years of history subsumed in six months.

Then with 19 minutes still to play, worse got worser. Vieira found Parlour in the centre-circle, who, with the outside of that magic wand of a right foot, put Anelka in a race with Stam. Doing well to keep up, Stam couldn't get close enough to block the shot, and with Schmeichel wandering too far off his line and too far from his near post, the ball was soon over one and inside the other.

"The force is still with Arsenal," declared Martin Tyler at full-time, and he was right. Fergie, meanwhile, was just making stuff up. "It's almost a new team and I have to shape it," he explained. But it was not remotely new, and it wasn't much of a team either.

Nor were things right in the dressing room, with Keane and Schmeichel in conflict. Antipathy between the two, already decent, progressed when Cantona left, Keane inheriting the captaincy and winning an eventuating scuffle. Then, when he injured his knee, Schmeichel took over and was disinclined to relinquish the role on his return, retaining it for the pre-season tour. "I wasn't too pleased," Keane later wrote, and even less so when nothing changed prior to the Charity Shield. "No welcome back, Roy, here's the armband. No fucking chance with Peter. In the end the gaffer had to order him to stand down. He sulked. Arsenal got two soft goals... Afterwards the gaffer called a meeting and told Peter to grow up."

A thoughtful birthday present for Keane, perhaps, but otherwise, things did not look at all good.

*

That same Monday, MUTV began transmitting, in its early years not quite the defiling marriage of anodyne and doctrinaire that we see today. Which isn't to say that there wasn't suspicion – of course there was, United were involved, and particularly so because the club had recently admitted participating in talks about the formation of a European Super League.

In the meantime, they made do with the Champions League, and the following Wednesday, United had a qualifier with LKS Lodz. "I had thought about turning down the invitation," Fergie later wrote, "because I had always felt that the competition should be for what it said – champions! But it was only a fleeting thought which lasted a millisecond. Europe figures so high in the priorities of both the club and the fans that we simply had to take part, however ironic from my point of view."

Qualifier or not, the funny little pyjama polo shirt kit got an outing, as did yet another new pitch. The first of its kind in the northern hemisphere, its supposedly springier grass replaced the previous season's mess that was, of course, responsible for the capitulation necessitating the game in the first place.

Lodz had interest in nothing beyond hiding-aversion; though the match to which United had sent a scout was postponed, there was little about them worth knowing. The club had been recently been taken over by a local millionaire, who, as a young man, was refused a place on the board of local rivals Widzew – whom he'd supported – on account of insufficient richness. So, after making his money, he purchased their rivals instead, implementing a policy of recruiting players from Brazil and Nigeria.

As against Arsenal, Scholes and Cole started up front, and Giggs was United's brightest attacker. He missed the first opportunity of the game with a low shot directed too close to the keeper after excellent link-up play between Cole and Butt, but after a quarter of an hour, put United ahead with a lovely goal. Phil Neville hit a long diagonal ball towards target man Scholes, who headed down for Giggs to skip inside and skim around the nearest defender, sending him sprawling, before a skilful piece of right foot avoidance saw him finish with the little toe of his left.

Very little happened during the remainder of the first half, the Lodz back four aimlessly rolling the ball to and fro like Liverpool in their glory days. Stam had an effort cleared off the line following a post-corner ricochet, there was the now-curious sight of a midfielder breaking into the opposition box, and Beckham unveiled a new free-kick, sending an effort around the outside of the wall to clip the outside of the near post.

Soon after half-time, Cole missed a pair of handy chances, first rolling his man beautifully only to see his shot saved by the keeper's feet, then failing to connect with Giggs' whipped low cross. Though the manner of his movement gave him the appearance of looking sharp, so too did his work subsequent to it, though the balance of the team, especially against inferior opposition, wasn't quite right.

Then, with ten minutes remaining, United constructed another excellent goal. Irwin, on the left touchline, snapped a ball infield for Giggs, who, facing him and 30 yards from goal, back-flicked a turn that lost his man, and with a second touch created the angle for a stabbed return pass. Irwin, now almost at the byline, allowed it to run slightly past his left foot in order to send over a cross that Cole nodded home, arching his back hard to impart requisite power. There hadn't been much else, but here was a second moment of crafted quality.

*

Everyone loves a good redemption tale, but few ever unfolded with as much swagger as that one about David Beckham, sent-off sillily in the summer. Of course, it was *entirely* his fault that England lost to Argentina, his split-second reaction far more blameworthy than, for example:

• Glenn Hoddle's egotism in omitting him from the first two group games, partially responsible for a second-round tie with Argentina;

• Glenn Hoddle's cowardice in omitting Michael Owen from the first two group games, partially responsible for a second-round tie with Argentina;

• Glenn Hoddle not bringing Eileen Drewery to France sooner, an error he acknowledged as his gravest in the pages of his World Cup diary;

• Alan Shearer's idiocy in elbowing the Argentina goalkeeper Carlos Roa, forcing the referee to disallow Sol Campbell's golden goal; and

• Captain Tony Adams' cowardice in shirking penalty duty.

For example.

But instead, and in the absence of a dead benefit thief, the country focused on Beckham, this time with phony fury rather than phony sorrow. "Still bitter? Take your fury out on our Beckham dartboard" implored the *Mirror*, while another headline read "Hate Mob Targets Beckham Family", and a hoarding outside Mansfield Road Baptist Church proclaimed that "God Forgives Even David Beckham".

Roy Keane took a more measured view. "He was playing a game of football," he wrote in his autobiography. "He flicked a petulant foot at Diego Simeone, who was intent on kicking the shit out of him. The press got on his case, priming the pump that spews out the vile chants Becks had to listen to up and down the country all season. Stuff about his wife and son that is sick. Who's letting the country down?"

If nothing else, though, the country concentrating its deliciously impotent rage on him – and by extension United, the culmination of several years of deliciously impotent animosity – was a highlight of one of the "long summers, those" described by Ryan Giggs as following all trophyless seasons.

"It winds you up," he would reflect more than a decade later. "You go away on holiday, you're lying on the beach trying to enjoy yourself with the kids, and you do, but then you have a quiet moment, it comes back to you what happened and… I'll say it: You're pissed off. You're on holiday and you're just pissed off."

At the time, it was the avoidance of this feeling that motivated him, what he termed "fear of failure". In his dotage, he's either found or learnt a more positive outlook, one more in tune with that of a supporter – "just craving that feeling of winning the title" – but back then, the horror of defeat easily outranked the pleasure of success.

*

On the morning of United's first league game at home to Leicester, Aston Villa conceded that Dwight Yorke was likely to leave the club, despite their rejection of a faxed offer from United earlier in the week which declared itelf the last. This was not cheering; everyone knew he wasn't of the required class, same as that posing spoofer Sheringham, and just another example of managerial idiocy.

Leicester had won at Old Trafford the previous season, United's distress componded by the almost unbearable ignominy of being labelled "arrogant" by Tony Cottee. Often, teams who've played competitively before the league season starts find themselves at a competitive advantage, but not here; Leicester were good and United were miserable, deservedly falling behind after seven minutes when Muzzy Izzet bustled past Gary Neville to pull Johnsen out of the middle and finding Emile Heskey, who scored.

The only real highlight was the support offered Beckham at every wasted corner, which would later manifest in one of the better but less heralded songs of the period: "David Beckham went to France as a national hero, got sent off he came home, reputation zero. England fans, they're all twats, they get so excited, stick your England up your arse coz we are Man United."

"They put us through the mill and we got very nervous," said Fergie afterwards, accusing his players of "lethargy" and "bad defending", thoughts communicated in less measured fashion during the interview. "I met Alex at pre-season and everything was relaxed," recalled Stam, "but when the season started if you did something wrong he came in at half-time and was very angry. He was expressing himself in his way and I was a bit surprised because he was a different man."

Bother with a thigh muscle meant that Stam remained in the dressing room, replaced by Berg, as United continued to huff and puff. But the stodge was no particular surprise; in 17 league games since the turn of the year, they'd managed only 24 goals, five of those once the title had departed. Then, on 76 minutes, they fell further behind, and to Cottee, too, also scorer of the winning goal for West Ham in a game more than 12 years earlier which crystallised an entire decade: United play well, Robson scores, Robson dislocates shoulder, United lose.

In response, Sheringham was sent on for Gary Neville, with Beckham moving to wing-back. Almost immediately, the two of them combined for a goal, Sheringham coiling under and into Beckham's long-range drive towards the rear post and heading an undeserved livener in at the far with his first touch. Then, in the third minute of injury time, Izzet fouled Scholes ten yards outside the box, just left of centre. Everyone knew what was coming, everyone assumed that it wasn't coming, and then it came, Beckham arcing an improbable parabola into the closer bottom corner with impeccable geometry. Disorder did thus ensue, the unrelenting pace of the season set. Life: what happens to you while United are busy making other plans.

Of course, Fergie was still unhappy, not with his role in the impoverished performance, but that of the referee, complaining that United were due eight and a half minutes' injury time – "my watch is never wrong," he insisted. This carping was not universally enjoyed. "It's become a joke, an embarrassment," wrote Mr Spleen in *Red Issue*. "Mad old Fergie muttering on the touchline, staring manically at his watch."

The long summers, those, looked like extending well into autumn, winter, spring and summer.

*

The following Tuesday, Old Trafford staged the obscenely overdue testimonial for the Munich families, a game which also saw the return of Eric Cantona. Sporting a dignified paunch, he scored a typically outlandish goal, though the circus behaviour of Pascal Olmeta, the goalkeeper he brought with him, attracted almost as much attention.

Then, on the Thursday of that week and after very much tedium, Dwight Yorke arrived at Old Trafford for a fee of £12.6million, forced to go crying to Doug Ellis to secure the move. Very few people were impressed – Brian Kidd particularly not, likewise Arsène Wenger. "He is a very good player," he said, "but we would not pay that kind of price for anybody." Two years later, he spent even more on Sylvain Wiltord, in a largely unchanged market.

United had first tried for Yorke in 1995 only for him to sign a new contract with Villa. But by the autumn of 1997, he was resolved to leave, and had been promised by Brian Little that he could do so in the summer, only for Little to resign in February. The following month, he was alerted to United's interest, but John Gregory did not consider himself bound by his predecessor's agreement, and publicly accused Yorke of not trying in their season's opening game. In the end, he had little choice but to go along with the sale.

"Dwight openly stated to me a couple of weeks ago that he wanted to play for Manchester United and that he didn't want to play for Aston Villa," Gregory told the press. "If I'd have had a gun at the time I think I'd have shot him."

Were he to say that nowadays, he'd no doubt find himself accused of encouraging gun crime, and even then, it didn't go down well with Fergie, who lectured his attitude and patronised his youth. To his credit, Gregory paid not the slightest.

Yorke then turned up to the introductory press conference in blazer, tight white t-shirt and belt with silver buckle; he was going to have to go some way to prove himself. And prove himself he did, soon replacing the outfit with the suave cool of suit teamed with baseball hat, earning himself the title of Britain's Best Dressed Man in the process.

"There was something about Yorke that always worried me when we played him," Ferguson explained later in the season, "and there's not many I can say that about in English football. I used to say to Pallister, watch him, watch he doesn't get in behind you, watch he doesn't turn you. I tried for him two years ago and he signed a new contract, which was a big disappointment. So I wasn't going to lose him this time."

But there remained scepticism that his contribution to the combinations would amount to little more than a nickname to fit snugly alongside Coley, Teddy and Olly.

The following morning was Yorke's first training session, and of course he came in grinning. And, of course, Keane stuck one on him immediately. "As soon as I got out on the training pitch, he put in one of those tackles of his to test me," he recalled. "I think it was his way of saying, 'Let's see if you really want that money, and to play for United.'"

And that wasn't the end of it. Shortly afterwards, arrived a typical short pass drilled into his shins, Keane scoffing, "Welcome to United. Cantona used to kill them," when it bounced off. But the grinning continued unabated, and in time the two would become friends, their polarised personalities characterising the team.

Like Stam, Yorke was given no guarantee of a starting slot, told he was just one of four strikers, but that he should "express himself", do what he'd done for Villa, and everything else would follow. The other three, though, felt differently: Sheringham had already lost his place, and both Cole and Ole Gunnar Solskjær expected Yorke to be first pick, so were focused on proving themselves his best partner.

But in the days leading up to his debut at West Ham, the fuss was instead about Beckham, the home crowd easily the most gutted, disgusted and disgraced by his role in England's World Cup exit. Then, on the morning of the game, the *Daily Mail* broke the story that Ole Gunnar Solskjær would not only be joining Spurs, but "after dramatic chairman-to-chairman negotiations", no less. Ennio Morricone was set to score the film adaptation.

The principal concern of all right-minded individuals was, of course, for the children, following the *Mail*'s shocking but lyrical revelations at the effrontery of a football club not informing them of its plans.

"Ole Gunnar Solskjær yesterday signed for Tottenham from Manchester United in a £5.5million deal which once again exposed the ruthless side of soccer," it sniffed. "Despite the bare-faced denials perpetrated by both Spurs and United, as the camouflage was pulled across the transfer in what appeared to be a deliberate attempt to mislead," it hyperventilated, "the deal had, in fact, been set up since Thursday. Is it any wonder, when clubs of the stature of Tottenham and United are so economical with the truth," it snivelled, "that the image of the game is smeared in duplicity?"

Smearing himself in something else was a spokesman for the Tottenham Action Group. "We cannot get too excited about signing a player who has become little more than a reserve fixture at Old Trafford," he knowingly insighted.

Before the United coach left the hotel to drive to Upton Park, the police advised Beckham not to sit next to the window, and when the team arrived, the car park was full of West Ham families, foaming their indignation. But inside the ground the atmosphere was muted, and not even the menace of Michael Jackson's favourite song could rouse any genuine hostility, the United end chanting "Argentina, Argentina!" in provocation as much as retaliation.

As far as United's team went, Berg replaced the injured Stam and Butt came in for Scholes with Cole given the first opportunity to partner Yorke, who was aiming to score past his old friend, Shaka

Hislop. He would be protected by, amongst others, was Rio Ferdinand, but West Ham were without their new signing, Ian Wright, suffering from a dead leg.

The home team enjoyed the better of the opening stages, but then, after three minutes, the game's principal moment of controversy. Giggs swayed down the wing and crossed to the back post, where Cole was waiting to tap home – but somehow Neil Ruddock elevated both self and arm to paw the ball away, somehow escaping the concession of a penalty. He did, though, manage to refrain from deliberately inflicting serious injury.

West Ham's best opportunity of the half fell to Hartson, denied a goal from two yards by Keane's horizontal block, the attentions of Berg enough to deny him in the aftermath. Berg then prevented a certain goal after Schmeichel parried Frank Lampard's drive from distance, an extended foot forcing Eyal Berkovic to direct his shot over the bar, before Cole drew a smart save from Hislop.

United improved in the second half but created little, a Cole–Yorke link-up resulting in a blocked shot and a Butt effort whooshing over the top. For the second game in a row, Gary Neville found no life in his legs, forced to concede that he was wrong after ridiculing a warning that he was given before the World Cup. So he was replaced by his brother and sent on holiday to Malta for two weeks after a couple of days' treatment. Otherwise, Schmeichel did well to deny Sinclair following the kind of classy through-pass eventually to be coached out of Ferdinand, and Hartson headed narrowly over but that was about it.

In the circumstances, a draw was not a terrible result, with no team but that was about it in the league winning both opening games. And Yorke, though he'd not played well, now knew something of the challenges he would face. "I was up against players I'd been playing against for years without a problem," he observed. "Suddenly I found these same guys trying extra hard. The difference astounded me."

*

United then flew off to Poland, for the return against Lodz. With Yorke ineligible, Sheringham was allowed to start up front, and Phil Neville also came in. On a pitch resembling an old couch, in a ground that was half closed and almost completely uncovered, nothing much happened apart from a lot of rain, a banner proclaiming Lodz's Crazy Cannibals turning out to be an idle boast.

Niznik shot narrowly wide after 20 seconds while United's best chance came just before half-time with Johnsen and Beckham ganging up on Zuberek to set Giggs away. Speeding along paying not the remotest heed to a ball skipping unevenly under his feet, he waited for Beckham to draw alongside before playing him in. But, forced a little wider than was optimal, Wyparlo pushed the eventuating shot over the bar.

Shortly after the hour, Kos saw his free-kick deflected just past the post, and then Butt blootered narrowly over the crossbar, but otherwise, that was about it for a sordid mess of a match. The introduction of Solskjær, who had rejected the move to Spurs on managerial advice, livened things slightly, and he came close in the closing stages, but his effort was saved. United were through, Fergie blaming the lacklustre performances until now on the lack of a sensible pre-season in the aftermath of the World Cup.

There was a two-week break before the next fix of United, during which Chelsea beat Real Madrid to win the Super Cup and England lost to Sweden in a European Championship qualifier. Elsewhere, poor Kenny Dalglish was sacked by Newcastle after a run of 11 wins in 40 games, and then, on the Friday, came the draw for the group stages of the European Cup. The competition wasn't quite the protection racket that it would become, and accordingly, United could not be allocated a group more favourable than, say, the team who beat them to the title. But Fergie was typically steadfast, warning that "Manchester United not being a seed will make it more difficult for two other teams."

In the event, they were billeted in the obligatory Group of Death with Bayern Munich, Brondby, and Barcelona – "The team which have most luck," predicted Bayern's manager, Ottmar Hitzfeld, "they will be first in the group."

*

At United for barely ten days, Dwight Yorke found himself in hot steam when the *Sun* ran a story detailing an evening he'd spent with four girls, an unnamed man, and Mark Bosnich, the three men dressed up in dresses and Bosnich lashed with belts. Yorke, it transpired, had secretly rigged up a video camera before throwing away the recording, which was then "found by a *Sun* reader, who took it home believing it to be a blank tape."

No one ever got to know what Fergie made of it all, but John Gregory was amused. "We have been having some contract talks as you know," he said of Bosnich, "and I told him this morning that I'd like to tie him up for five years." Then, when signing Paul Merson – who turned up in beige double-breasted blazer done up to the sternum – he was asked about his various addictions. "He said that he's been having one or two problems… but we got one or two players that like dressing up in women's clothing, and having their backsides spanked now and again… I think he'll fit in quite well."

Yorke would later serve as Bosnich's best man, organising his stag for the night before the wedding and presiding over the groom's arrest. He was married only after posting bail and two days after signing for United.

SEPTEMBER

September did not start well. First, on the second of the month came the death from cancer of Jackie Blanchflower. Converted by Matt Busby from forward into centre-half, he was seriously enough injured at Munich to be read the last rites, and forced to retire from football when he recovered, August's testimonial coming far too late to help him.

Like most players at the time, Blanchflower lived in a club-owned house. "It was made pretty clear we had to leave," his wife Jean recalled. "United were very cold, very harsh, after the crash." And within a year he was signing on, unwilling to load pies onto lorries for Louis Edwards and spending the next period of his life working in a variety of jobs. He then studied finance to become an accountant before enjoying success as an after-dinner speaker.

Next, the following week, the potentially devastating news that BSkyB had agreed a deal to buy United. Only a few months earlier, the words 'football club' had been expunged from the club crest, a symbolic moment in its bastardisation into a brand, and here was one of many practical manifestations of the same. "They wanna win the league, we wanna win the league, they wanna win the Cup, we wanna win the Cup, they wanna have the most talented players and the best manager, and so do we. They wanna compete at the highest level, and so do we," went Mark Booth's revolting press conference rhetoric.

And of course, Martin Edwards, supported the wheeze – but definitely not because he stood to make lots of money from the sale, as he had when imperilling the club with the original flotation, and as he'd hoped to but hadn't when imperilling the club by trying to sell it, first to Robert Maxwell and then to Michael Knighton.

As fan groups mobilised to prevent yet another desecration of their heritage, so too did politicians concerned by the obvious conflict of interest inherent in a major broadcaster owning a major club. Consequently, Peter Mandelson, the Secretary of State for Trade and Industry, gave an assurance that any takeover would be investigated carefully by the Office of Fair Trading.

The next day, the sop: the club announced plans to expand Old Trafford, by way of a second tier built on top of the stands at either end. Increasing capacity from 55,300 to 67,400, it would replace Celtic Park as Britain's biggest football stadium.

So it was that the home game with Charlton was ·not quite the main event it was expected to be, even less so for Andy Cole. Unable to contain himself after learning he'd be a sub, he stormed in to see the manager. "I have yet to be convinced there is a partnership to work on with you and Dwight," Ferguson told him. "I can't see you two doing it, so I have got to look at my options."

The two teams hadn't met in the league since May 1990, as Charlton were relegated shortly afterwards. But in the four seasons that they had played in the same division, United had contrived to lose to them at Old Trafford in August 1986 – Charlton's only win in their first eight games – and then in both April and November of 1989.

Buoyed by an incredible win in the play-off final, 7–6 on penalties after a 4–4 draw, Charlton had started the season well. They'd drawn their first game away to Newcastle, thrashed Southampton 5–0 at home, and then drawn 0–0 at Highbury – a game in which Emmanuel Petit received the first of three red cards he would collect during the season, Arsenal finishing with a grand total of ten.

Like United's two previous league opponents, Charlton started well, their neat passing game keeping things fairly quiet, and then, on 32 minutes, they went ahead. Redfearn knocked a free-kick into Mendonca, backing into Stam, and his attempt to lay the ball back was inadvertently directed by Phil Neville into the path of Mark Kinsella, 25 yards from goal, almost dead centre. His shot went straight down the middle and would've been easy for Schmeichel to collect, until it took a deflection and deviated just enough to leave him with no option other than to fall backwards.

But they held the advantage for only six minutes. Johnsen sent the ball right to Neville, who loped over halfway and squared to Scholes. Quickly assessing his options, he rattled a pass low and hard at the unmarked Solskjær, dropping off, who turned and attempted to play in Yorke ahead of him, a deflection off Eddie Youds knocking the ball straight back into his path. Where others might have shot immediately, Solskjær dipped inside Redfearn, and from just inside the D, flayed high past Saša Ilić with the aid of a slight deflection.

Scholes then almost put United in front with a trademark vaporiser from 25 yards, before, in the first minute of injury time, United won a free-kick on the right, close to the corner of the box. Taking great care, Beckham pulled back on his delivery, stubbing a lightly curled cross to Yorke, alone in the six-yard box. He headed easily into the far corner to complete a combination that would become a feature of the season, before running into the crowd to seriously threaten its safety by way of celebration.

And three minutes after the break, Yorke, his collar up in homage to Cantona, scored again. Moving towards his own goal, Blomqvist – out with a foot injury until this point, clearly not match fit and enduring a dodgy debut – knocked a pass back to Irwin who in turn sent the ball forward to Yorke. Floating inside, he opened his body and laid off to Scholes, who measured a cross-field, inside-out pass to precisely where Beckham wanted it. This time, his cross was low and to the near post, evading Solskjær but continuing into the path of Yorke, who quickly adjusted his feet to score with ease.

Just when the various vesteds would have been praising the calming effect of football taught by Matt Busby, onto the pitch came a streaker, "Takeover my arse" scrawled on his back. Just a gesture, but a pointed one, and it took a phalanx of stewards to crowd his sidestep.

There was still almost half an hour remaining when United scored a fourth, Keane curving a pass into Solskjær, perhaps ten yards outside the box, who took a touch before finding Yorke, just square of him. Also taking a touch, Yorke then zipped the ball wide to Berg, on for the injured Irwin, and he produced a cross every bit as good as Beckham's, the forehead of a diving Solskjær wrong-footing the keeper and sending it into the bottom corner at the near post. He and Yorke had stood out in training as the best early combination, and now they had proved their compatibility in a game.

"This is a new dimension, this is the future," proclaimed Yorke afterwards, without clarifying quite what that meant. He did, though, admit that for the only time in his life, he'd felt nervous, unable to sleep the previous night. It did not show.

Elsewhere that evening, Chelsea and Arsenal played out a goalless draw at Stamford Bridge, and again Arsenal had a man sent off, this time Lee Dixon. They were fifth in the table with six points, four behind joint leaders Aston Villa and Liverpool. United were ninth, on five, but had played a game fewer.

Momentum suddenly acquired, the next game could not come quickly enough – at home to Coventry at the weekend. They too had won only once so far, but against Chelsea, and were far from useless, the same side that had beaten United and finished 11th the previous season.

After heavy rain and hail in the morning, it was back to being sunny again by the time the ground filled up, and there was additional cheer to be found in the team news; though Denis Irwin was absent, Giggs and Gary Neville returned to the starting line-up.

In order that the players be inspired to represent the famous Man United with dignity and pride, before the game they received a visit from Martin Edwards and Peter Kenyon, to advise them that the takeover would probably not go through until the new year, pending the approval of the Monopolies and Mergers Commission. There was nothing to worry about, they were assured, and they shouldn't bother reading the papers, because everything therein was rubbish – like those reports about selling condemned meat to schools, for example, or unsolicited toilet-sniffing. But really, there was no need; Fergie said nothing, and the players weren't sufficiently interested even to discuss it amongst themselves.

Though United controlled Coventry from the start, they didn't take the lead until the 21st minute, Solskjær roving down the left side of the box and retreating, before spreading wide to Giggs. His cross on the run was too high for Yorke at the front post, and for Beckham at the back, the goalkeeper coming between them and missing it too, finishing up in a heap on the byline after falling while back-pedalling. In the meantime, Scholes arrived at the loose ball and drilled it across the face of goal to Yorke, who mishit into the net from exceedingly close range, the chain of events deemed worthy of a name-pointing celebration – a narcissism yet to proliferate, but an inevitable consequence of adding them to the backs of shirts.

United's passing was just too much for Coventry, Beckham causing particular problems, and provoking David Burrows into a foul that earned him a yellow card and abuse beyond that which he was already receiving. But the lead remained at one, before, two minutes into the second half, United won a corner on the right. Somehow managing to retain his composure amidst the shock of Giggs swinging it directly onto his head, Johnsen glanced against Marc Edworthy, the rebound arriving directly at the feet of Yorke, by the penalty spot. Falling into a low, strong shot, he was surprised to see Gary Breen waiting by the post to clear – but only into the path of the advancing Scholes, who hammered at goal from outside the box, Johnsen sliding out a leg to divert the ball past Magnus Hedman.

The remainder of the game passed quietly, United taking it easy before their midweek encounter with Barcelona. Afterwards, Fergie was pleased enough, but Coventry manager Gordon Strachan was not. "We didn't relish the challenge until it went to 2–0. We were like somebody going to the dentist's, taking the painkillers and waiting until it was all over."

Also that afternoon, Arsenal required a last-minute equaliser to sneak away from Leicester with a draw, their fourth in a row. The goal was the first that they had managed in the period, its scorer, the notorious Stephen Hughes, celebrating by cupping his ears after not being singled out for abuse by the notorious Filbert Street crowd.

The following night, United supporters held a meeting at the Bridgewater Hall, to discuss how Murdoch could be defeated. "It's no good talking about wait and see, it's now we've got to stop it," said Jim White, then of the *Guardian*. And unlike the later battle against the Glazer family, which ultimately required mass action, here the intense commitment of a dedicated few could just work.

*

United's decision to enter the 1957 European Cup against the order of the authorities was a seminal moment in English football, advancing the game as much as any on-pitch accomplishment. But when *L'Equipe*'s Gabriel Hanot conceived the competition, he had not the remotest inkling of what it would become. "Even Hanot himself on occasion regretted letting loose what he felt was rapidly growing into a Frankenstein monster," wrote Geoffrey Green in *There's Only One United*. In 1978.

Hanot's particular concern was the immorality to which teams and supporters would stoop in order to win, though it's unlikely he would have felt much more comfortable with the financial machinations that he did not foresee. But in 1998, these were to the benefit of the actual sport, the golden goose of club football at its most delectably plump a season prior to its depressing descent into forcefed, overfed obesity. Each matchday was an event and each one meant something, because the organisers still understood that this was still the point.

United's priorities were different too; the aim was to confront the finest teams around and see what happened, not to win at all costs. The obsession was growing – in the mid-90s, league titles were as much about earning another go at Europe as anything else – but a group including Barcelona and Bayern Munich, with only one team guaranteed to progress, was accepted and attacked with alacrity.

But it was with reference to the takeover that Clive Tyldesley opened commentary of the first game. "Some will try to persuade us that there are weightier issues for football fans to consider at the moment," he trilled, "but when all the shares and all the diaries have been bought and sold, it's who wins matches like these that really matters."

Almost aggravatingly, the two teams then did everything possible to prove him right, chasing the rainbows from ITV's opening montage and crystallising the inherent problem that is destroying elite sport: it's so good that people will tolerate almost anything in order to enjoy it.

Though they boasted some outstanding players in Rivaldo, Figo and Enrique, Barcelona – we were not yet on nickname terms – had started the season poorly. Mallorca had beaten them in both legs of the Spanish Super Cup and they could only draw at Racing Santander in their first league game, before scraping by Extremadura at the Nou Camp.

Because Barcelona's home and away jerseys both clashed with red, United played in white rather than in the special kit – yet managed to start well nonetheless. In the very first minute, Neville put Beckham in behind Sergi, and the ground responded raucously.

But Barcelona were unconcerned, twice hustling Scholes into conceding possession, and then Boudewijn Zenden almost played in Rivaldo, already sharking the width of the pitch. United responded straight away, Beckham zoning a crossfield pass for Giggs who pulled a shot against the bar.

Encouraged, the speed of United's passing, thought and movement increased, crafting a racing amphetamine of a goal. Irwin zipped a low, hard ball into Solskjær, who moved it onto Yorke, who sent it wide to Beckham. Incapable of beating his man, he drew his man, then beat – nay *pasted* – him on the outside, contorted his body implausibly, and, as he fell, calculated an ideal cross for Giggs, who hovered for no short time before easing a difficult header past Ruud Hesp.

As soon as Barcelona kicked off, United jumped them again, the zeal and zest of their play underpinned by a work ethic so extreme as to be almost undignified. "You have to choose between a gradual build-up to try and cope with their attacking play, or going for it," Fergie explained. "We are no good at stifling teams anyway."

So after 25 minutes, it was no shock when they scored again. Solskjær's chasing presented possession to Beckham, and incapable of crossing with his left foot, he stepped inside and picked out Yorke with a perfect left-footed cross, of juddered at goal by way overhead kick. Pushed out by Hesp, the rebound cannoned off Enrique, unable to get out of the way, and fell for Scholes, who couldn't miss. Barcelona were getting beaten up and beaten down.

"There was a bit of personal relief involved", Scholes later wrote, "because I had missed a sitter against Barcelona four years earlier." That he was referring to a chip from the edge of the box is a testament to his absurd standards.

As chants of "Kluivert, Kluivert what's the score?" and "You should've signed for a big club" chortled around the ground, Barcelona improved, and United were lucky to escape just after the half-hour mark when Rivaldo saw his shot deflected past Schmeichel, the officials incorrectly deeming Sonny Anderson offside.

Despite the warning, Fergie sent United out to play exactly the same way after the break; "I think we can score more goals", he told Gary Newbon in the tunnel. Likewise, his last order to the players was to "keep playing the ball forward, don't sit back".

Louis van Gaal, on the other hand, altered various aspects, the most significant pushing Figo infield and Luis Enrique further forward. Whether he was clever for making them or thick for needing to, and whether United retreated or were forced to, within minutes the deficit was only one. Figo found Rivaldo on the burst and consecutive ricochets diverted a pass meant for Enrique into the path of Anderson, who shot high past Schmeichel, cueing the eerie silence of an away European goal. On the bench, fury.

So the decision to replace Solskjær with Butt was curious in context, and suddenly spooked, United withdrew, leaving Yorke isolated up front and Giggs wandering around the middle of the pitch instead of supplying the width that had been so effective in the first half. Soon after, Rivaldo nutmegged Keane – a stunt it's doubtful John O'Shea ever attempted – and racing into the box to collect Enrique's return, managed to convince the referee he'd been fouled by Stam, launching into a dive and roll when already tackled fairly to his knees. Up stepped Giovanni to dispatch the penalty beyond Schmeichel, who became angry enough to boot the ball into Figo when he dashed after it to hasten the restart.

But from the kick-off United jazzed back into action and Cocu was forced to foul Yorke just outside the box. Everyone knew what was coming, everyone thought it wasn't coming, and then it came, Beckham astonishing a free-kick just inside the post. And whatever else was said about him, no one could deny that he celebrated his goals thoroughly and in the proper manner, with none of the affectation of Giggs' "celebration that's not a celebration", the reverse of their media images. He was happy and he knew it.

Almost immediately, Barcelona brought on some "Xavier Hernandez Cruz" kid for his European debut, and almost immediately after that, Anderson bobbed Enrique's cross onto the bar. Then, Schmeichel saved from Rivaldo, but Butt, who'd narrowly avoided a red card in the Lodz home game, handled Anderson's follow-up on the line to make sure this time – "a bad decision", hallucinated Fergie afterwards – and Enrique knocked in the penalty, this time Schmeichel booting the post.

As Barcelona pushed for the win, Stam imposed his first performance of particular quality; bought as part of an attacking strategy for his ability to defend one-on-one, he proved himself equally comfortable in a rearguard action. And had Yorke not been on his heels when Beckham arced over his final cross, United might just have snatched a win, but the result was a fair one.

"The perfect football match," reflected Fergie later. "Both teams trying to win with scant regard for the consequences. That's how football should be played and in a sense this match was a throwback to the days before detailed organisation of teams."

But the approach, though quintessentially United, was a departure from the previous season, "with two sitting in midfield at all times, not over-committing and leaving us open to the counter-attack"; the lessons taught by previous away nonsense had been absorbed, for a year at least. In the following morning's *Times*, Kevin McCarra wrote that they "were forced to clutch the draw as if it were a gleaming prize", but that wasn't right: the draw was incidental, the gleaming prize was the night itself.

*

The following Sunday, United were at Highbury, and again, the teams gathered in the tunnel sporting classy, understated jerseys – though Arsenal's home version did have a slightly peculiar sheen. Meanwhile, grinning away with even greater fervour than usual was Dwight Yorke – or Mr Duracell, as he was known to a lady interviewed in one of the morning papers.

Arsenal were without the suspended Emmanuel Petit – he was replaced by Stephen Hughes – but otherwise, all was as usual. Though playing fairly well, they had only seven points from five games, enough only for tenth place, while Dennis Bergkamp and Nicolas Anelka had yet to score. Should they lose, they'd be four points behind United having played a game more.

United's line-up was peculiar. Johnsen was still out injured, his Ice Man nickname derived not from his unflappable style, but the cold compress to which he was always attached – so Henning Berg continued in his place. In midfield, Nicky Butt's solidity was considered more important than Paul Scholes' creativity, while on his left was originally to be found Ryan Giggs, with Ole Solskjær partnering Yorke, but a late change of mind led to Giggs playing upfront, with Blomqvist on the wing. And at the side was poor Cole, in collar, tie and scowl.

The alteration was presumably prompted by the unique dimensions of the Highbury pitch; during the Charity Shield, Martin Tyler mentioned that it was too narrow for Arsenal, such that moving European games to Wembley was "an all-round good decision". But the reality was different – Arsenal knew better than anyone how to find and create space on it, particularly against opponents lethargic after emerging from a dressing room in which the radiators were somehow, irreversibly and mysteriously, fixed at the highest setting.

"Manchester United left empty-handed last season, it must still stick in their throats that they let slip that 12 point lead to Arsenal," said Martin Tyler at kick-off, the start of another afternoon of measured partiality. And immediately, Arsenal worked the angles, Vieira, Dixon, Bergkamp and Parlour showing precisely how to get things done – quick, precise passing and movement – before Dixon let fly with a shot that was blocked to safety.

Then, after Beckham sent a free-kick too close to Seaman, Irwin misjudged a bounce that allowed Parlour to attack the space behind him and find Anelka. Choosing neither to go on nor shoot, he played in Bergkamp, having failed to notice that he was several yards offside.

United crafted little in response, and Arsenal attacked again. Feeding Overmars for the first time, Butt immediately sprinted across to help the back-pedalling Neville, but just teasing, the ball went back inside, Bergkamp's eventual and errant flick too strong for Parlour.

Keown then did well to head Beckham's cross away from Yorke, the only challenging presence in the middle, before Vieira pounced onto a weak but not weary one from Giggs and gangled off down the wing. Allowing Giggs to catch up, he then accelerated away to lose him and picked out Bergkamp on the edge of the box, his shot blocked by Irwin. Dixon connected well with the follow-up, but put his effort straight at Schmeichel.

United then threatened a break, Giggs picking up possession after a Vieira error and pacing into space, but Vieira was quickly back behind the ball to smother with his shins when taken on. Immediately, Arsenal countered, foiled in the first instance, before Irwin lobbed a pass to Blomqvist, and while he waited for it to come down, Dixon charged in to assume ownership, finding Parlour who rushed by Irwin. Stam kicked away the cross and the resultant throw went back to Dixon who knocked off to Vieira, Blomqvist darting over to foul him anyway.

This gave Arsenal a free-kick on the right touchline, perhaps 25 yards from goal and ideal for Hughes' swinging left foot. He whipped a cross into the middle of the box for Adams, up early and leaning over the top of Stam, Schmeichel belatedly jumping towards a ball he could never hope to make. Accordingly, all it needed to beat him was a flick from Adams to score, off parading himself in the corner while the arguments began.

United did improve marginally after that, connecting a pass or two but without the merest menace. Arsenal, on the other hand, continued to press with imagination and verve, Overmars leading a shimmering break and Bergkamp only just miscueing a volley on the turn after Anelka's scoop over the top.

Next, United's nearest thing, Yorke taking Blomqvist's throw-in and finding Beckham, over from the right. Sidestepping the ball into his stride, he set himself for a shot flighted between Adams and Hughes, dipping low past Seaman before it clipped the inside of the near post, the spin then taking it past the far. Then, in United's best move of the game, Keane chested down a clearance for Beckham, who arrowed a pass from the touchline to Yorke. Pulling it out of the air, he diverted the ball to Blomqvist behind him, probably by mistake, and turned on the return inside the D, before dragging back from the sliding Adams and rolling it on for Giggs, to his right. Only for Giggs to be offside for no reason, with no one between him and goal.

Giggs was then foiled by Keown's excellent tackle, and when Vieira shoved the loose ball forward to Overmars in the centre-circle, no one was around to stop him looking up and wedging a pass over the top for Anelka. Away from Stam, he took it deftly on his laces, delivering it into his stride from behind as he hovered into the box on its right-hand side. Again he went for the near post, Schmeichel saving superbly with his foot. But just as it had for Wreh, the rebound fell handily, and as a grounded Schmeichel attempted a desperate dive, he rammed the ball past him and jogged off. Meanwhile, Parlour headed over to the bench, Winterburn to the crowd and Giggs to whinge at the ref, indignant that he chose not to penalise what was clearly a very good initial tackle. Then it was half-time.

Almost as soon as the second period began, Hughes inserted his elbow into Beckham's face with the ball already gone. This earned a booking, as Beckham going down and remaining there for the requisite time.

Next, Anelka won a flick-on to send Bergkamp into the box ahead of Berg but wider than he would have liked, and he could only screw a shot wide of the near post, before, in the next passage of play, Beckham's revenge. Taking a pass from Winterburn towards the touchline, Keane drew up alongside Hughes and toppled him with a shin bump. The referee's attention diverted in that direction, Beckham seized the opportunity to improvise a donkey bite by trapping a hunk of tender inside-thigh, hard, between studs and grass – easily United's most inventive and incisive contribution to the afternoon.

Vieira then caught Butt in possession, midway inside the United half and right of centre. Freeing Anelka to thrust the ball to one side of Stam and glide by on the other, he paused when Butt buffeted him from behind and waited to be overtaken by Vieira to his right, rolling into his stride as he stepped at pace towards goal. This forced Butt to slide a leg in front of him just outside the area, the ball well inside, his subsequent fall deemed by the referee to merit a red card. This news was received with quite some distress by his team-mates, trapping referee Graham Barber on the touchline, tempers in *dishabille*. There'd been a shirt-pull, indicated Berg. "He got the ball!" shrieked Irwin. "It was a dive!" threatened Keane. None were remotely close to so, though Stam's proximity suggested that he would most likely have inserted himself between man and goal prior to any shot. Keane was booked.

There existed now a contemplation of quite how bad things could get, though the kind of asinine, indolent softness that results in 6–1 kickings remained a scientific impossibility. But it might have got worse immediately when Overmars came in off the left and fired a low shot straight at Schmeichel with Bergkamp loitering in the middle. "Arsenal revelling in this!" growled Martin Tyler, revelling in this, and so were the crowd, taking advantage of a game already clinched to address Sheringham.

And United ought really to have conceded again after Yorke passed backwards to Bergkamp. Spotting Anelka escaping Berg, Bergkamp slid a pass down the side of Stam to meet Anelka's run and a touch took him clear, but he dragged his shot wide of the far post.

Stam would consider this afternoon the lowest point in his United career, the game prompting him to decide that his settling-in period was over. He determined to move the ball quicker and forget the self-imposed pressure to prove wrong all who doubted him after watching him play barely a handful of times.

With 11 minutes to go, Wenger made a change, "the situation such that Fredrik Ljungberg could be given his debut for Arsenal". Moments later, Overmars accelerated through the centre-circle, slowing until Parlour made his way outside him. The two then exchanged passes, Overmars jabbing in to Hughes, who in turn lifted over the top seeking Bergkamp – but the ball went straighter than intended, bouncing between keeper and defence. Schmeichel could not reach it in time to avoid his lobbing by Ljungberg's first touch.

There was still time for a Keane – Vieira confrontation, foreheads pressed after Overmars was toppled. They separated, but couldn't help but get back at it when Barber called them over in an effort to assert authority, Vieira sniggering to himself at Keane's impotence.

Fergie was not at all happy with what he'd seen, provoked even into reflexive pronoun. "I shall examine the reasons why we were up against opposition more determined and hungrier than ourselves," he wrote. "It's quite unusual and something that will always register with me."

But though Arsenal's greater need to win was unarguably in evidence, so too was their superior quality. And so too their smugness in that superiority, hard to take at the time, magnificent in hindsight. There's a Hebrew principle, *gam zu letovah*, generally used by religious people to excuse all the horrendous badness visited by God upon the world. Roughly translated, it means 'this is also for the best', and works by applauding an overall plan unintelligible to human minds – and is applicable to every single misfortune that befell United during the season, all contributing to the perfect outcome and each of which can be loved with a great and overwhelming affection. *Gam zu letovah*.

The following evening, Chelsea were 3–2 down at Blackburn with eight minutes to go, before Tore Andre Flo, on as a substitute, scored twice in five minutes to give them the win. *Gam zu letovah!*

*

The defeat at Arsenal suggested a team uncomfortable in itself, lacking the magic to detect goals where there appeared to be none. The three against Barcelona had arrived when things were functioning properly, but every team produces a few good days a season, and still United hadn't won. Meanwhile, they had already failed to score on four occasions and were tenth in the league, six points behind leaders Villa, two behind Arsenal and three shy of Liverpool – who, to help both teams prepare for the following week's European fixtures, had agreed to the double-rare treat of a Thursday night game.

At the time, Liverpool had joint managers, Roy Evans yet to sulk off at having Gérard Houllier – originally meant to take over as coach from Ronnie Moran – encroach on his job. This was actually a fairly decent development for those of a United persuasion, Evans responsible for the 96-97 anomaly of a side more attractive and enterprising than United's title winners. "They play good football and they play the right way," Fergie would say after the game – not a compliment he would feel obliged to issue once Houllier had assumed full control.

After the travesty at Arsenal, Gary Neville replaced Berg at centre-back for the first part of his "annual cameo". The specific theory was that his pace would combat the threat of Michael Owen, as would familiarity with his game gleaned whilst away with England, but in general there was managerial concern at a lack of communication in the middle of the defence. In midfield, Scholes was back in and Butt dropped to the bench, suspensions only coming into immediate effect after the ludicrous manipulation of the system afforded to Arsène Wenger in 2001–02. Up front, Solskjær also returned, with Giggs was sent back to the wing instead of Blomqvist, yet to properly get going.

Liverpool brought Brad Friedel in for David James, while Jason McAteer played at right-back with Phil Babb in the middle, suddenly Britain's most expensive defender after a couple of good World Cup performances. Also playing was the returned Steve Staunton, his 1991 sale to Villa on account of David Burrows one of bountiful signifiers of imminent decline. Not quite there was Robbie Fowler, back on the bench after returning from a cruciate ligament injury in just seven months, his importance less significant since the emergence of Michael Owen. Owen had outed himself as himself during the previous season's run-in, via a hack at Ronny Johnsen, eventually explained as simply of a consequence of the bad mood he was in that day. So, when he

followed it in August with a hand-rubbing celebration that was indisputably the most unbearably smug of all time, it was already easy to
be relieved that he played for them, even though he was quite good.

The principal chatter before the game concerned Paul Ince, visiting
Old Trafford for the second time since his banishment in the summer
of 1995. And Fergie clearly considered this insufficient retribution,
deciding to publicly, purposely and purposefully insult him in a docu-
mentary about his career, screened the Tuesday before the game and
showing footage of a team-talk prior to the teams' previous meeting.
"If he tries to bully you, fucking enjoy it… don't let him *attempt* to
bully you. Right? You just make sure you're ready for him tomorrow.
And that's all you need to worry about him, his fucking big-time
Charlie bit. He's against fucking men, am I right? And that's all you
need to worry about him. Is he gonnae do me, Redknapp? That is a
problem for them by the way. We get the ball transferred into these
areas there, I don't think they've a *chance* against us… I don't think
they've a *chance*, what youse have got."

Given his stellar and influential contribution to United's success,
and, just as importantly, his attitude at Anfield in May 1992 and
Selhurst Park in January 1995, this was, on reflection, more than a
bit churlish. "I used to have a saying," Fergie related in happier times,
"that when a player is at his peak, he feels as though he can climb
Everest in his slippers. That's what he was like."

On the other hand, the animus did a handy job of nurturing
additional needle, and was accordingly lapped up. Though most
backed the decision to let Ince go, it was celebrated by very few, and
though most thought him not good enough to come back, no one
was remotely chuffed at where he then appeared, even if it was the
best option available to him. One best way of reconciling it was to
go on the attack, so the attack was gone upon.

The course of Liverpool's decay could be charted through their away
strip, altered from smart yellow, to ridiculous silver, into inexplicable
green, followed by white with green, green and white quarters, insipid
ecru, a brief sojourn back to yellow, and finally, the spice boy white
in which they now appeared. The way it set off Jamie Redknapp's
eyes was quite something.

And despite their decent position in the table, Liverpool, top after
four games, had not enjoyed a good couple of weeks. First, they'd lost

to West Ham, a game for which Houllier left out Riedle to accommodate Steve Harkness, and were then forced to come from behind three times to earn a home draw with Charlton. "Never mind sex and lies in Washington DC, Liverpool should be required to squirm through a video scandal of their own today", chided the *Independent*, going on to describe the "ill-starred alliance of Phil Babb and Jamie Carragher" and "peculiar arrangement" between Evans and Houllier.

So it was no surprise when United started at a decent lick, Stam soon hurtling into Riedle with the extreme speed to the ball and power on arrival more common in a linebacker than a centre-back. As the *Independent on Sunday*'s interviewer observed later in the season, "If Stam says he will do something, his commitment is total" – a characteristic with which Liverpool were already familiar. They too had attempted to sign him in the summer, but discovered only his determination to move to United regardless of how much more money they offered him. In the event, the demands made by PSV forced him to forgo his contractual cut of the transfer fee, more than a million pounds, and he also agreed with his wife that their first child be induced, so as not to disturb the pre-season tour of Scandinavia.

Five minutes later, Liverpool mustered another attack, McManaman waving and pointing at Riedle, who had the audacity to look elsewhere. That he remained unnutted by Zinedine Zidane in two years together at Real Madrid is testament to the potency of Marco Materazzi's insult.

Straight back came United, Irwin's ball running through to Friedel who sliced his second goalkick, the mess tidied up by Babb. Then, two minutes later, the best move of the game so far, Scholes and Yorke twice zipping the ball between them before Scholes was rolled over by Jamie Carragher as play progressed. He was booked.

Liverpool had been permitted hardly a touch in the first quarter of an hour, and on 16 minutes, Keane was only just unable to reach Scholes' pass at the end of a painful break, his shocking spryness evidence of returning fitness, new perspective and renewed dedication – both to home and professional life – resulting in a generally less parched individual. "Now my tolerance level was zero," he wrote in his autobiography. "Only one thing counted in football: winning, actually achieving. For that I was hungrier than I'd ever been."

But a moment later, he was beaten twice by Patrick Berger and staggered in the process, only for Berger to whump a shot straight into Riedle. Immediately, United responded, Solskjær preying on a weak Carragher header and shooting, relatively weakly. But, like almost all of his attempts on goal, it was on target, and when it bounced in front of Friedel, he could only fumble behind before tottering under Beckham's left-wing corner, slicing his knuckles across the underside of the ball, and retreating towards his line. This left McAteer to deal with the situation, and under slight pressure from Scholes, he was left with every option but to knock it away with his hand, then knocked it away with his hand, the camera showing a coupon bewildered by its own unfathomable stupidity. The consequent penalty was easily dispatched by Irwin into his preferred bottom-right netting, following customary slow walk and immediate turn precursor.

With Old Trafford rattling out a healthy din, United resumed the boust, those watching on telly shown a banner reading, "God gave us his son, then he gave us Manchester United – what more could we want?"

Liverpool came a little more into the game after that, appealing for a penalty of their own after a ball struck Giggs on the arm – but it was by his side. Next, McManaman stotted forwards like a shackled deer and found Ince, Stam launching into a definitive block almost before the pass had been considered. Neville then flattened McManaman and a combination of Giggs and Keane fouled Berger, McManaman joining in the telling-off. Redknapp's free-kick, taken from just left of centre, was pawed around the post by Schmeichel easily enough.

Minutes later, further aggravation: first, Giggs held back Redknapp who for him was so unhappy, he really was, a top, top unhappy person, and then Ince dug into Solskjær from behind, the ground avenging him with a further rendition of "Fuck off Charlie", seguing into "Charlie, Charlie, what's the score?"

But Liverpool continued to press, Owen trying his luck drifting wide. Stam, though, was brave enough to go with him and skilful enough to shut him down. Shortly afterwards, Phil Neville was booked for blackening McManaman's ankle, and then Berger was too, complaining after experiencing Stam.

A minute before half-time, Stam, Keane and Gary Neville blocked Riedle so Redknapp plunged into Scholes, Keane breaking up a row between Stam and Ince that Stam was keen to pursue. And there was still time for a further Liverpool attack after Schmeichel tipped away Redknapp's free-kick, Berger feeding Ince and the ball moving through midfield via Bjørnebye, McManaman, Redknapp and then back to Ince. A bad first touch took him into the box on its left side, allowing him to set for a shot driven low and deflected across Schmeichel, who sent his save to his left and Riedle, following in. Next second, McManaman found Owen in the box, Gary Neville sitting down into a two-footed tackle with perfect timing, after which it was half-time, McAteer hectoring about the penalty award all the way off.

The second half opened with a typical Giggs final ball, aimed towards the hitherto absent Solskjær and Yorke. Then, on 47 minutes, he skived shooting with his right foot after Yorke's delicious pass nutmegged Carragher, instead slithering across the face of the area and finding Solskjær, whose shot faded agonisingly wide.

Liverpool looked to build again, but Gary Neville cleverly dropped back to deny Owen space to run into, forcing him instead to turn and take him on. Ineffective against a player with skill as well as speed, like Overmars, it was more than enough to flummox a one-dimensional sprinter.

Next, it was Stam's turn, Keane winning a tackle with Riedle and the ball breaking to Owen who had ventured into his sphere of influence. Champion of the legal teeth-rattler, he cruised through him following preparatory hop and skip, shorts rearing up to reveal a shark fin of ingotflesh that screamed silently perpetrated violence.

Then, on 53 minutes, a medley of crashing tackles: Riedle on Giggs then McAteer on Giggs, both trumped by another Stam hop and skip special. Owen then raced by Phil Neville who achieved the merest tickle on the ball, lucky to concede only a corner, and shortly afterwards, Berger could find no power in his finish after McAteer's cross was slowed by Gary Neville's head.

Just before the hour, Ince diddled Keane on the right touchline, drawing him in and knocking the ball right while nipping left, the transference of weight forcing a slip – but, alone in the middle, Owen could only miss the ball. Still, Liverpool were on top, Keane not yet fit enough to do the running and tackling of two and Scholes not yet a game-controlling superbrain.

On 64 minutes, a minor rumble developed between Beckham and Redknapp, before Berger shot straight at Schmeichel, who managed to plant a palm by his foot but still fail to hold it. Though Riedle tapped in the loose ball, he was clearly offside, Schmeichel shaking his head at his own incompetence.

Looking to alter the flow, United replaced Solskjær with Cole, who had played only 20 minutes in the previous five games. "Now a chance to re-establish himself and perhaps formulate a partnership with Yorke," said Martin Tyler.

Cole was a relative rarity: a United striker who succeeded ultimately but not initially. Like most players he improved significantly in his time at the club, growing from finisher into footballer and swapping a shoal of tap-ins for a wider variety of goals and assists, testament to the coaching of Brian Kidd. Illustrated by his streak through autumn and winter of the previous season and in particular a display of complete centre-forward play at Barnsley in the Cup, his movement, already exceptional, had improved too, the eagerness that resulted in some accomplished first-time finishes manifesting less frequently as nervous snatches at easier ones.

And he made an immediate impact. His speed forced Liverpool's defenders deeper, making it harder for them to find midfielders and allowing him room to turn and run at them – far more taxing than simply trying to stop Solskjær from shooting. In particular, Cole's sprinter's start was almost impossible to counteract, and in the 74th minute, Beckham somehow directed a through-ball towards him between Bjørnebye and Babb, who collided and collapsed in comic fashion, Friedel out only just in time.

As Liverpool pursued the equaliser, inevitably they left gaps for United to exploit, and in the 77th minute Beckham made a sharp break down the right, his crossfield pass to Yorke moved quickly into Cole, whose shot was blocked. But Liverpool then broke, Fowler – on for Riedle – extracting a foul from Stam and earning a free-kick just outside the D that he curled just over the bar. Then, a minute later, a loose touch from Beckham forced Scholes to accidentally career into Owen, for which he received a yellow card. "He needs to tidy up the bookings", advised Martin Tyler as if it were possible.

Then, on 79 minutes, Liverpool forced a corner. From Bjørnebye's cross, McManaman headed back and Giggs headed up, Stam and Fowler pursuing the loose ball which came off the latter's shoulder to Yorke, just outside the box. Swivelling to clear and missing his kick entirely, suddenly the pitch opened up and he had time to pick a pass to Cole who convulsed along the left touchline and into the Liverpool half. Heading staright at Babb, he stuttered and feinted a double-kneed crouching waddle before scurrying past him on the outside, to the byline and turning in a low cross. The ball then evaded Yorke but not Berger, marking him, the latter's slight touch diverting it at reduced pace along a line between the seven defenders in the box and precisely to where a coiled Scholes was waiting to unwind his entire body into a leaping left-footed curler that rocketed past Friedel into the far top corner.

That goals of this ilk were no longer surprising is a precise testament to the genius of Fergie, his first title-winning side the progenitors of the genre. And the innovation brought with it new pleasures, the exhilaration of the speed and excitement of predicting the next pass like doing a crossword on a roller-coaster. Of course, the counter-attack itself was nothing new, but never before had there been a side genuinely feared when under pressure, the ability to turn defence into attack in an instant now in the armoury of all decent teams.

And the approach applied not solely to football. Speaking to Tony Blair and Alastair Campbell a week before the 1997 General Election, Fergie's advice was clear: "Take it a bit easy. Let them come after you more and watch them make mistakes and then punish them for it." Or in other words, hit them on the break.

Scholes' goal inspired first more Ince abuse then more generic abuse, a guttural Old Trafford devouring the joy of ten minutes' guaranteed victory. But Cole was after more, thoroughly refreshed with confidence. First he banged a shot into the side netting when once he'd have meekly passed, then played a long one-two with Giggs, who found Scholes to slice a lash wide. Then, with two minutes to go, Yorke and Scholes combined to set him up for a mishit, before he capped a splendid display by accidentally wiping his studs across the midriff of a furious, spluttering McAteer.

The win took United into third place in the table, ahead of Liverpool, who, though they had enjoyed a decent amount of posses-sion, had managed fewer shots and fewer shots on target; the margin of two goals was a fair one, beyond its crucial existance.

Man of the match and deservedly so was Gary Neville, who admitted afterwards that "the fans would've had something to say to us" had United not won. Reflecting not just his ability but his application, his performance was that of a man who spent hours shadow defending, always determined to improve. "Some people said it was my best game for United," he later wrote. "I don't know about that because I was in awe of Jaap." This was the same attitude that made him unwilling ever to apportion blame elsewhere, his response unequivocal after missing three good chances in two games the previous season: "It's unacceptable. I'm a Manchester United player and I should be able to handle any situation put in front of me."

The least naturally talented of his contemporaries, Neville committed everything to football on the basis that he could get qualifications and fun later, if necessary. "He was out at three in the morning," he said of the teenage Ryan Giggs. "Me and Phil were worried about facing him the next day."

And he really wasn't joking, the maintenance of old relationships, generally taken as a sign of groundedness, entirely eliminated. "I was willing to ditch everything in my life apart from football and family," he explained in his autobiography. "So much for my wild teenage years. If there was a game on Saturday, I was in bed by 9.15pm every Thursday and Friday night. I was a robot. I cast off all my mates from school, never saw them again. I decided, ruthlessly, that I was going to make friends with my new team-mates, who shared the same goals as me. As far as I was concerned the lives of athletes and non-athletes were incompatible. Between the ages of 16 and 20, I dropped women completely. They were always going to want to go to a cinema or a bar on a Friday night." Cynics might simply deem this an elaborate money-saving scheme for someone legendarily obsessed with financial micromanagement, another facet of his compulsion to control, but his dedication was unimpeachable.

After an assured entry into the first team in 1994–95, he soon lost his place to his younger brother, forced to endure uproarious quips about briefly being the finest full-back in England, before not even being the best in his own family. But because his perspective was different to the usual he remained calm, proclaiming that, "if United signed Roberto Carlos and he was better than me, or if Phil and Denis Irwin were playing better than me, I wouldn't complain about not making the team. I've supported Manchester United all my life and they should always have the best players available. If that means me, good; but if it doesn't, hard luck."

This equanimity permeated his play. Rarely flustered, he clearly thought hard about how to maximise his assets and how to defend against particular opponents, his organised, sensible style a product of his personality. "I like to plan things," he explained after retiring. "I like to know what I'm doing, the next day, the day after that."

And this aided his defending, his contribution measurable not just in tackles made but in influence. Initially restrained on graduation to the first team, losing the title to Arsenal prompted him to ponder how he might improve, so he increased his vocal contribution accordingly, playing a particularly important role in directing the runs of Beckham.

Off the pitch, Neville was involved in every conceivable activity; a "busy cunt" as Jaap Stam succinctly put it, far more affectionately than was inferred. Along with Keane, Stam explained, he was the principal dressing room motivator, "making sure everyone is desperate to win" – which, given the company, evidences an exceptional obsession.

Of course, the same talents now manifest in his work as an analyst. As a young player, he criticised the "camera talk" of some of his contemporaries, and still insists on speaking as honestly as he would in private.

And he also retains the self-critical inclination: "Sometimes I'm disappointed with the things I say," he told *The Times*. "The other week, Ed asked me a question at half-time of Aston Villa v Sunderland and I said the three goals in the first half were sensational. They weren't, they were good. Where do you go from sensational? If there's one in the second half that's better, what do you say? I get disappointed if I use the wrong word, when people at home won't even have realised."

But perhaps most importantly of all, he has never had illusions or delusions as to his position in the scheme of things. "You try and be as right as you can, or as detailed as you can," he asserts, "but the important thing is the football… we're there to support the *football match*, the game itself is what everyone is interested in."

Like many attributes, though, it brings with it an accompanying downside. Despite a youth spent on the Old Trafford terraces, this devotion to the actual game led him to see it as football's only aspect. So, when those supporters who felt compelled to stand found themselves in conflict with stewards, his advice was that they pipe down to avoid losing their season tickets. Similarly, he was supportive of the proposals to form a European League because it would raise standards, in favour of the Sky takeover because the club could spend more money on players, and unfussed by the Glazers' pillaging because it had no impact on how the players played.

As for United, they were still getting by, close enough to the leaders to be relatively satisfied. Of course, in subsequent seasons, that would no longer be the case, but prior to José Mourinho's arrival at Chelsea, it was possible to take the first half of the season off – in 1981–82, for example, Liverpool were 14th on Boxing Day, before a run of 20 wins in 25 games burned off the opposition. Similarly, there was broad tolerance for Fergie's cliché about the New Year heralding a run of form, as though not bothering to supply it previously was some kind of loveable quirk.

But change was already underway. The previous season Chelsea could call upon Zola, Hughes, Vialli and Flo, and now Fergie had four strikers too, the first to make the system of rest and rotation really work. Now, injuries, suspension and loss of form were less crucial, and, most importantly of all, in games where his team were level or behind, he had options, not just of other players, but of different ones, presenting opponents with an entirely different challenge. A more extreme version of the method would be a principal factor in his success once priced out of the top end of the market by the Glazers.

*

While United prepared for Munich, there emerged the season's most controversial moment so far, during Arsenal's game at Hillsborough. A stramash between Paolo Di Canio and Martin Keown, prompted by Patrick Vieira chucking a punch at Wim Jonk – he would later do the same to a policeman in the tunnel – led to their sending off. This caused Di Canio to become so angry that he pushed the referee, "Di Canio sparks day of shame" and "Di Canio is facing end of his career" two of the more restrained headlines that followed. He was banned for 11 games, five more than was David Batty after shoving David Elleray just a few months earlier, the only difference between the two offences a nationality, a complexion and a pratfall.

And the furore managed to deflect attention from what happened in the final minute of the game, Wednesday's left-back Lee Briscoe scoring the winning goal with a brilliant, implausible chip from the corner of the box, his first in five years at the club. Arsenal had already squandered the advantage gained in beating United.

*

"A night wrapped in a shroud of history", warbled Clive Tyldesley at the start of United's first return to Munich since the 1958 air disaster – a fact not lost on a group of 50 Leeds fans en route to Madeira, who, in the airport at the same time as the players, took the opportunity to remind them.

After the cowardice of previous seasons there was no guarantee of football taught by Matt Busby, but it was there, alright, Fergie now confident that United could go anywhere and play like United – producing, no doubt by strange coincidence, what he adjudged to be the best such performance under his management.

On the morning of the game, the story had broken of an alliance with Belgian side Royal Antwerp, which would become a feeder and nursery club. The aim was to circumvent legislation put in place by the Department for Education and Employment as regards the recruitment of overseas talent – it was far easier to obtain a work permit in Belgium, explaining the country's prominent role in football's slave trade. Those who did well there would then be invited to move to United, while promising domestic players would also be sent the other way to play first-team football, without a thought for the entirely expendable integrity of the Belgian league. The scheme was a resounding failure, Ronnie Wallwork and Danny Higginbotham given long bans after attacking a referee who they felt had scuppered their promotion bid, and a grand total of one player sent there and no players from there progressed to become United regulars.

Also that morning, reports emerged of injections administered to England's World Cup squad. Specifically, Fergie had written to the FA wanting to know why Gary Neville had been given "vitamins and minerals" before the Argentina game. "I was tired coming into the World Cup," wrote Neville at the time, "but the injections are kicking in and I feel really strong and sharp. All the lads have said the same thing." Oh, really.

The Bayern Munich side of 1998 were in a similar situation to United: not champions and boasting fewer European Cups than they felt befitted their status, without one in a generation. And they'd also thrown away an advantage in their opening group game, mugged by a pair of late goals to lose at Brondby.

But in the league they were six from six, so, despite missing Helmer, Basler and Scholl, fancied themselves against a United side still searching for itself. With Johnsen and Berg out injured, Gary Neville remained at centre-back, the selection of Sheringham partially motivated by the helpfulness of his height in defending set pieces. This, Tyldesley thought, placed "extra onus on Peter Schmeichel to come for crosses and free-kicks where possible".

Marking Yom Kippur with a white away strip, Munich in quilted bin liners, United started well enough, pressing high up the pitch, with Beckham fastened onto Lizarazu wherever possible. But after 11 minutes, the Germans compiled a move down their left in which Jancker was offside twice, before laying the ball off to Elber, himself at least a yard offside, and in front of goal. He beat Schmeichel for 1–0.

In what was now a twinkling waterfall of rain, Sheringham put a chance narrowly wide following a Stam pass, then saw a version of his Tottenham corner routine cleared off the line by Lizarazu. And with United increasing the pressure, it was no surprise when, on 29 minutes, they equalised. Matthäus, poor, unfortunate, ravaged Matthäus, by this stage of his career forced to intimidate his way into the team – misplaced a pass, intercepted by Beckham – too quick, too clever and too furious. He exchanged passes with Sheringham, moved towards the right touchline and rode the tardiest of tackles while dispensing a perfect cross for Yorke to diving-head home, in the pose that would become his Jumpman equivalent.

"Don't worry about his personality, he'll thrive on it," had said Large Rotund Not Racist Ronald when asked in commentary how ex-charge "Yorkie" would handle the pressure at United, and Andy Gray, who'd assisted him for a time, was also sure he was the right signing. Recommended to Fergie by members of his defence, the notion that anyone doing well against his side could only be good always tickled his arrogance, and was similarly significant in the purchase of Blomqvist, even though all he'd needed to do to look good was run past David May.

Before half-time, Beckham enjoyed a yellow card for fouling Effenberg in a bouncing swish of curtains – he'd miss Brondby away – and then belted half the length of the pitch to chuck an arm and a leg at Salihamidžić, doing well to stay on the pitch. Soon after, Bayern almost scored, Effenberg sliding a clever free-kick down the side of United's wall to Elber, who set Salihamidžić for a shot that went through Neville's legs. Already moving left, Schmeichel somehow thrust a right foot in its direction to deflect clear, Cossack-style, before Sheringham smuggled the loose ball away with his arm as Babbel lunged. Half-time.

"What's your advice to the players?" asked Gary Newbon of Fergie in the tunnel. "Go and win it," he replied, and within three minutes of the restart, it looked like they might, confluence of happenstance allowing Scholes to mosey through the German defence to score for the third consecutive game – "like a man cutting corn", wrote the *Guardian*'s David Lacey. Scholes later surmised that Oliver Khan "might have squeaked out of the challenge a little bit" – odd, on the face of it, for a man nicknamed Der Titan and with the appearance of a DDR discus throwette. The reputation of tough Manchester gingers had clearly spread.

Most of the rest of the game involved United defending, relatively well in the main, and again Stam excelled, an obelisk on skates. If Vidic and Ferdinand were an ideal combination of strength and stealth, so too would be Stam and Stam, with added marauding inclination. He had arrived.

"In the beginning, when they pay a lot of money and you're over in Holland, you try not to think about it," he said later in the season. "But everyone is talking about it, everyone is watching you and if you make a little mistake they ask whether you're worth the money or not. My agent came to my house and said he'd seen a shopping centre built for a little less than what they'd paid for me: £10m. Of course it's absurd, it's too much money for a footballer."

And he also experienced the usual difficulties settling in. Though his English was good, he found dressing room slang hard to grasp, reporting the two most popular terms to be "mingin'" and "freebies" – closely followed by "pre-millennial tension" and "antidisestablishmentarianism".

Unsurprisingly, the criticism and pressure had an effect, his appearance belying a smalltown childhood in which he was spoiled into softness by his mother and three older sisters.

"You start reading about it and I started thinking about it, which made my game harder. You can only do bad things in a game. But

I talked to Alex and Brian Kidd and they just said, 'We know what you can do, just play your own game as you did in Holland and everything will be OK.' When people at the club have confidence in you that really helps."

But Bayern could not be entirely shut down, their tempo that of a side which could not afford to lose. On 72 minutes, Irwin played Elber onside, presenting him with a chance that he benevolently sliced across, then Schmeichel saved well from Jeremies and Ali Daei missed a presentable chance, Oktoberfested Reds hollering ever louder.

With only injury time remaining and the points almost secure, pressure persuaded Phil Neville to welt into touch a ball already on its way behind for a goalkick. Lizarazu then lobbed in the throw, and, from nowhere, appeared a Schmeichel extra-onused up to the eyeballs and diving over the top of his defenders to not clear, Elber thus able to force Sheringham, extra height and all, into scoring an own goal. "I'm not making any excuses for that, that was plain stupidity," said Schmeichel of his plain stupidity.

Yet even then, there was time for Sheringham to force a handy reaction save from Khan – "never a dull moment with Manchester United in Europe", Tyldesley asserted, and for a while, there wasn't.

"Bayern Munich, they never give in... they keep going right to the end, the boss told us that this morning," lamented Gary Neville in the tunnel after the game.

Let's just leave that one to marinate.

OCTOBER

If the players weren't sufficiently distraught at conceding such a late goal, which they were, along came the extra aggravation of a plane with a fault, disquieting too, in the circumstances – particularly so if reports alleging that trees were hit on arrival at Lodz and a seal broken on the way home were true. Forced to stay in Munich an extra night prior to the weekend's hike to Southampton, this presumably went down least well with Peter Schmeichel, quietly absorbed in the absorption of his own misery.

Nor could he play himself out of it immediately, a stomach injury forcing his replacement by Rai van der Gouw. With Scholes and Giggs also unavailable, Butt and Blomqvist played, but the most important decision was the pairing of Cole with Yorke, immortalised by the first public utterance of the dreaded "freshen things up" phrase.

Excluded against Bayern principally on account of being less tall and less old than Sheringham, Cole's impact against Liverpool had not been forgotten. Throughout the summer and even into the early stages of the season, there were rumours that he would leave, possibly as part of a swap deal with Yorke, and though he was reassured as to his future, in the first instance, it was hard for him to ignore the possibility. "I was the striker United could have sold for the most and my fears were realised as I was on the bench a lot," he recalled.

But he quickly decided that he couldn't live with the fear and if he was sold, would just have to cope. And if he wasn't, then Yorke would improve the squad, which could mean only good things. So, recalling his own loneliness when moving clubs – "the life of the hermit" – he went out of his way to be welcoming. "I remembered my own isolation," he later explained, "and I didn't want anyone else to suffer the same way."

Southampton had managed to lose seven of their first eight games, scoring only three goals one of those a penalty. Already four points adrift at the bottom, they were also missing the suspended Mark Hughes, but United hadn't won at The Dell since 1993, losing on their last three visits. Had the unmarked Howells not headed Østenstad's cross wide in the first 60 seconds, perhaps things might have been different. But he did not, and they were not.

After 11 minutes, Butt swept a pass out left to Blomqvist, who advanced before stabbing to Cole, on the touchline. Jiggling inside onto his right foot, he drove a cross to the near post, where Yorke poked out a leg, catching enough of it as it bounced to send it dribbling past Jones. Quite what Lundekvam was doing during all of this remains a mystery.

Southampton possessed neither the quality nor the confidence to seriously threaten after that, the game another landmark in the restitution of Keane's authority. And United could have increased their lead before half-time, Cole shooting over, Yorke missing a header and Beckham going close with a free-kick. Then, on the hour, they did. Blomqvist ambled back into his own half, rolled the ball under his studs, turned, and sped off on a burrowing run, cutting past Ripley and inside Warner. Straightening as Cole ran across his path and in behind Monkou, he slid a pass outside the defender over which Cole dextrously flicked legs, accepting it on his inside, then opened his body and firmly side-footed across Jones as Palmer slid in, to no avail. "Manchester United have taken both goals with great economy of effort... and expertise as well," said John Motson with rare lucidity.

United's control of the game improved after that, even after three changes, Brown, Sheringham and Cruyff replacing Irwin, Yorke and the excellent Blomqvist, now fully integrated into both team and dressing room. And it was Cruyff who scored next, the goal his first in 18 months. Picking up the ball deep in the United half after Irwin robbed Le Tissier, he played it to Butt, who attempted to refind Irwin, instead smacking it against Cruyff's feet and directly into his stride. Allowed to run 40 yards without molestation, with Cole alone to his left he rolled him in, and watched as he paused for a second, then dragged outside of Monkou to drive a shot that Jones saved at the near post. But the ball looped up off his shin straight to where Cruyff was now waiting, and he sent a falling volley into the empty net.

But the major football story of the week came at West Ham's Chadwell Heath training ground, when John Hartson was caught booting Eyal Berkovic in the head. Naturally, Hartson was contrite; "Sorry about the tackle, happens every day, like," he offered. Magnanimously, he then told the *Daily Mail* that should Berkovic choose to leave the club, "that's up to him", and he, Hartson, "certainly wouldn't do anything to stand in his way" – like boot him in the head, for example. It was all rather sad, really, because he "used to like Eyal" – even while booting him in the head – but subsequently he "lost a lot of respect for him", a sanction too far even for this most heinous crime.

Without the leverage to threaten international retirement, he was banned by the FA for three games, and would move to Wimbledon later in the season – where he was again in the news after the crazy, hilarious, crazy Crazy Gang marked his arrival by burning his clothes. It is understood that Berkovic certainly didn't do anything to stand in his way.

*

After a debut of poise and composure against Leeds in the previous season's run-in and in the absence of Berg, Irwin, Johnsen and May, Wes Brown was given his first start against Wimbledon – whose manager, Joe Kinnear, claimed to have enquired about him in the summer, United later confirming receipt of fax headed "Wostley Blouse". With Butt suspended and Scholes on the bench, Giggs played in central midfield, though Beckham would wander inside too, and van der Gouw continued in place of the injured Schmeichel.

Wimbledon had started the season well, but United had done the double over them in the previous four, after struggling against the original Crazy Gang. Steve Bruce tells a yarn that he once told a newspaper that he wasn't scared of facing John Fashanu. A few days later, his phone rang, and on the other end of the line was Fashanu. "I hear you're not scared of me," he announced. "Well, I'll see you by the back post at five past three, where our heads will mince."

But now, they were a little different – better at football, worse at intimidation – and immediately United forced the issue. Keane stretched to intercept a pass in his own half, right of centre, before zipping over a challenge to pass fast and low to Yorke. The ball somehow went through him to Cole, who returned It fiist-time to Keane, somehow now at inside-right and legging it into the box. Looking up to see no support, he stopped and checked, billywrighting Kimble in the process, took a touch, and flagellated a delicate left-footed curler against the post.

Soon, though, the lead was taken. Beckham was permitted time to survey his options before lancing a ball straight through the middle for Cole, on the half-turn. Gathering it onto his left foot, he turned, and from the edge of the box, power-passed a shot beyond Sullivan with his right.

United spent the remainder of the first half creating and wasting a succession of chances, the pitch slick with drizzle and aiding the developing style. Getting forward quickly was nothing new, but the incisive, rhythmic passes and unpredictable movement were different to the aimless turns and turgid puffing of recent times. And after Brown cut in and cut across a shot from distance that whistled over the bar, the best of the opportunities. Keane, who'd scored for Ireland in midweek, was picked out in the middle of the box, but opening his body to side-foot a low cross from close range, insufficient elevation allowed two converging bodies to get it away.

Nonetheless, his was another excellent display; somehow he'd improved during the course of being injured. "He began to direct and distribute brilliantly, and was invariably in the right place at the right time," Schmeichel later recollected.

Then, out of nowhere, and with their first genuine attack, Wimbledon equalised. Cunningham's cross allowed Leaburn to hold the ball up with Stam behind him, before laying it off to the arriving Euell. His shot deflected against Stam and in at the near post.

But, possibly conscious of a half-time sermon strongly rebuking the immorality of wastefulness, United regained the lead in added time. Blomqvist set Cole away in the inside-left channel and Sullivan came out a long way and unnecessarily, practically forcing Cole to round him. Steadying on the byline, he moved the ball onto his right foot and looked for Yorke, who had overrun the optimal position, so, hanging on a moment longer for the retreat, he cut back for a certain goal – except that the shot was somehow and brilliantly cleared off the line by Blackwell.

Immediately, though, United snatched back possession, Keane winning a header and Cole getting a touch to send the ball out to Blomqvist. He crossed to the back post, where Giggs directed a firm header into the net.

Though Kinnear made two changes at the interval, it was too late, and it wasn't long before United scored again. The initial damage was done by another straight pass, this time from Gary Neville to Beckham, but there remained work still to be done. Collecting it inside the centre-circle, he advanced moving left and then right, before zooting a precise shot across Sullivan from fully 30 yards.

Just six minutes later, Blackwell allowed a goalkick to bounce, the ball seized by the leaping foot of Yorke. Chasing it towards the box, he let it bounce again and then again, swaying inside past Perry after shaping to go outside. Ten yards from goal, he cleverly sent Sullivan towards the far post as he slotted in at the near, wearing Blackwell's slide at the same time.

Wimbledon were now playing to keep the score social, and Brown, confident enough to race forward again, found Yorke, carried on past him, and accepted a ball from Cole lamping a second left-footer high and wide. And this was just another feature of another impressive display, deemed worthy of a *Match of the Day* recap and why not? Confident, classy, Mancunian and called Wesley, there was simply nothing not to like.

Next, on 54 minutes, Scholes met a weak goalkick with his chest, thrusting the ball forward to Cruyff who set Cole away in the inside-right channel. Waiting for Blackwell to come close, he then sprung at him, put the ball through his legs, finished into the far corner and ran off in celebration all along the same diagonal, diverging only to give the corner flag a firm shake. Though there was still more than half an hour to play, 5–1 was how it finished, the players slowing with Europe in mind.

Kenny Cunningham later explained that Wimbledon had tried to condense the play with a high line, only to find the adaptability of Cole and Yorke left them bereft of options. "You are always aware of Cole's pace over 20 to 30 yards if United play the ball in behind you. And Yorke can hurt you with the ball at his feet because he can roll you and bring others into play," he said, and he was half-right: both had shown the ability to do both.

But good performance or not, Fergie was still smarting from almost a month earlier. "I think the Arsenal game was one game which you get and I think we're back on the rails and we're playing like Manchester United is expected to play."

This was not lost on Brondby manager Ebbe Skovdahl, who was in the stand. "I can't shut my eyes without seeing United score goals!" he semi-joked – and he'd have been as well enjoying the daytime respite, because come Wednesday evening, opening them would yield identical results.

*

Travelling to Brondby for a meeting of Denmark's two best-supported clubs, United were without the injured Irwin, Johnsen, May and Sheringham, and the suspended Butt and Beckham. Giggs took Beckham's spot on the right, with Blomqvist stopping on the left, and Scholes coming in, while in defence, Gary Neville partnered Stam. So Phil was at left-back and Wes Brown made his European debut on the other side, the pleasure of watching a young player develop unhindered in the absence of several thousand blogs claiming defini-tive authority as to his potential. "He's got the temperament," said Fergie, "and that sometimes makes your mind up for you."

It was also a big night for Peter Schmeichel, returning not only to the team but to his former club, with whom he still trained when visiting Copenhagen. Brondby were without John Jensen, suspended after being booked in both previous European games – the second time in the Nou Camp – for diving in the area. But they were with Ebbe Sand, who, between scoring the World Cup's fastest ever goal by a substitute and appearing in this game, had recovered from testicular cancer.

Live television coverage was a reward for living in the Granada area – for those elsewhere, there wasn't even radio commentary – and came with the fringe benefit of Steve Bruce and a beige-suited Bryan Robson in the studio, discussing the role of Scholes. "This fella, as Bryan and I know, is a terrific footballer," said Bruce. "He always has been since a kid... got an unbelievable football brain."

Though United were now in exceptional league form, the game was expected to be a taxing engagement – despite hammering Brondby in pre-season, they'd taken a hammering themselves for the first part of that game. And now, bottom of the group, they were in severe need of a win in this one, "there's no question about that".

The pitch looked like a mowed 3g effort, but inhabited by moles, and the weather was just as much a mess, parky in the Parken. And the sheeting rain, swirling wind and cold would only get worse, Stam, Keane and Gary Neville showing themselves as the dignified conscience of the team by retaining their short sleeves nonetheless.

With only two minutes gone, Brown galloped down the right and tossed over a cross that was easy enough for the keeper to collect – except, in front of him, Rasmussen made to clear before diving underneath it when there was no need. Still, and despite the heavy tracksuit bottoms weighing him down, he ought to have collected – but instead, he fumbled into the path of the onrushing Giggs, who couldn't help but score on the half-volley.

As they ought not to, United barely noticed the conditions, the confidence harvested in Munich sustaining. On 11 minutes, Yorke, Scholes, Blomqvist and Phil Neville linked up on the left, patiently exchanging passes until Scholes was ready to move things on to the advancing Keane, who touched off first time to Cole on his left. His shot across the keeper was pushed away, but not without difficulty.

Brondby were still to construct an attack of note – they "seemed nervous, in awe of us even", wrote Gary Neville – and on 18 minutes United ought probably to have scored again. With his back to goal and just right of centre, Cole flicked a pass towards a pumping Keane, whose low cross picked out Yorke. Rather than roll the ball on one more to Blomqvist, he elected to shoot, dragging wide.

But United pushed forward again, Yorke winning a throw down in the left corner. Taken by Phil Neville back to Blomqvist, his deep cross was perfect for Giggs, leaping at it early and hard to thud a header beyond Krogh, his third such goal of the season and an upgrade on the weekend's, taking him ahead of Bryan Robson and Mark Hughes in the club's all-time list.

Immediately after the goal, a first of many: Brown premiering the skill that would later take his name, wesleying Jensen onto a stretcher and down the tunnel, all within the laws of Association Football. Having announced himself against Leeds the previous season with a Cruyff turn, in his first incarnation, he was a silkier technician than would be his ultimate reputation but following a few injuries and errors, he focused principally on the joyous abandon of the wesley. This, along with a wondrous performance against Barcelona in 2008, would be his lasting contribution to the tradition.

Next, another United break. Giggs ferreted infield, and found Scholes outside him, and, from an acute angle, cut across a shot that skidded just wide of the far post. But Brondby could not get away with it for long. Scholes picked up a loose throw-in just outside his own box, weaving some space before feeding Keane, who knocked off immediately to Giggs, on the right. There was still little danger when he wafted a pass at Yorke, but one leaping clavicle control and turn later, he was easing away from the substitute Da Silva and pushing forwards for Cole, close to his left. Wriggling back inside a mystified Rasmussen, he opened his body and punched in yet another difficult side-footed finish. "This looks like a combination doesn't it, now, Yorke and Cole… they're bedding in nicely together," inadvertently observed Clive Tyldesley.

Prior to the game, Brondby's keeper Mogens Krogh had been in the papers telling them that he didn't rate Cole, who would never score past him. After the game, Brondby's keeper Mogens Krogh had been in the tunnel telling the United players that he'd been misquoted, after Cole had scored past him.

Game effectively decided, it was time for the exhibition stuff, and on 31 minutes Scholes dived in on Ravn, avoiding a booking, before stroking his studs across Colding's ankle, again without due recognition. But this gave Brondby a free-kick near the right corner of the box, Lindrup's left-footer taken too quickly for the referee's liking, which, deemed deserving of a card, meant that he would miss the return. Daugaard then took over kicking duties for the retake, and with his right, dribbled a minorly awkward, bouncing effort around the wall towards the near post, Schmeichel flopping to pat the ball down and past him, first crowded by the woodwork and then half wrapped around it.

By the time the second half began, the wind was baying into the faces of the United players, but they continued to press, Cole electing to shoot after turning on the edge of the box and Giggs dangling a foot at a Stam pass, outraging Ian St John in the commentary box. Then, a few minutes later, Lindrup nutmegged Stam along the left byline without having contemplated what he might do next, suddenly befuddled by circumnavigational issues.

United's next break was led by Yorke, finding Blomqvist, who did well to move infield and nudge to Giggs. With only one defender attending the middle, it looked as though another goal was unavoidable, but the cross was too long for Cole, and Giggs was unable to resolve the ensuing scramble. "There's never a dull moment with Manchester United in Europe these days," Tyldesley asserted, and for a while, there wasn't.

Then, on 55 minutes, the highlight. Cole plucked Brown's lofted pass from the air and spread to Blomqvist, his cross was headed clear by Da Silva to Keane, 50 yards from goal, right of centre. His first touch was perhaps a little heavy, in the absence of a tackle, he moved the ball perfectly into his stride and ducked inside a wild attempt at a block after feinting to shoot. Taking another touch, he then jabbed a pass right to Yorke, hurdled another attempted block, and moved onto the return, slotting hard past Krogh to score off the post. It was his first goal in more than 13 months.

Immediately, United launched into a further attack, Giggs locating Cole's feet, and with his back to goal. Turning his man on the outside, he took a further touch before punishing a shot straight into the keeper's visage. The fifth goal was not, however, far in the distance. Gary Neville headed a clearance to Cole who transferred the ball wide for Blomqvist and wider still to Phil Neville, pegging down the line to flight a left-footed cross on the run – precisely the skill he was told to improve when ejected from England's World Cup squad after being assured that he was in it. It met Yorke's movement perfectly, and a leaping, thudding header, too strong for the keeper to hold, made the score 5–1.

Giggs and Cole then departed, the former by earlier arrangement, to be replaced by Cruyff and Solskjær – and a minute later, United scored again. Keane loped a pass into Yorke, which he allowed to hit his knee, turning it slightly to coincide with the stride of Solskjær. It was still barely a chance, but from just outside the box he scudded a glorious first touch into the bottom-right corner with minimum fuss and maximum prejudice.

The remainder of the game was relatively quiet. Mark Wilson came on for his debut, in the absence of Beckham, Irwin and Giggs, Keane got a go at a free-kick, and after Schmeichel was late to get down to a shot from distance, he consoled himself by allocating Brown his first going-over. Then, in stoppage time, and just after Keane had tanked back half the length of the pitch to double-team Bagger with Stam, United conceded another goal, Sand tapping home after Bagger's initial shot was palmed into his path.

Though it had been another iffy night for Schmeichel, it didn't really matter – the team was now good enough to absorb individual errors. It had enjoyed a similar run the previous autumn, but thanks to excellent finishing more than irresistible combinations. But now, though, with a spine fortified by two ideal signings and the returning Keane, its other elements could function at a high level regardless of who actually comprised them. The consequence was hidings of this ilk, ones that didn't just look pretty but prompted re-evaluation of what was possible, and even likely; while the finishing had been exceptional, the passing still had plenty of room for improvement.

*

And there was more good news from Munich where Stefan Effenberg's goal on the stroke of half-time was enough to give Bayern a win over Barcelona. United were now top of the group.

*

The weekend's trip to Derby was harder than it seemed, United with only one win over them in the four games since their promotion. They'd had an odd start to the season, drawing three in a row, winning three in a row and losing three in a row, which prompted a change in approach. Configuring his team in a 3–4–3 formation, Jim Smith ordered his forwards to pressure United's defenders in possession and gave Deon Burton his first start, following a goal as sub the previous week. And alongside him were Wanchope and Sturridge, both capable of troubling accomplished defenders, particularly those on the downside of a midweek European schlep. But the back four remained the same, United's only changes coming in midfield where Beckham and Butt replaced Blomqvist and Scholes.

Kick-off was delayed 15 minutes due to congested traffic, and the game took a similar form, with little of note created in the opening quarter of an hour. After two minutes, Yorke had a shot deflected behind, and on ten, Schnoor was booked for fouling Beckham, to immense local rage. Things improved a little after that, Brown blocking Sturridge's shot and the returning Stimac just off with a header from the resultant corner, before Brown belted over from distance, narrowly, and Schnoor belted over from close, unnecessarily. Then, Cole was shown a yellow card after encroaching at a free-kick and was fairly fortunate not to incur a second for obstructing Sturridge just outside the box.

Derby created various opportunities in the second period, aided by the half-time introduction of Tony Dorigo, newly signed from Torino. Wanchope headed straight at Schmeichel when he might have done better, and two more Brown blocks – one to a shot from Burton and one to a header from Wanchope – kept the game goalless.

But just when it looked like Derby were out of juice, missing the guile of the injured Bohinen, they scored the goal that their superiority deserved. Delap, under no pressure in the middle of the pitch, was allowed to move the ball wide to Dorigo, who approached Brown, pushed towards his outside and back-heeled for Powell at the left corner of the box. He crossed immediately, and Stam, drawn out of the middle, was unable to get a head to it, leaving Phil Neville with both Wanchope and Burton to mark. Opting to stand around instead, he finished marooned between the two, and Burton tapped in.

Going behind was precisely the catalyst for which United were aching, and after it, they generously elected to start playing. With nine minutes to go, a triple substitution: Giggs, who hadn't looked fit and wasn't, went off – he'd miss the next month – and so did Butt and Gary Neville. On came Blomqvist, Scholes and Cruyff; "When you're down you have to do things like that," said Fergie afterwards.

And with the fresh legs came fresh impetus, United moving the ball faster and wider, Cruyff managing to block Blomqvist's goal-bound shot. Then, with four minutes to play, Stam hared into the Derby half and slid a ball down the line for Brown. Protecting it by keeping his back to play, he feinted to follow it before stepping back the other way around the corner to fool Sturridge and enable a cross with his left. But seeing Cruyff on the edge of the box, dead centre, he dinked a ball for him to cushion down for Yorke, close by. A touch to control and a return tap, then a touch for Cruyff to set himself as the ball rolled across his body, and he dragged a deceptively decent shot across Hoult and into the far corner.

Reserve team aficionados had been praising the form of Cruyff for a while, a man described by Fergie as "one of the most talented players I have handled." While that might have been generous, things might have worked out differently; he was, by all accounts, a nice boy, and had inherited some genes from his father though his refusal to wear the family name on the back of his shirt spoke badly of his ability to succeed under pressure. But the problems were of comfort and conviction. He had no desire to leave Barcelona, and even the inconceivably nice Phil Neville ribbed his proclivity for exaggerating injuries and the desire to protect them by not playing – perhaps the same lack of confidence that hindered his play.

Despite the little time that remained, United almost skanked a win, but it would have been undeserved. "I wish Derby had scored 25 minutes earlier," said Ferg, "because our reaction was good." Instead, pointed questions were raised on the terraces about the team's away form, Yorke's ability to score away from home, and the manager's ability to time his substitutions properly.

*

Despite the self-righteous bleating and parliamentary questions that followed nobodies like the fledglings Neville, Butt, Beckham and Scholes being picked to play in the 1994-95 League Cup, using it to give young players a chance is now accepted as a clever innovation. Obviously, it's nice if they happen to be good enough, but even those who aren't get the chance to improve and earn a move elsewhere – and it was that ilk playing for United against Bury, though Phil Neville was convinced that Erik Nevland would become a great player. But he was on the bench, as was Scholes – starting were John Curtis, Michael Clegg, Mark Wilson, Jonathan Greening and Phil Mulryne, with van der Gouw, Phil Neville, Berg (c), May, Cruyff and Solskjær making up the numbers.

Bury, meanwhile, had Dean Kiely in goal, making his second appearance at Old Trafford – the first was for York in what shall forever be known as the McGibbon game, one of the most vivid nightmares that the ground has ever witnessed. Managed by everyone's favourite and least favourite anagram, Neil Warnock, they would be relegated at the end of the season, an injustice for which he held Morph and the Hoover Dam jointly responsible.

Despite a downpour that stood out even in Manchester's wettest October on record, 52,000 people turned up – 8,000 of them Bury fans, 3,500 more than their average home attendance for the season. And they were treated to a thoroughly forlorn game, on a pitch that was sick and tired, despite the 50,000 blue-nosed worms (really!) scattered onto it in the summer in an effort to improve drainage having no apparent effect.

Of the United youngsters, Greening was easily the most impressive, testing Kiely with a cross-shot and tricking his way into the box to chip goalwards, an effort almost headed into his own goal by Manchester City hero Steve Redmond. In between times, Johnrose surprised van der Gouw with a volley, hooked only just wide from the edge of the box, but otherwise, Bury were mainly forced onto the defensive.

Nevland replaced Mulryne at half-time, missing a good opportunity from close range, and then on 69 minutes, Brown and Scholes came on for Clegg and Wilson. But at full-time, there were still no goals, visiting a further half-hour upon everyone. Then, just as they were wondering whether it was legitimate to hope for the relative excitement of penalties, United scored the kind of goal that caused them to wonder what they'd been playing at during the previous 105 minutes. Neville broke through midfield and away from Johnrose, finding Greening wide on the right. Unchallenged, he advanced, but towards goal, squaring to Solskjær in the D, who whipped a finish past Kiely, in off the base of the far post.

Greening ought really to have sealed the win, easing past two defenders before hitting the post, but, with four minutes remaining United scored again. Brown exchanged passes with Neville down the right and stunned a low, diagonal cross that ran all the way to the back post, where Nevland slid home.

The following day, a victory – or partial victory – of far greater significance. Peter Mandelson announced that Sky's bid to purchase United would, on the advice of the Director General of Fair Trading, be referred to the Monopolies and Mergers Commission, scheduled to report its findings in March. This was not at all what Sky or the board had expected when they announced the deal, giving Rupert Murdoch no choice but to experience a tantrum during a press conference – though, of course, he had no involvement in the scheme. And a month later, Mandelson, the one Cabinet member sympathetic to his cause, was forced out of office after failing to declare a loan accepted from the Paymaster General. Oh, how they wept.

Next, United travelled to Goodison Park, a ground on which they had been unable to win between 1981 and 1990, before embarking on a run of seven from nine, as Everton slid. Avoiding relegation the previous season by virtue only of a goal difference superior to Bolton's, the club fired Howard Kendall and replaced him with Walter Smith, who had retired, but found the lure of the job too strong.

And Smith made an inauspicious start, Everton 15th in the table with only two wins, top of the bookings table, and yet to score at home. An *Observer* headline later in the season would pair "Boring, boring, boring, boring, boring, boring, boring Everton, (that's one boring for every 0–0 draw at Goodison Park so far this season)," with "nil satis nil-nil", acumen that would earn Smith an Old Trafford coaching gig in the spring of 2004.

But, within seconds of kicking off Everton created a scoring opportunity, Ferguson forcing a smart save from Schmeichel and seeing his follow-up blocked by Stam. "Always a menace to Manchester United!" exclaimed Ian Crocker, his sentence double the necessary length.

United's passing then took over for a period, but the next opportunity of note also fell to Everton, Bakayoko fooling Brown and laying back for Collins to shoot, foiled by a perfectly-timed Scholes tackle. Short was then booked for barrelling into him and Materazzi avoided the same despite hoofing Cole.

Shortly afterwards, Schmeichel attempted to find Keane with a lofted pass which went over his head into touch and resulted in a concerted barney. Unfinished as play resumed, Keane was forced to attempt an amputation on the nearest man to him, in order to get back on with it. For this he received a yellow card, the defence that it was his first yellow card-deserving offence failing to persuade the referee into clemency. "One of the biggest tempers I've ever met in my life," went Lee Sharpe's perfect personification.

Within minutes United were ahead, Scholes spotting Cole dropping off and firing a pass into him, popped off to Blomqvist. Accepting a return by the left corner of the box, he turned and flighted a clip over the Everton defence to where Scholes was now deep into its opposite side. Dangling the softest of side-foots, the ball went square and squarely into the path of the arriving Yorke, who poked at it awkwardly and unnecessarily with his right foot, straight at Myhre, who saved – but presented it straight back to his left which this time he used to slam into the unguarded net.

"Nobody realised Dwight Yorke was such a prolific scorer!" marvelled Crocker, as though he'd been at it on the sly all along. But the reality was that this was a new and unpredictable development, aided by every chance occurrence proceeding in his favour.

And United set about Everton once more, Keane sparking a Cole–Yorke one-two that featured movement beyond the comprehension of their markers and drew a brilliant tackle from Unsworth as Cole prepared to shoot. Like Yorke, Unsworth had forced a move from Aston Villa once the season had started, his on account of homesickness, which was also not appreciated by John Gregory. "We sent him home today, from training," he told the press, "because I think his wife said he had to be home at one o'clock for his dinner… something like that, so we let him go."

Unsworth then bungled a cross as Everton attempted a response, Stam collecting possession and finding Scholes, who angled quickly into Yorke. Turning, he set Keane away through the centre-circle, who slid a pass inside Cadamarteri for Blomqvist. Feinting to centre and cutting inside, sending his man sliding off the wrong way, though he then pulled his pass, it carried all the way to Beckham on the opposite touchline, who redirected it back to the middle, where Watson leapt to clear, and missed. Consequently, the ball hit the unprepared Short behind him, and dropped into the net, the ground filled with confused silence and a giant Roy Keane grin.

Keane was then penalised for a foul on Cadamarteri, out on the right touchline but well inside the United half. Typically, he delegated the marking of Ferguson to himself, but Ball's cross was perfect and Ferguson met it on the run, too much even for Keane, and stuck a header past Schmeichel. That would be his last goal of his first spell at Everton – he would play for them only three more times before being sold, to his vast distress and without the knowledge of Walter Smith, by chairman Peter Johnson.

And Ferguson nearly scored again, rising alone to meet Cadamarteri's high cross and heading narrowly wide. Then Scholes, increasingly influential, leaned back and snapped a dink to Beckham on the touchline, who, spotting Unsworth racing in to tackle, nipped the ball left and dashed right to collect. With his man prone in a scrotum-splitting star-shape, he turned to share with him a wide-mouthed cackle at what had just come to pass before continuing on his way.

But Everton began the second half well, and when Cadamarteri was felled, Collins took the opportunity to curl a free-kick towards Ferguson at the back post. The task of supervising him had passed to Stam, who in his eagerness to keep the ball out of harm's way, craned his cranium into a back-header, diverting the ball against the post – and wide.

Back came United, Yorke drawing a foul from Watson on the left touchline, the free-kick taken quickly to Beckham on the right. Quickly, Unsworth ignored the ball and stamped over it, studs meeting foot and elbow chin, earning himself a booking, while Beckham flicked a substantial gob in his direction.

As the half wore on, Everton assumed the ascendancy, so United scored another. Keane and Stam double-teamed Dacourt just outside the centre-circle, the ball breaking for Scholes to advance and slip left to the unmarked Blomqvist. Spotting Cole's run towards him, diagonal and in behind the defence, he stepped into a pass to meet it down the side of Watson, eliminating a stride to ensure perfect timing. This allowed Cole a moment to assess his precise position, wait for the ball to arrive, and sweep a finish across Myrhe in off the post, for his fifth goal in five games.

And still Everton attacked, winning a corner taken short to Cadamarteri, whose cross was headed away by Gary Neville and dropped straight to Collins on the edge of the box. Shaping to unleash a left foot volley, the very instant he missed his kick, Beckham and Keane were onto him like wild dogs – as Fergie once said, Keane wasn't the fastest player, but he was the fastest to the ball.

But it was Beckham's initial touch that won possession, Keane first securing it by rotating his legs at the knees as he ran and then transferring it from behind to in front, spinning his body in the process before righting to set Beckham free. Gauging the precise elevation and force necessary, and with Yorke also available, Beckham chipped a pass over the top onto Blomqvist's left foot, but Myrhe was out quickly to block his shot – but the ball reared up behind him, and Blomqvist caught up. From an acute angle, he cleverly nodded it across the covering Watson and into the far corner, bouncing on the spot in delight at his first United goal before waving his sleeved arm about a bit.

Now full of confidence, Blomqvist was even wandering inside, facing Dacourt in the centre-circle and dancing right without the ball, then dancing left and taking it with him, leaving Dacourt seated on the grass. His reluctance to leave Parma had been no secret – perhaps only Cruyff had wanted to join United less – and after the game, he would have the brass neck to inform *Match of the Day* that until he joined, he "didn't really know the players were that skilful, individually good". But, for the first time in some time, United had a genuine locum for Giggs, whose extended absence coincided with the destruction of the previous season.

In stoppage time, with the Park End half-empty, the Gwladys chucked a selection of bottles towards Schmeichel, causing a short pause, before Keane directed Beckham and Brown into some keep-ball that worked a chance for Scholes, bouncing through midfield and clumping a low drive against the bottom of the post. At the start of the season, many felt his best position was behind a striker, another reason for the antipathy towards Sheringham, and for England he had excelled as the most attacking of a midfield three. But this game offered compelling evidence that he was best deployed right in the centre of the pitch, not playing on the half-turn but with the play in front of him, to make best use of his extensive expertise: shooting, timing, range and subtlety, as well as the rare ability to make others perform better. Though he would not quite come of age as a dominator until Keane declined, he was now a proper footballer.

NOVEMBER

Start of the season's busiest month so far, Champions League group game, at home, against opposition whose dinner money you brutally taxed in shocking fashion just two weeks previously: one change from the weekend. One fine day, momentum outranked rotation, and with the win at Goodison taking United to second place in the table, a point behind Villa, Irwin regained his place at the expense of Brown, and that was that. The consequence was another hiding.

Things had not gone well for Brondby since their first encounter with United. First, they'd lost in the league to Denmark's bottom team, and then watched local rivals FCK give a much more sensible account of themselves in a narrow Cup Winners' Cup defeat to Chelsea. Expecting further victimisation, they added a midfielder and subtracted a striker, John Jensen back from suspension and the nickname "Faxe" on his jersey – the name of a local beer poured over him as part of an initiation when he was a young player – with an "I saw John Jensen score" t-shirt underneath. Elsewhere, goal-keeper Krogh skived, replaced by Andersen, and the splendidly-named Aurelijus Skarbalijus also got a go. Refereeing was Lubos Michel – at 31, younger than plenty of the players, and who would preside with distinction over the 2008 final.

For the first time in the season it was now thoroughly cold, forcing Schmeichel to team his donkey top with a pair of tracksuit bottoms, and he was barely involved in the opening exchanges, United knocking the ball around patiently before injecting a little more tempo. With six minutes gone, Scholes found Cole, and when he was held by Rasmussen, Beckham approached to take the free-kick, 30-odd yards out and parallel to the left edge of the box. Though Brondby had wound themselves up pre-match by watching United's shooting prac-tice, it was felt that a three-man wall offered adequate protection. So

Beckham's effort curved where a fourth would have stood and away from Andersen's dive, dipping sharply and hitting the ground as it passed – not dissimilar to his equaliser against Leicester.

Then, on nine minutes, the rarity of a Roy Keane error, casually accepting possession in his own box, losing it, and having to watch as Schmeichel scrambled the loose ball behind. But United cleared the corner comfortably enough, after which Scholes filched Jensen with a sliding tackle, knocking the ball into Cole who squared for Yorke to skid a searching pass forward for Keane, pacing along the left wing in the manner of billy-o. He flighted a return cross to the penalty spot, where Nilsen's desperate defensive header hit the post and arrived at the feet of Cole, whose shot was blocked by Bagger's desperate midriff.

But Brondby could not survive for long, and on 13 minutes, Scholes again won possession in United's half, this time finding Keane, whose pass went through Coling to Blomqvist. Running away from Ravn, he checked to survey his options before firing low into Cole, who stepped over to leave for Yorke, ahead of him but on the same diagonal – and thoroughly hoodwinking his marker. Yorke then allowed the ball across his body to rebound off his foot, its path the second side of a triangle and Cole's run the third, the two meeting in front of goal where a gentle right-footed touch set up a delicately chipped left-footed finish, over the keeper's dive and between his body and the near post, for another majestically crafted goal.

And there was more. Two minutes later, United won a free-kick in their own half, bumped wide to Phil Neville and one further to Beckham, Neville continuing his run and checking behind him to see a return ushered his way. Moving it into his stride, he adjusted to move infield and accelerated into space, another wall-pass off Yorke eliciting another perfect return, this time with added spinning flourish. It allowed him to take one more touch, advance into the area, drill past Andersen and carry on running, high-stepping and arm-waggling before winding up flat on his back by the corner flag. Which was where he met Keane, who acquainted studs with thigh and toe with arse, to remind him.

With red shirts darting all over, Brondby knew not what to do, waiting 23 minutes to manage a shot. And after Bagger sliced wide, United took over again, Andersen tipping Cole's header over the top, his first save of the evening.

Phil Neville soon departed with a hamstring strain, replaced by Wes Brown. Before he could adjust, Rasmussen broke forward and crossed low for Sand, Schmeichel diving the wrong way but managing to save with his feet. This encouraged the Brondby fans, who spent most of the rest of the game chanting "yellow blue army" responsively, interspersed with English renditions of "Stand up if you hate Man U" and "Who's the wanker in the black".

Fergie would later assert that the first half was the finest of his time in charge, which, given a bedraggled opposition as yellow as its shirts seemed a bit much. Nonetheless, the savage manner in which they had been obliterated, in another extreme burst of competence, ambition and invention, was worthy of note.

It was certainly the finest half that Blomqvist would ever play for United, withdrawn at the interval and replaced by Cruyff, precipitating what Ron Atkinson described as "a second half sleeping-in period". Brondby did improve, though without accomplishing much beyond that, and it wasn't until 52 minutes that United had a proper shot, Beckham catching Jensen in possession 40 yards from goal, motoring past him, left past the next man and right past the one after, before curling a shot just wide from the edge of the box.

Solskjær then came on for Cole as ITV showed Yorke's goal, overwhelmed by the confusing nature of the situation, and Jensen tried chipping Schmeichel to hilarious hilarity, by which time it was also caning down with rain. Then, just after the hour, Scholes allowed a Beckham free-kick to roll down his right side and set off, using its pace to flick outside the first man towards the right side of the area, managing the deviation when it clipped his heel, then feinting to shoot and stumbling inside the second, now cutting across the box and retaining complete control. Approached by a third man, again he feinted to shoot, ducked outside and turned back in, before picking a finish inside the near post with the keeper forced to forsake it. A deluxe version of his goal in Munich, Scholes had now scored against all three group opponents and United had now scored a Champions League record 16 group stage goals, with two-and-a-bit games still to play.

"It was a true team display and you can't fault it," said Fergie in the tunnel afterwards, and even Roy Keane thought things were going well. Though he still rated the 93-94 side as the best he'd played in, on the Friday of that week, he told the press that the squad was the strongest he'd ever known. "The fear factor is there," he said, "a fear that you will lose your place if you let your standards drop even a fraction."

*

The Newcastle game, on a Sunday 4pm, marked the 12th anniversary of Fergie's appointment. "I am the last of a dying breed," he said when asked for his thoughts. "I just can't see another manager lasting 12 years in a job."

United were now four points behind leaders Villa, who had beaten Spurs 3–2 the previous day, midweek signing Dion Dublin scoring twice on his debut. Elsewhere, Liverpool lost at home to Derby, and at West Ham, Chelsea's Pierluigi Casiraghi suffered a career-ending injury. Then, in Sunday's early game, Nicolas Anelka's early thump was enough to give Arsenal a win over Everton, putting them just a point behind United.

Newcastle were now managed by Ruud Gullit, some supporters still turning up in wacky dreadlock wigs, and he surprised Fergie with his team selection, picking as many quick, tough players as he could deny them time and space.

Though the only change from Brondby was Brown for Phil Neville, United never really got going – and with limited excuse, given the ease with which that game was won, at home, and by half-time. As against Derby, they wasted the majority of the first half and were lucky not to concede a penalty six minutes before the break when Irwin careered into Dalglish as he pursued a Shearer flick-on. Then, at the start of the second and under pressure from Shearer, Wes Brown played a back-pass without checking who was where, Dalglish intercepted and set off towards goal – but was denied by Schmeichel.

United stirred after that, Cole chesting down Brown's chipped pass to shoot over the bar before overhitting a pass that would have provided Scholes with an easy opportunity. Even so, Johnsen for Brown was a peculiar first change, and he was soon nailed by an already-booked Shearer, vaulting into him with studs up and putting him out for the next four weeks. But an angry letter to *Red Issue* wanted to make clear Johnsen's responsibility for his own demise, spurning the gift of a challenge 60–40 in his favour and with it the opportunity to hammer Shearer into the North Stand, all good and legal. "I use the word 'tackle' lightly," it chided, "because I can at best describe it as some old tart testing the water in the bath with her big toe." This allowed Shearer to do the same to him – illegally, and without due punishment – but luckily, Keane was on hand to address the issue, crumpling him not before time and not long before time.

In between, Beckham spurned United's best chance, at the end of their best move. A quick Keane pass found Scholes, who squared to Neville, charging through the centre-circle. Measuring a perfect through-ball, he put Beckham in on goal, but moving left and on his left foot, he attempted a deliberate finish into a small gap between goalie and post, the effort going just wide. "I'm not really the man for one-on-ones," he would admit a few years later after preferring to chip the Birmingham keeper from 25 yards, rather than carry the ball close and beat him in any one of the numerous easier ways available.

"That performance begged questions about playing games after European matches," said Fergie afterwards, not indicating how he expected this purported problem to be overcome. But he also praised Gullit for a "brave selection" and his team for how well they played, observing that "they were terrific… for a side that is supposed to be struggling, they showed great confidence."

*

The 10th of November. Ah, the 10th of November. On the 10th of November 1998, Manchester City lost to Wycombe Wanderers, who had only been in the Football League since 1993.

The next evening, Nottingham Forest visited Old Trafford in the League Cup fourth round, United needing 57 minutes to take the lead. Greening, on the right flank, came inside and invited a challenge, rolling a pass into Cruyff when it arrived, dead centre and 35 yards from goal. Spotting Solskjær moving off the shoulder of his man and across the defensive line, he allowed it to come onto his left foot before sliding a diagonal ball between the centre-backs to meet his run. A touch to control and consider, a pause to look Dave

Beasant up and down, the ball then slotted in at the near post as the keeper dived to the far, just like that.

Then, three minutes later, Butt broke from deep and found Cruyff, still in the United half and just to the right of the centre-circle. Moving inside, he noticed Solskjær wide on the left and pulling away, so zipped him a canny ball inside the right-back, manoeuvred expertly into his stride from just behind, before it was, again, deposited smack-bang into the onion bag.

The goals were a perfect illustration of what Rio Ferdinand once said of Solskjær: "He had a clear picture of the game, no grey areas… black and white, bang: this is the way I see it." Some players are good when required to act in the moment, but given time to ponder, find it harder, while to Solskjær it made no odds. He never foxed himself and never panicked, his finishing the perfect combination of instinct and intellect. He described his footballing identity as a composite – "take the best out of everyone and mould it into me" – so, natural, focused and composed, he needed no time to play himself in, and no less a judge than Peter Schmeichel rated him the best finisher he played with.

With 22 minutes remaining, Steve Stone thumped one into the top-left corner from 30 yards, but United were able to see the game out. Meanwhile, at Anfield, Liverpool were eliminated by Spurs, their predicament clearly caused by the bloke who was doing fairly well until a partner was foisted upon him. Accordingly, the board accepted Roy Evans' resignation the following morning, dumping Gérard Houllier in sole charge.

That same day and to the shock of his team-mates, Peter Schmeichel announced that he was to leave United at the end of the season, his body no longer able to cope with the strain. Oddly, though he was the only unarguable all-time great in the squad, he was its weakest player in its best season, and though he never let on, you have to wonder whether this was what really prompted him to leave. In spring, he claimed to have been untroubled by the grief he'd justifiably attracted through autumn and winter, but it's hard to believe that the arrogance underpinning his talent subsumed his grasp of reality, rather than forced it home.

But either way, his overall contribution to the club was of rare brilliance, oddly enhanced by perviousness to error. To make the mistakes that he did and still be perhaps the best that there's ever been speaks even more highly of the brilliance of his brilliance.

Far from an unknown when he signed, his remaining at Brondby until 27 was odd even then, though to United's advantage – he later cited his gradual progression as a reason for how good he became. Though United had tried to sign the previous season, they'd baulked at an asking price of £1.2m, but, as he would in different circumstances with Ruud van Nistelrooy, Fergie travelled to Denmark, assured his man that he remained his man, and Schmeichel responded by playing the best season of his career to that point.

So the confidence with which he turned up was probably only to be expected. "I'm Peter Schmeichel and I'm as big as Man United", was how Steve Bruce described it, and it was an attitude probably necessary to succeed in the circumstances, if not one that was necessarily endearing. "Between you and me, I actually don't think I have any real weaknesses," he confided in his autobiography.

Even as a young player, the journalist Niels Rasmussen, who played with him at Gladsaxe, remembers someone with "an enormous amount of comfort in himself" – or, as John Jensen put it, "he believed in himself so much it was unbelievable". But this was tested when he was picked to make his professional debut – for Brondby against Porto, in the quarter-finals of the 1987 European Cup and in front of 80,000 people, after having previously played in front of not many more than 8,000. Hoping that somehow the game would be cancelled and he could escape, a moment of clarity led him to vow never to experience nerves again, the capacity to banish negativity in that manner a rare strain of mental strength.

Goalkeepers, like wicketkeepers, are often categorised as falling into one of two personality types – the obsessive weirdo, or the obsessive lunatic, and Schmeichel was very much in the latter category. Brian Kidd dubbed him "the Mad Mullah", while Andy Cole wrote that "from morning til midnight he was a complete nightmare" – and yet both did so with affection, Cole calling him United's "single most important player".

His combustible nature did, though, almost end his United career five years earlier, following a dressing room discussion with a manager unhappy with the concession of a three-goal lead at Anfield. Given that Fergie was attracted to his "enthusiasm and fanaticism" when signing him, and given the quality of the rows that were sometimes had, and given how they were generally forgotten by the coach ride home as a serious matter of policy, and given his nature, and given how good he was, it can only have been of truly spectacular proportions. "He was towering over me and the other players were almost covering their eyes," recounted Fergie. "I'm looking up and thinking 'if he does hit me, I'm dead!'"

"We've both got temperaments," was Schmeichel's deadpanned summation.

But despite his ego and even after being advised that he'd need to take his business elsewhere, he retained the humility to apologise properly to the squad. Luckily for him, Fergie was listening in, and now furnished with an excuse to forgive, did precisely that.

Just as well. His unparalleled skill at saving one-on-ones was not only useful but necessary in teams that ceded too many such opportunities, and he was also an integral attacking cog, the speed and accuracy of his throwing crucial to their epochal speed on the break.

In particular, his contribution in 1995–96 was crucial: "Cantona and I had a standing agreement which went more or less as follows," he recalled. 'Peter, I score one and you keep a clean sheet, OK?'" Though his display at Newcastle in March of that season was most significant, the one at Anfield in December was every bit as valuable, not in points, but in mental health; any other man in net that day, however good, and the 0–2 margin of defeat would've more than doubled. He'd have reinvented the art of goalkeeping but for the fact that no other man will ever be able to do it as he did.

Like Stam, Schmeichel was genetically blessed with the rare combination of immensity and dexterity, his ability to manoeuvre his hands up and down a piano as incredible as anything he accomplished on a football pitch. But they were hands that could also crush tracheas should they see fit, part of a presence as intimidating psychologically as physically.

And yet, of all United's Treble winners, Schmeichel is recalled with perhaps the least fondness. Some were suspicious of his spat with Ian Wright, and, more recently, he referred to Paolo Di Canio's fascist sympathies as "the political stuff the media's trying to catch him out on". And then there was his physical removal of celebrating United supporters from the pitch at Villa Park in 2002, followed by his later transfer to City – not that easy to understand in terms of his career. Accordingly, he was bracketed with Mark Hughes and Andrei Kanchelskis, rather than Denis Law and Andy Cole, whose moves were unrelished, but understood. He may now claim to have experienced no highlight in his time there, but that was not remotely how it appeared on 9 November 2002.

But fucking hell, did he keep some goal.

*

With the news about Schmeichel more bothersome with every mention of Mark Bosnich, Blackburn visited Old Trafford, a ground at which they hadn't won since 1962.

Ireland had a game away to Yugoslavia in midweek, so Irwin was left out and Keane on the bench. Consequently, John Curtis came in on the left of defence with Phil Neville on the right and Gary Neville continuing alongside Stam. In midfield, the two gingers were paired for the first time in the season, a reminder of the inordinate joy to be wrought from the fact that off Prestwich's Scholes Lane can be found Butt Hill.

Blackburn, meanwhile, were in trouble. Only two months earlier, Roy Hodgson had rejected an approach from the German FA, seeking a replacement for Berti Vogts, and Jack Walker had also been busy in the press warning off potential suitors. But neither show of faith altered the fact that their team were third from bottom with nine points from 12 games, following a run at the end of the previous season in which they lost nine of their final 14. And they arrived in Manchester without the injured Flitcroft and Sutton – a hindrance, apparently – and also Tim Flowers.

They did, however, have Kevin Davies up front, fresh from a spell at Southampton that caused his younger brother to be bullied at school on account of his uselessness and also including a predict-able winning goal against United. "He may look soft but he's a hard player – though not in a nasty way," wrote Phil Neville. Within three minutes, he had arrowed in on Scholes, two-footed.

It was about the only thing that happened in the opening stretch, United's passing not quite on-point on what was now a patchwork pitch, various strips pasted across its various bare bits. On 11 minutes,

Scholes fizzed a pass into Cole which he again let run for Yorke, who might have gone on – but instead, laid back a return pass, Henchoz managing to block the resultant shot.

Then, Beckham hit a searching diagonal ball towards Cole, Henchoz waving a head at it intending a diversion back to Filan, but Cole was able to scramble it away. With supporters behind the goal already celebrating, he somehow marmalised a finish against the near post, so hard that the ball went out for a throw on the opposite side.

But United were into it now, the combination of quick legs, feet and brains overwhelming. On 32 minutes, Dailly dallied and had the ball pinched from him by Yorke who shook him off to the horizontal, advanced to the edge of the box and slid in Scholes, free to his left – a pass obvious yet disguised by a prematurity that prevented Henchoz moving across to cover. Predictably, Scholes finished with precision, pulling across goal and into the side netting so perfectly as to force Filan to receive treatment, while Dailly audaciously went round clapping to gee up his less culpable team-mates. Scholes celebrated as best he could, successively hacking Johnson and punting Sherwood before play could stop, earning a yellow card.

Shortly afterwards, Filan rolled out to Kenna, only for Blomqvist to pursue him and win the ball. As Johnson came over to help and did not, he found Curtis, who squared for Scholes to move on to Phil Neville and then back inside to Beckham. Inspecting the lie, a feint bought him the angle to feed into Yorke who took a touch to control and then sent it back from whence it came. The next pass into him was immediate, so he hopped over the ball and skipped away, Butt turning it around the corner and into his path for him to panel across Filan and into the corner, completing yet another minor classic; has any team ever scored more?

Almost immediately after half-time, Davies lobbed a gentle kick at Stam as he returned a pass to Beckham, whose heel was clipped by Sherwood, playground-style. His rush to remonstrate was met with a forearm twitch to the sternum, Beckham electing to collapse clutching his face when he might perhaps have clanged him into the crowd and been done with it. A minor skirmish followed, both Nevilles upset, Schmeichel out of his goal and Damien Duff clearly aggravated by his captain's behaviour. "This is very unsavoury," sanctimonised Jon Champion.

As Beckham retained a low profile, now in dead lion pose, referee Mike Reed – of Erland Johnsen ghost penalty fame – waved the red card. But for Blackburn, this was a small price to pay for the services of a man who once prompted Jack Walker to wonder why Kenny Dalglish wanted to sign Zinedine Zidane "when we have Tim Sherwood?" In February, he left for Spurs.

But Gary Neville was not happy, later writing that "Every time we've played against him, there seems to be trouble. I didn't appreciate him spitting at me on his way off either." Accordingly, when he got home he insisted that his mum ring Mrs Sherwood to complain about her son's behaviour.

In the meantime Hodgson replaced Duff with Dario Marcolin, on loan from Lazio, while the crowd voiced its appreciation for Schmeichel, before, on 58 minutes, United scored again. A goalkick was taken short to Beckham and returned, the ball moving through Curtis, Gary Neville and then back to Beckham who fired a low pass crossfield to Blomqvist. Laid back for Butt, possession then went wide to Phil Neville and short for Beckham, whose lofted cross was back-headed clear by Kenna but only to Blomqvist. He sent in another cross which was again back-headed away by Kenna, the second ball nodded only as far as Beckham, now outside the box on the left. His touch to control was either too heavy or a perfectly cushioned pass for Cole, who, with his back to goal, flicked around the corner for Scholes to control on the half-turn, moving away from Peacock and across the face of the box. Playing a one-two with Yorke, he shaped to shoot and moved off again, making his way around the outside of the defence and arriving on the right of the box, swivelling to screw a low drive into the corner – another difficult finish executed with obvious ease for another minor classic, whose essence he'd reprise against the same opposition, at the same end and in more crucial circumstances, almost nine years later.

Once asked to recall the most important piece of advice he'd ever received, Scholes cited Eric Harrison: "always know where you are on a football pitch" – and this goal was a perfect illustration – but it was a lesson that probably didn't need teaching. "I've been born with the ability just to relax and be in the right place at the right time on the pitch, to be in the space that I create for myself," he explained. "I'm not the quickest of players so I need to have some other kind of ability and thankfully I've been born with a bit of ability to pass the ball and just be able to show a bit of patience."

Game considered over, United lapsed into immediate shoddiness, relieved to see Marcolin hook into the crowd after Croft's cross, before he headed in following a short corner. And Blackburn kept at it. Davies poked a ball through to Dailly, whose shot was blocked behind by Stam, precipitating a Schmeichel fit. The corner was again taken short, preparing for a cross aimed at Blake, recently signed from Bolton, and he sent a diving header into the net. Suddenly, United were hanging on, with 16 minutes still to play.

But Cruyff, on for Scholes, pulled a hamstring and departed for Keane, his influence preventing Blackburn from exerting too much pressure. Accordingly, the closing minutes passed without any major threat on United's goal save for a cross from Blake that missed everyone and was missed by everyone.

United remained second in the table, Dion Dublin's hat-trick against Southampton keeping Villa top. Also that afternoon, Leeds came from behind to win at Anfield, thanks in part to Alan Smith's first-touch debut goal, which left Liverpool in the bottom half of the table.

The following week, Blackburn were after a new manager, a spokesman announcing that "Jack Walker and Roy Hodgson have agreed that Roy will be leaving the club". Never one to mislay an opportunity to shtech, Fergie went in hard. "I wonder about it," he wrote in his review of the season. "Surely if there is one team to lose to without feeling disgraced it's Manchester United" – though Blackburn were beaten once more before the change. "Yet we have this kneejerk reaction and you wonder if there is a jealousy that gets through to a lot of people like Jack Walker and makes them react illogically."

Hodgson, meanwhile, blamed Sherwood's desire to leave for Spurs, and subsequently nurtured a complex as regarded his reputation in his home country, where, curiously, folk were not especially minded to recognise the enormity of his achievements at Halmstad and Malmö. "Of course, my track record, if people bothered to study it, would put me in the same category as Ferguson enjoys today," he told the *Independent* in 2002, "but people don't talk about what I've done outside England." Fortunately, he has since been able to add Liverpool and the national team to his list of abject triumphs.

The day before England's game with the Czech Republic, Andy Cole finally voiced his vex with Glenn Hoddle, who had left him out of the squad for that game and also for the World Cup, because he needed "five chances before he scores". Only a year earlier he had paid £7.5m for Kevin Davies.

"His behaviour towards me has been cowardly," Cole told the *Sun*. "He is a bad communicator. His comments about me are disrespectful. Is he a man or a mouse?"

The answer to the question, of course, depends on whether one is talking solely about this life or those which preceded it too, but either way, Hoddle's attitude towards Cole was bizarre, even for him. The logic of measuring a goalscorer not on the goals he scores but on those he does not is a particular peculiarity, and very much missed the point – Cole did miss a few chances, as all strikers do, but so many came his way by virtue of the alertness, anticipation and imagination that separated him from contemporaries. Nonetheless, Hoddle selected Emile Heskey and Dion Dublin ahead of him; "Dion Dublin was impeccable," he would tell the press after the game. "Anyone who suggested he is not an international player should be embarrassed."

Hoddle's position on Cole was and is shared by plenty, though he boasts a record matched by few; only Alan Shearer has more Premier League goals, and if you subtract penalties, Cole's per-game record is superior; and only Ryan Giggs and Dennis Bergkamp have more open-play assists. Or put another way, Cole was proper; of his generation, and without quite the same caustic pace and improvisational instinct, perhaps only Dwight Yorke could claim similar completeness, this the substructure of their equal partnership. His winner in the 2002 League Cup final, for Blackburn against Hoddle's Spurs and from only his third chance, was a genuine pleasure.

*

On the Friday of that week, United held its AGM – in the middle of the working day, of course, thereby excluding a significant swathe of regular folk. The meeting also featured the peculiar aspect of United's owners – a number of small shareholders – being evicted by paid employees, their agents – for distributing leaflets opposing the Sky bid.

As expected, Martin Edwards came under particular fire. Claiming that the 1,700 who showed up were not representative of those with minor stakes, when challenged as to the £88m he stood to make from the sale, he claimed, to much derision, that "money had nothing to do with" his desire to sell, on the basis that "once you get beyond a certain figure, money does not mean anything."

Michael Crick, of Shareholders United Against Murdoch, told the board that it had failed in its duty to inform shareholders of an option to dismiss the bid, whilst Adam Brown, one of the principal figures in the resistance, also spoke. "You are insulting our intelligence," he said, "if you suggest that the best thing for Manchester United is to become a subsidiary of a TV company," and another speaker harangued Edwards for his callousness. "We want to continue the traditions of Sir Matt Busby," she said. "Without us, you are nothing."

In the context, it was tricky to become too agitated by United's next game, at Sheffield Wednesday – a fixture capable of donating the willies to anyone old enough to remember 1985. And United had won only one league game at Hillsborough in the previous decade, a particularly spineless performance the previous season spurring a particularly ruinous run.

As was the custom, the Friday before the game saw the award of the pally – a yellow jersey presented to the day's worst trainer, and named in honour of legendary malingerer Gary Pallister. But when Dwight Yorke was announced as the winner, he launched into a vehement justification of his performance and then, in the shower, confessed to Peter Schmeichel that this was now one of the worst days of his life, almost reducing him to tears. Later on, as the team made their various ways to Sheffield, the manager was overtaken in dangerous fashion and both car and owner met Yorke's description. He was fined £500, though it later transpired not to have been him, and after the players decided that all this contributed to the game's outcome, it was also decided that yellow didn't suit his complexion.

A grey day at Hillsborough forced a strange light through the portals between the stands, "the old enemy Manchester United" drawing a near-capacity crowd some 6,000 above the season's next highest mark. Without a win since beating Arsenal, Wednesday were sixth bottom of the league with only 13 goals scored in 14 games. But they were not rubbish, and though Paolo Di Canio was still suspended, boasted the class of Benito Carbone and Wim Jonk. In goal, penalty king Kevin Pressman was injured, so Pavel Srnicek donned the famous dirty yellow and rust for the first time, while United made two changes, Irwin replacing Curtis and Keane returning for Butt.

The game started slowly, the only action worthy of note a lustrous pass from Keane, on the right touchline, that picked out Blomqvist on the left of the box. He controlled, turned inside Sonner, and curled over the top.

With neither side able to assert itself in the opening quarter of an hour, Scholes determined to intervene, catching Jonk minding his own business and sliding in to rap him across the shins. From close to the touchline on the Wednesday left and level with the bottom of the centre-circle, Hinchcliffe punted the free-kick towards Booth, but both he and Gary Neville missed their headers. This allowed Alexandersson to collect, who lost Irwin and moved infield, clubbing a shot from the edge of the box almost straight at Schmeichel, who caught it easily and then dropped it into the net, subsiding in pursuit to no avail.

But United came straight back, Cole heading wide from Blomqvist's cross, before another fallow quarter-hour, before an equaliser. Passes moved from Gary Neville through Stam, Phil Neville and Scholes then back to Gary Neville, and seeing a gap, he moved through it before finding Cole, left of centre and moving infield across the edge of the box. He laid off and inside to Yorke who performed a version of his signature trick, shaping to move the ball wide but instead stubbing a flip the other way, through the defence and back to Cole, who, eight yards out, hopped into a controlling touch with the little toe of his right boot and snaked across Srnicek, opening up the bottom corner of the net, found with another firm side-footer for another minor classic.

And United maintained the pressure, Blomqvist retreating deep and exchanging passes with Irwin, ahead of him and tight to the touchline. Accepting the return, he turned his back to Jonk – a move of preference – and spun into a pass, lofted into space for Yorke just inside the box, his thigh control taking it into Irwin's path. He controlled, squared up Alexandersson and dragged the ball past on the outside, tempting him to dive in with no hope of tackling fairly. "A legitimate penalty," admitted Danny Wilson afterwards, Fergie was reduced to impotent laughter when David Elleray saw nothing untoward.

It seemed for all the world that United were racking Wednesday up, more lovely football starting with a Yorke and Scholes one-two in midfield that expanded into a Scholes and Cole one-two, the ball zipping wide to Beckham whose cross forced Walker to head behind. From the corner, Stam headed back and good honest pro Scholes pushed it in with his hand – but unlike in the 2008 Super Cup, he'd somehow avoided an earlier yellow card, enabling him to escape a red here. But the incident triggered a light kerfuffle, Cole and Thome nuzzling foreheads.

At half-time there was a lot of shouting. "Keano began ranting and raving before we even had time to sit down", related Yorke. "He was having a go at Peter for having given away a soft goal. My team-mates were at each other's throats. Schmeichel and Keano had to be separated before coming to blows."

And Fergie wasn't exactly thrilled either. "What the fuck are you lot playing at?" he inquired. "That is the biggest load of shite I've ever seen. Not one of you can look me in the eye, because not one of you deserves to have a say. I can't believe you've come here and decided to toss it off like that crap you're playing out there."

So United were immediately on the attack after the restart, ball speeding between Keane, Yorke and Beckham, whose cross forced Des Walker into a desperate slide that inexplicably became a slice clear.

But then, on 55 minutes, Rudi, under no pressure, played a square pass to Alexandersson on the right wing, and his slow, low cross forced Schmeichel to dive at Booth's feet, loose ball arriving at Jonk, seven yards out, who tucked away an easy finish for Wednesday's second goal. Only Stam had been seriously concerned with its prevention.

As United chased an equaliser, a curious change saw Butt replace Blomqvist, United left with no pace out wide and not coming all that close to resolving matters. Cole knocked down an Irwin centre for Scholes whose shot was deflected away, and though Brown made an attacking difference when he came on, Schmeichel was soon forced to tip away Booth's chip. Yorke's shot from distance then went over the top and Beckham curled a low one just wide, before Wednesday scored the clincher.

Alexandersson, the obligatory boyhood United fan, rolled a ball into Carbone, who cleverly flicked it up and aimed an overhead pass towards Rudi. Beckham was there to intercept, nodding back to Stam but catching him on the wrong foot, moving right and his weight all on that side. This resulted in a heavy touch, and as he lunged in its retrieval, Alexandersson arrived, breaking through it, rounding Schmeichel, and rolling in.

Seventeen minutes still remained, but Wednesday came closer to a fourth goal than United did to a second. Jonk forced Schmeichel to tip over another chip after Keane was caught in possession, and Booth then lost Neville and went through on goal, forcing another save when really one should have been impossible. With the crowd cheering each home pass, it was no small relief when the final whistle arrived.

But full-time brought some good news: Arsenal had lost at Wimbledon. Elsewhere, less good news: Robbie Fowler's hat-trick had helped Liverpool to a 4–2 win at table-topping Villa, and Chelsea's win at Leicester by the same score allowed them to close the gap. They sat fourth, two points behind United, but with a game in hand.

"Unrecognisable and unacceptable," said Fergie of his team's effort, a sanitised version of thoughts shared in the dressing room and disproving once again the cliché that he never criticises his players in public. And referring to the midweek game in Barcelona, he added: "This was not on the agenda and you wonder whether we're a big-game team now because on Wednesday night we will probably excel."

*

"Four years ago Manchester United retreated from the Nou Camp stadium with their tails so far between their legs that the team could have been renamed Manx United," wrote the *Guardian*'s David Lacey the morning before the team went there again. But for the current expression, any lingering fear had been usurped by strut, and the morning after, his paper would salute a team of "cultured braves".

"We plan to have a right go at them," Fergie told the pre-match press conference. "We've got to give their defence a thorough examination. I won't be satisfied if we don't."

And there was no reason not to; United knew they were a hard night for anyone, home advantage irrelevant provided the players remembered who they were, a surprise visit from Eric Cantona helping with the process. This attitude was fortified by Barcelona's defensive disarray: their centre-backs were the midfielder Celades and the right-back Reiziger, with Samuel Okunowo, who'd end up on trial at Northwich Victoria while still in his twenties, in Reiziger's usual role.

But United's attacking form was reason alone – especially the partnership of Cole and Yorke. Writing the previous season, Phil Neville took pains to praise Cole's sunny demeanour even at the worst of times, but Peter Schmeichel's more experienced analysis was enlightening. "Extremely sensitive, but a person I liked enormously from the moment I met him," he wrote in his autobiography. "He has always taken things personally, even though he's tried to hide it and show a brave face. But now he's so much stronger; practically everything glances off him. Yorke's arrival at the club strengthened Cole, no doubt about it. It hasn't made a new man of him – and thank goodness for that – but it has changed him noticeably. He's not so vulnerable, though not in Yorke's more boisterous (and charming) way."

But they were very different people, as Cole explained. "Dwight was, 'Look at me, I play for United, I've got a nice bird and car'. I'm the opposite. I bought a Porsche one year but was so self-conscious that I couldn't drive it. It took me two months to drive it to training. Yorkey had no such worries."

Born within 19 days of one another, Yorke was another man of colour in a dressing room that prior to then had only Wes Brown, a youngster. Particularly sensitive to issues of race, Cole devoted time later in the season to anti-racism initiatives, and the pair would also help launch a book telling the story of Arthur Wharton, Britain's first black professional footballer.

Their connection was also based on a shared culture, Cole explaining that though he grew up in Nottingham, his Caribbean heritage was central to his identity and upbringing. But he also noted Yorke's sunny demeanour as "different from the English mentality", and acknowledged its influence on him. "Accepted, he does smile a bit more often than me," he wrote, "but I've got more into practice with him around."

And they genuinely did do everything together. "He phones me in the morning, gives me a wake-up call," Cole told the cameras – inordinately elaborate when a shake would do the trick just as well – but either way, four defences had been mercilessly animalled. "Southampton, Wimbledon and Brondby might have been ripe for a mangling," surmised Lacey, "but someone still had to turn the handle."

In United's favour in Spain was their position in the group; Munich, absorbing the momentum presented by Schmeichel, had beaten Barcelona home and away. This left them needing a win to have any chance of progressing, and consequently any chance of reaching "their" final – in their hundredth year, on their home ground. So the mood in the city was not good: two days earlier, one local paper, *El Periodico*, pictured five generations of players staring dolefully at the camera, along with the headline "The silence over the Centenary". On the other hand, United knew that even if they lost, a home win in the last game would see them through.

"We're here coz we won fuck all" dissipated from the away enclosure up amongst the cirrus and stratus, and then, a minute later, Barcelona had scored. Giovanni clipped a ball in from the left, Irwin headed weakly clear, and Neville ran past Anderson, who beat Schmeichel with ease. Unsurprisingly, it prompted a lot of noise and arm-waving, a collective "Gol!" sounding far better than a collective "Yes!"

But United didn't panic, their riposte a bout of composed rat-a-tat passing that came to nothing. Before minutes later, they almost fell further behind. Figo, driven off the pitch by buggy after taking a knock, sneaked back on to rob Blomqvist before feeding Rivaldo, who shot just wide.

Though Cole and Yorke did have a shy at an ambitious stepover-one-two routine that was far too elaborate to work, United found it difficult to find a way into the game. Xavier Hernandez Cruz was back, "just keeping Barcelona ticking over", while Rivaldo and Figo did the fancy bits and van Gaal glared on, an unholy mix of skin and grease. But United, and Stam in particular, had learned since the game at Old Trafford. "If you let a player like Figo run at you," he wrote, "there's no one better at punishing you... I make a point of closing him down as soon as possible, once he comes into my zone, and at that stage I leave someone else to pick up my striker. That's essential, as you can't give Figo any time to get in motion."

Then, after 24 minutes, Schmeichel was forced to save from Anderson, through one-on-one, before, suddenly, United were level. "Unformed and void" is the best the Bible can do in describing pre-creation nothing-ness, but that would be to praise United's prior offence, until Blomqvist burgled Celades and found Yorke 25 yards from goal, who found an ideal first touch to deliver the pass into his stride. "Great chance" rapped

Tyldesley, which it was not, but it didn't matter; a split second later, the ball rattled past Hesp low to his right, and there was light.

Perhaps with no player signed by United has there existed a wider discrepancy between what was thought was being got and what was actually got. Even the players in the squad hadn't all been sure, Roy Keane admitting as much in his autobiography and Giggs in the *Observer*: "He has surprised me a little, to be honest. I didn't realise how good a player he is until I started playing with him. It was a bit like Eric Cantona all over again. I'd seen him playing for Leeds without being unduly impressed. I don't mean I didn't rate him, but he didn't strike me as exceptional, yet as soon as we were in the same team it was obvious from the start the man was a genius. I suppose that shows I had better stick to playing, but it probably also demonstrates that the quality we have here brings out the best in players. I'm sure that is what Dwight is finding."

But Yorke had known he was up to it all along on account of the confidence that enabled him to prove it, and quickly; for a period, even his mis-touches resulted in goals. Though he lacked a necessarily outstanding attribute, this was offset by excellence in every department. His louche liquidity was aesthetic and deceptive, a contrast to the frantic, fidgety, angular explosiveness of Cole. He was stronger than he looked, much better in the air than expected, and though he had only one trick, that one trick – drifting one way then sliding the other, reminiscent in a way of Chris Waddle – seemed to fool all of the people all of the time. When you're described as "one of the most imaginative attackers in the game" by Scholes, one of football's most magical realists, you know that things are very right indeed.

Yet, as much as anything, Yorke's contribution was spiritual, thoroughly rejuvenating a dressing room and team that had mislaid its serotonin somewhere in 1995. Well, that and what Phil Leotardo would call brass tacks, the Talmud *tachlis*: 29 goals, including the only one in league games against Derby, Charlton and Middlesbrough; two against Chelsea in the Cup, one in league and Cup against Liverpool, goals away to Munich and Barcelona, goals against Inter and Juventus – and 23 assists. Or put another way, the same number as Beckham in the most productive season of his career. It didn't last, but for nine months and perhaps alongside Andriy Shevchenko, he was the finest striker in existence.

United were not, however, clear of mither. On the half-hour, Figo grooved away from Beckham and clumped a shot that Schmeichel couldn't hold but probably should have done. As the ball escaped, Rivaldo stood poised to accept the eventuating tap-in, until from nowhere appeared a giant paw, majestically swiping the ball to safety, and United survived.

"They never seem to disappoint, these two," rhapsodised Clive Tyldesley at half-time and then, they didn't.

The second half of this game remains one of the best in which United have ever been involved. In its first minute, Cole and Yorke had a shy at an ambitious stepover-one-two routine that was far too elaborate to work, and soon after, Irwin, abandoned by Blomqvist, sliced through Figo.

Then, suddenly United were dictating, Yorke not far away with a snap-shot after chesting down a Blomqvist cross and Scholes obliterating one wide from 20 yards. After a quiet first period, his influence grew in the second, and he later wrote of his determination not to let the opportunity pass him by. "I knew I had to concentrate like crazy to try and make my mark", he recalled. "There are that many great players around you that you could easily spend all your time worrying and never get anything done yourself. But you never forget that these immense footballers can make you look silly at any moment, and that forces you to concentrate still further."

Presumably playing next to Keane was also handy in sharpening focus, his captain now very close to his best. On 53 minutes he sent a brisk, brusque fizzer towards Yorke, who initiated an ambitious stepover-one-two routine with Cole that was far too elaborate to work except that it worked, an improvised dialogue of sickening slickness refined yet one step further to put Cole through. He took a touch, looked the keeper up and down, picked his spot, and put United ahead. Though they'd pulled off an abridged version at home to Brondby and used versions of the same move in almost every game, this was of another level entirely, the centrepiece of a performance that Gary Neville later praised as "the best attacking performance in terms of a pair that I've ever seen".

On the bench, Ole Solskjær was equally impressed. "Never seen anything like it, just one of them things. I do sessions nowadays with the link-up with two strikers and it's 'let's just do the Cole and

Yorke'... They made a couple of patent plays: it's now called the Cole and Yorke."

Individually, each had capacity for brilliance, but as a combination they were verging on genius.

"I didn't fear anybody," Cole said some years later. "You can call it arrogance... it was a case of right, how many we gonna get today. Everyone was more worried about what we were doing." And yet, the two generally played on opposite sides in training, their moves genuinely spontaneous. "We didn't work on anything," he said. "It was just two natural people doing what they believe was right to do on a football pitch and that was why it worked... When we started playing together, it was like meeting a special woman and falling in love. Everything felt right. Whatever he did, I did the opposite."

But the imperviousness to pressure that facilitated Yorke's success and made him so different to Cole could not exist in a vacuum, part of a liberal lifestyle and philosophy that ultimately hindered his career; within a year, he was finished as a serious player. "Dwight is from a small Caribbean island and I'm of Caribbean descent," Cole explained. "I know the mentality – when you reach the top, you relax and ease off. What more could Dwight do? He'd won the Treble."

Though Yorke later acknowledged in a newspaper interview that he "could have done things differently", he didn't mind that he didn't. "Would I give up the women and nights out for another year at United? Would that make me happy? Would that make me the person I am today? I'm not sure. I have no regrets. I went to United to win things and I achieved that."

The remainder of the game was a mixture of colour, speed and geometry, heavyweights moving like lightweights and swinging for the fences, United's lead lasting just four minutes. When Barcelona won a free-kick 30 yards from goal, Schmeichel humbly assumed that he knew where Rivaldo was aiming, the same as he had against Robbie Fowler in December 1995, and wandered off in that direction. It transpired, again, that he did not, this time the ball deflecting the other way into the net. Ah well, *gam zu letovah* – no way he'd be thick enough to do it again, on the same ground, at the same end, in the same competition, in the same season, *in the fucking final.* Two-two.

Fergie was now on the touchline imploring his players to "please defend properly", but United didn't pause, a Keane–Cole–Scholes combination almost putting the captain through. Then, Gary Neville was forced into a last-ditch clearance to prevent a Zenden cross leaving Giovanni with a tap-in.

Back came United, Scholes shooting high with only Hesp to beat, then Yorke and Cole lowered themselves to a simple one-two, earning space for Beckham to cross, one bounce. Hesp somehow ushered Yorke's header behind, before, two minutes later, that useless Yorke from useless Villa – why couldn't we have signed Kluivert instead of that grinning idiot? – launched himself headlong into a Beckham cross that Hesp couldn't hope to cut out, reclaiming the advantage. In the ten games Yorke and Cole had played together since Southampton away, they'd scored 16 times.

Before Barcelona could react, United stepped-to once again. Keane and Beckham linked to good effect, then Cole and Yorke broke, only for the latter to stray offside unnecessarily, depriving himself of a probable one-on-one. His carelessness was costly, because within minutes, Barcelona were level again. Leaping, Rivaldo controlled Sergi's cross high on his chest, then *placed – placed!* – a bicycle kick past Schmeichel to his right, Stam and Neville turning away with what-can-you-do impotence. "Where, where, where is all this going to end?" cried Tyldesley.

Not here was the answer, as two minutes later Rivaldo almost did it again, bow-leggedly arrowing a fantastical shot from miles out that left the crossbar quivering. Next, Barcelona swarmed forward, then Keane pounded through midfield, bodies scattered in his wake, before Barcelona stormed back the other way.

And so it continued. Cole had a header from a Beckham corner, Stam managed to impound Celades' cross before it reached Rivaldo, Schmeichel's charge foiled Giovanni, through after Rivaldo's back-heel, Irwin intervened to stop Reiziger, Hesp thrust out a foot to deny Cole, Irwin foiled Anderson. And so it ended.

"After all we've been through tonight, let's just sit back and admire and remember a night of the most thrilling 90 minutes of football that you'll see this or any season," sang Clive Tyldesley. "We'll be back again in May" sang the United section. Such is the power of football taught by Matt Busby.

Meanwhile, at Wembley, Arsenal – there, because, in the spirit of the competition, it made "financial sense" – had been eliminated.

They'd needed a goal from each centre-back to beat Panathinaikos in the first game there, and that after conceding a late goal in Lens that cost them two points. Then they could muster only home draw and away defeat against Dynamo Kiev, which made the penultimate game with Lens one they could not afford to lose, but they did. Luckily, Wenger had got his retaliation in early claiming from the outset that no English club could possibly win the competition given the relentless nature of the domestic schedule.

Which next served United a game against Leeds, who, after winning only two of their first 11 games, had seen George Graham leave for Spurs and a deal with Martin O'Neill fall through. So they were left with David O'Leary, who, despite sporting the horizontal sideboards of a loony, had won his first four games in charge as he gradually slotted in the innocents who would charm a nation. They were in sixth place, with only one defeat in the 14 games played so far, while United were third, only four off the lead with a game in hand – and ordered by Fergie not to fall further behind the leaders.

It turned out that the full five days of sunshine conferred upon Manchester in the summer were insufficient for anyone looking to dry out a lump of new turf so that it might take root. Consequently, the Old Trafford pitch had been relaid once again after the Blackburn game, the grass coming from Yorkshire and its consistency that of shagpile.

Leeds were still without Radebe, who was injured, and also Molenaar and Bowyer, who were suspended; in came Haaland, Ribeiro and McPhail. United left out Irwin, with Phil Neville coming in, Beckham was replaced by Butt, and Blomqvist's place went to Solskjær. Included on the bench were Giggs, absent since Derby, and Sheringham, out since Southampton.

Despite a private warning sterner than the one delivered in public, United's passing was careless to begin with on an admittedly unhelpful surface. They were, however, unlucky not to be awarded a penalty after forcing a throw deep inside the Leeds half. Taken short by Phil Neville to Yorke, he held possession and retreated before squaring to Solskjær, on the edge of the box. Immediately bright, he nipped a pass into Cole, his back to goal, for him to lay off for Scholes. Crowded out in the first instance, he won the ball back and pushed it into the path of Yorke, who was then eased to the ground by Haaland. Referee Graham Poll was uninterested in the ensuing protestations.

Gradually, United assumed control, almost taking the lead when Schmeichel's long punt was headed clear, directly to Butt. Patting it wide, Brown then sneaked a pass into Cole, supervised by a man on either side, but on the half-turn, and when Harte missed his kick, surprising Woodgate who was then hit by the ball, Cole snatched it away. With Hiden seeking to avert the danger, Cole swayed inside, and instead of shooting with his left worked back onto his right, opening his body to arrange a more deliberate finish. But with Woodgate sliding in from behind, he was forced to shoot under pressure and with the ball now under his feet, Nigel Martyn, The Affable Cornishman, was able to push away well.

But United increased the pressure. Unmarked in the centre-circle, Cole rose to flick a goalkick on for Yorke, who cushioned the ball and returned possession, Cole moving wide, checking, and finding Butt. Immediately, he raced a pass into Yorke, who, back to goal, sent the ball wide for Phil Neville to cross, picking out Butt, now in the middle of the box. Leaping early, he cranked his neck into a header, but somehow, Martyn, flying to his left, realised that he couldn't reach it with his nearer arm so reached over his head with the other, Rick Stewart-style, to claw the ball away – injuring his back in the process. That's where affability gets you.

And then, on 29 minutes, Leeds went in front. A mis-touch from Butt, meeting a goalkick, diverted the ball towards the touchline on the Leeds left. But Butt was over quickly, recovering possession from Hasselbaink and swerving by Harte as he got up, before McPhail slid in, followed by Scholes, and suddenly Hopkin was moving out of the centre-circle towards goal. Feeding into Kewell, who shielded from Gary Neville, he found Hasselbaink running at Phil, for some reason at right-back. Allowed to cut in, Hasselbaink then cracked a trademark low, early shot in off the near post – "question marks will be raised, *once again*, about the Manchester United goalkeeper," said Alan Parry, and he was right – Schmeichel had gone down late and feet first.

Moments later, Leeds were in again, Woodgate winning a header and Ribeiro flicking behind him to McPhail, out on the left touch-line. With United's back four stepping up, one straight ball lifted into space, between Stam and Gary Neville, left Kewell clean through, a kindly bounce leaving him the relatively simple task of lifting over the star-jumping Schmeichel. But somehow, he sliced his instep across the shot, sending it wide of the near post.

Then, in the final minute of the half, Kewell's punishment. Stam's bouncing back-pass forced Schmeichel into a long punt, missed by both Yorke and Woodgate, and Cole headed the loose ball out to Scholes on the right. Leaning back into a long, driven pass for Butt, Wetherall nodded away and Yorke tapped back to Keane, who returned it – but now, there was space to turn. Indicating to Wetherall that he was going right, he did his drift left and waited for Hopkin to arrive, then found Solskjær, who laced a measured finish into the far corner before Woodgate's tackle could interfere.

Leeds were forced to replace Martyn at half-time, a thin-faced Paul Robinson coming on for his debut, and within 22 seconds, he was extracting the ball from his net. Running at a lofted clearance, Keane glanced a header for Butt, just to his left, who scholesed an imme-diate pass to Scholes, on the right. Poking outside the approaching Harte, then running inside and across his path, the eye in his elbow alerted him to Keane's arrival, so he cut back a pass into his stride. Allowing it across his body, he'd learned from his Wimbledon error, slamming a left-footed finish into the roof the net with his left foot Cole and Yorke raising it in celebration.

Then, Stam came a long way to meet a goalkick but was beaten to it by Hasselbaink, Hopkin waving a leg at the loose ball ahead of Butt. Headed forward by McPhail, Brown – now at centre-back so that Neville could handle Hasselbaink's tendency to drift wide – missed his header, and Kewell was clear. This time, he shaped to curl low into the far corner and delayed, brushing over Schmeichel as he went to ground in pursuit of the expected finish.

Back surged United, Butt dictating an attack with tackles and passes, then losing Hopkin and poking to Yorke, who spread left to Neville. His cross hit Halle and was picked up by Keane, surging ahead of Wetherall, who, already committed to the tackle, wound up whacking shin across back of knees. When Graham Poll refrained from awarding a penalty, Keane set off after him, Haaland appearing to suggest he was all mouth. But his reasoning was sound – they were, after all, playing football, in public, and on television – Keane simply had no scope to seriously retort.

Chasing a winner, Fergie sent Giggs on for Cole, Solskjær vacating the left to move up front, and then replacing Scholes on the right when he departed for Sheringham. But it was Leeds who created the next opportunity, Haaland clipping forwards for Hasselbaink, who saw Brown coming, and turned him the moment he got too close. Immediately, Kewell drifted across the United line, away from Stam and left to right, inviting a pass which met his run. Inexplicably opting to aim for the near post, he screwed his shot wide.

Then, with 13 minutes remaining, Phil Neville collected a clearance and found Giggs. Drawing Haaland towards him, he returned it, while Butt moved across the D and stopped, the defenders behind reacting too slowly to follow, those in front too slowly to move back. When Neville fired in a pass, there was no immediate threat – but Butt feathered a drag-back to move the ball onto his right foot and turn his body towards goal, then battered a finish high to Robinson's left as momentum dragged him to the ground. A brilliant goal, and perversely, one that almost obscured a brilliant all-round performance.

There was still time for Haaland to scissor into Keane before the end, totally safe in his safety as Poll sprinted over to intercede – but again, Keane was calm. Then it was full-time.

"Usually they defend here," said Fergie, "but they had a positive approach and will take a lot of credit out of this. It was so exciting it made your nerves tingle."

DECEMBER

With the Champions League decider coming up, plus two league games against Chelsea, one away at leaders Villa, one at Spurs and then two more, the League Cup quarter-final was not exactly a December priority. Yet at the same time, it was a quarter-final and Spurs weren't up to much.

Chelsea, the holders, had been knocked out at Wimbledon the previous night, with Sunderland the other team through to the semis after a 3–0 win over Thatcher's Luton. Happily, Mitchell Thomas had been sent off, gratifying given his role in the various Kenilworth Road annoyances and two goals, overhead kick included, that he scored in a horrendous 4–0 evisceration at White Hart Lane in May 1987.

There had been much speculation in the days preceding the game about Brian Kidd leaving United to manage Blackburn, and Richard Keys enjoyed a tizzy on Sky when he didn't arrive with the club party. Fergie then reiterated his hope that he'd stay, before Kidd showed up drenched in sweat, telling the players that he'd been stuck in traffic and forced to run three miles through the streets.

United fielded a relatively strong team, Phil Neville and Butt remaining from the weekend and forming a central-midfield partnership, with Giggs returning on the left. Behind them, Berg made his first appearance since the previous round with Johnsen alongside him, available for the first time since September. Up front, Sheringham partnered Solskjær.

Spurs dropped goalkeeper Espen Baardsen in favour of Ian Walker, and scarred by the sleight, he would eventually retire at 25 to go on holiday, before taking a job in asset management – which tells you just how much fun it was in N17. Elsewhere, Darren Anderton made his 13th consecutive appearance, the first time in three years he had attained such a feat, and with Les Ferdinand fit enough only for the bench, Chris Armstrong, who already had three goals in the competition, started up front with Steffen Iversen.

On a sharply cold night the game started slowly, a Butt shot United's only real attempt of note in an opening stretch notable for little more than two exceptionally angry faces made by Neville. Otherwise, Greening and Clegg coped relatively well with Ginola, and no one else threatened anything.

Not until the midway point of the half did United create the semblance of a chance, Giggs controlling Clegg's crossfield pass on his chest with dismissive, disgusting ease and smartly lifting the ball into the box for Neville, who sliced a left-footer wide of the near post. Then, after more evenness, Johnsen's slip allowed Nielsen to break. With Iversen to his right, Armstrong to his left, and very little in the way of defence, he opted to dawdle, Berg tackling and Calderwood welting the loose ball over the bar.

Shortly afterwards, Solskjær located his non-existent yard to fire a shot across Walker, just wide. Then, on the stroke of half-time, Ginola bounded in off the left and larruped a curler towards the far top corner from the far top corner of the box – identical to his goal in the St James' Park 0–5, save for its not going in. And just before the break, Nielsen took advantage of Greening's loss of possession to dash through the middle once more, again deceived by the multitude of offensive options but doing nothing, a Tory in a recession.

At half-time, and out of both necessity and inclination, George Graham replaced Calderwood with Fox, which paid off almost immediately. On 48 minutes, Nielsen wedged a pass into the box on its left-hand side for the unmarked Fox, who back-headed his first touch square for the unmarked Armstrong, ten yards from goal. There was plenty still left to do, and it was done, a standing leap and nod somehow imparting the necessary purchase to get by van der Gouw.

Despite missing the obvious facilitators, United came straight back, Solskjær flashing a shot just wide after Butt's pass was set for him by Sheringham's thigh, the game instantly acquiring its missing rhythm. Then on 55 minutes, the ball reached Ginola on the left, and slowing to a walk, he drew Greening into a mismatch, rolling, stepping over, showing and leaving the ball before quickly dragging it in front again to wrap his foot around a cross, coinciding perfectly with Armstrong's arrival at the near post, his forehead again doing the rest.

Needing a goal, United increased their intensity, Butt in particular maintaining his weekend form. And just after the hour, he missed a decent chance created by Giggs' lofted pass, opting to stretch into a volley when a header might have worked better. Spurs then squandered an even better opportunity a few minutes later, another Ginola cross missing Armstrong but reaching Nielsen, there before Johnsen but managing to poke wide from five yards.

Play restarted with van der Gouw rolling out to Curtis to his left, and allowed to halfway, he found Greening who laid back for Neville, moving past the centre-circle to its left. Pushing hard into Giggs, ahead and facing him, it went back to Butt, more central, who eased a lob over the defence to meet Neville, now on the far left of the box pelting towards the byline – and he cut an awkwardly bouncing ball back onto the head of Sheringham, who guided a hard flick across Walker for another minor classic.

Curiously, Butt, who had been United's outstanding player, was then removed – in preparation, it appeared, for the weekend game at Villa – until he began it on the bench. He was replaced by Alex Notman, making his debut, but United created very little for him, and on 86 minutes, Ginola finished the game. Sauntering into the centre, from the right this time, when Giggs declined to close him down until he was sure it was too late, a thunderous drive whipped straight in at the post a third of the way up, for a very acceptable goal.

But post-match, all he wanted to do was whinge about his absence from the French squad, and Fergie was equally narked. "We've lost three goals in the second half and we were the better team," he told Sky. "Nothing was serious about the game in the first half." Hoping to lighten the tone, the interviewer set him up by wondering whether he'd found the game "a useful exercise". He had not, because no such thing existed. "We've lost tonight, we're out the Cup. I thought we could win it."

*

Two days later, Brian Kidd was unveiled as the new manager of Blackburn, from beneath a cloth of purple velvet. This ground Fergie's gears to a noxious dust, prompting him to claim that Kidd had never expressed a desire to be anything more than an assistant – because, of course, bosses are renowned for taking well to their subordinates coveting both their position, and those available elsewhere. So, when he was approached, and the board refused to guarantee him a future that met with his satisfaction, blaming the takeover, he felt it too good an opportunity to miss.

His departure was a significant loss for United. Respected by the players as a great bloke, a great mate and a great coach – no less august an authority than Keane called him a "straight talker" – they enjoyed his sessions and knew how crucial they were to the success that followed. They were made to work harder than anyone else, though generally for shorter periods of more extreme and focused intensity, and as a direct result, were fitter than any other side; if Fergie conditioned their minds to seize so many late goals, Kidd prepared the legs and honed the skills able to carry them there.

And the training was not only hard, but unforgiving, too. There's a drill known at United as boxes, and a favourite at most clubs, in which a group of players try to keep the ball away from a man or two running in between them. In most places, it's an exercise in improving the teamwork of those on the outside – but at United, those players would be trying to make each other look stupid, as well as whoever was in the middle. This was a spirit they took into England training sessions too, chastising whoever performed badly. "To talk about one individual player being competitive is unremarkable," wrote David James. "But to apply the same label to generation after generation of players from one specific club is unheard of" – an obsessive focus honed at the Cliff and Carrington. "Some managers are 'pleasing managers'," Fergie once explained to a class at Harvard. "They let the players play eight-a-sides or ten-a-sides – games they enjoy. We look at the training sessions as opportunities to learn and improve. The players may think 'here we go again' but it helps to win. The message is simple: we cannot sit still at this club."

But though the players could be cruel to each other, part of a bullying culture that he encouraged, Fergie did not expect the same of his staff, there to make them feel comfortable enough to produce their best, not so comfortable that they forgot it was important. "There is no room for criticism on the training field," he said. "For a player – and for any human being – there is nothing better than hearing 'well done'. Those are the two best words ever invented in sports. You don't need to use superlatives."

And that training field was Kidd's domain, though his job did not end there. It was he who spotted Butt and Scholes playing locally, and he who visited other teams, sometimes in other sports, to study their methods and see what he could learn – the advantage of a boss not too entrenched to re-evaluate. When United lost the title to Leeds in 1992 after tiring during the run-in, Ferguson hired a nutritionist. In 2007, when they limped over the line in the league, were smashed out of Europe by Milan and barely able to move by the FA Cup final, he built a squad of talent, not a fixed first eleven.

Nor was he too paranoid or too arrogant to delegate. In the same way that Matt Busby relied on the coaching, scouting and pastoral skills of Jimmy Murphy, Joe Armstrong and Bert Whalley, Ferguson trusted Kidd and Eric Harrison to get on with things. "Put the blinkers on," Fergie once advised Tony Blair. "Don't let anyone into your space unless you want them there. If someone says only you can deal with it, give them a few seconds and if you decide someone else can solve it, move on."

This trust in his deputies – appointed by him, after all – bought time, and the ability to switch off away from football. "You have to get the game out of your system quickly or it becomes an obsession," he explained. "Win, lose, or draw." In similar vein, if there was a decision to be made, it was made quickly: "Why should I go to my bed with a doubt?"

In 1997, he even suggested to Alastair Campbell that Labour employ a masseuse on its campaign bus, and still, when ribbed for it years later, insisted that his reasoning was sound. "Well, maybe that was a step too far. But the point I was making was that mental and physical fitness are two sides of the same coin. You have to build rest into any programme. That's another thing that applies in all worlds, not just sport. I don't think you can do high-pressure jobs now without being physically fit."

And in those periods of rest, he pursued a selection of other interests, on the look-out for fresh perspective as well as the simple pleasures of boozing and spieling – Abraham Lincoln's, for example: "What was fascinating," he told Alastair Campbell in an interview for *New Statesman*, "was how he held together all these big personalities, the ones who had tried to stop him becoming president, to make sure they stayed roughly on the same track. Now, he was president of the United States in a totally different era. I am a manager of a football team. But I can learn about the art of team building and team management from all sorts of places. It's all about managing people and relationships, in the end."

*

At the weekend United travelled to Villa Park, a point behind their hosts at the top of the table. Though Dion Dublin had continued his run of goals, now one of only six men to score in each of his first four games for a new club[1] since Sky invented football, defeat to Liverpool was followed by a 2–2 draw at useless Forest. They would need to do better, not just against United – without the injured Paul Merson and suspended Stan Collymore – but in their next two games, against Chelsea and Arsenal.

Though United had a big game of their own in midweek, there were few concessions to it. Giggs returned to the bench, Blomqvist playing on the left, and Phil Neville was replaced by Irwin. Otherwise, Scholes was preferred to Butt, and everything else was as expected.

Running out of the tunnel – then a dying, now a dead art – the players were greeted by kids forming a guard of honour, purple baseball hats atop their little heads. This failed to inspire them in a dull first half.

Yorke amused the home crowd when he ran onto Cole's header and trickled a shot well wide from 20 yards, then Joachim snatched at a loose ball after it bounced off Gary Neville's chest. But the first real chance was missed by Ehiogu, heading wide at the near post after a corner, Schmeichel messing around elsewhere. "He wasn't himself, he came and missed about two or three crosses, he didn't look at ease, and he was making his defenders uneasy," wrote Paul Wilson in the *Guardian*.

Next, Joachim found Hendrie with a clever pass. He skipped around Stam, then lost control fiddling for a better shooting angle, so Taylor took over – but Schmeichel extended a hand to flick the

---

1 Mick Quinn (Coventry City), Ian Marshall (Ipswich Town), Darren Bent (Charlton Athletic), Emmanuel Adebayor (Manchester City)

ball from his laces. Cole then had a soft header cleared off the line by Barry, and Joachim sprinted past Stam onto Taylor's pass, only to take the ball too close to Schmeichel.

At half-time, United replaced Blomqvist with Giggs, and within 90 seconds were ahead. Brown clipped a ball into space along the right for Cole, Alan Thompson chugging along behind. Squaring him up with feints, Cole then drove a cross that tempted Oakes to launch into an unnecessary clearing punch – which fell perfectly for Scholes to biff a leaping, left-footed drive into the far corner.

But it was Villa who improved subsequently, and drew level eight minutes later. Dublin chested down Wright's long pass, nominally for Taylor, but Joachim picked it up instead, 25 yards from goal, and veered past Scholes. As he shot from just inside the D, Irwin inserted a foot in front of him, sending the ball looping over Schmeichel and into the net.

For the next quarter of an hour, Villa stuck it to United, Joachim's shot from distance flashing just wide, Hendrie heading over from Watson's cross and Thompson battering a free-kick against the post. In the end, Fergie was happy to settle for a point, bringing on Butt for Cole – perhaps to spare Yorke the abuse that would have followed his more merited substitution – and admitting that Villa had been the better side.

Elsewhere that afternoon, Chelsea drew 0–0 at Everton and Arsenal drew 0–0 at Derby – a game that would cause the following refreshment to appear in *The Times*, a month later: "An Arsenal friend of mine had told me about something that happened when he'd travelled up to Pride Park to see his team play Derby County. He was in the toilets at the away end when a loud and lusty chant of 'If you all love Arsenal clap your hands' came from an impassioned North London voice behind him. Despite the impossibility of clapping his hands at that particular moment, he did manage to crane his head round to put a face to the voice – and it was none other than Charlie George, one-time darling of the North Bank (not to mention briefly a Derby player) and still an ardent Gooner, travelling home and away with his team. 'We'll never see his like again,' I wrote, but, after reading Gary Neville's column, I'm not so sure."

*

The night before United's decisive tie with Bayern Munich, Manchester City lost to Mansfield Town in the first round of the Auto Windscreen Shields Trophy, northern section – a game played in front of a rapt crowd of 3,007. It did, therefore, obviously follow that Manchester City Council should arrange to divert £22million of public money towards facilitating their residence at the City of Manchester Stadium, following the 2002 Commonwealth Games.

In the build-up to United's game, and as it had for much of the season, much of the pre-game patter concerned Peter Schmeichel, his form showing no particular signs of improvement. "We have studied videos of recent games to see United's weaknesses and strengths," said Giovane Elber, "and they show that Schmeichel has made a big mistake in nearly every match. We are all hoping that it happens again. It is clear that United are very strong in attack but they have problems in defence and we must take advantage."

The Germans were equally unimpressed with the state of the Old Trafford pitch, but were still confident. "We had a bad start in the qualifiers and if we can go through this so-called Group of Death as winner, it would be nothing short of sensational," reckoned Ottmar Hitzfeld. "In our current position, however, I am sure we can go through to the quarter-finals and win the competition."

United were certain of progressing with a win and likely to with a draw, in which circumstance they would be eliminated only if Galatasaray won in Bilbao and Rosenberg did the same at Juventus. Nonetheless Fergie's pre-match instructions were a little different, calling for "concentration" and "sensible play".

The team was that which played the second half at Villa. Wes Brown stayed in, with Gary Neville at centre-back, and Giggs started. On the United bench, Jim Ryan was alongside Fergie, like Brian Kidd a veteran of the 1968 European campaign, having played against Gornik in the quarter-final first leg.

Otherwise, Roy Keane appeared freshly shorn, his final haircut of the season, and Bayern again appeared in quilted bin liners, silver ones this time – but still without Scholl, who was injured, and Basler too. Already embroiled in a to-do with his national team manager over a late-night poker game, he'd been relegated to the bench after disappointing Hitzfeld with his attitude in training the previous night – not entirely surprising from a man who listed sleeping as his hobby in the club handbook.

Matthäus, though, was in the team, despite his recent bust for skiing in Switzerland when he was supposed to be resting an injured thigh. But his appearance on the pitch was not bad news for United, the errors he'd made in the first game a useful glitch in the machine. "Any sort of pressurisation, I think he'll go under," confided Large Rotund Not Racist Ronald.

In the Bayern end was a huge 'Stop Murdoch' banner, which United would play with their backs in the first half – fussing of an ilk rare in Europe, particularly given the unavailability of sun-in-eyes excuses. And it made no apparent difference, United knocking the ball around with confidence and Brown greeting Effenberg with Longsight kiss.

But Bayern's composed possession play made it hard for United to build momentum, their five at the back limiting the space for attacking. Accordingly, the first chance arrived via a break, Stam pursuing Zickler, sailing alongside and confiscating the ball with all the certainty of a primary school teacher extending a hand. He then moved possession onto Keane who found Beckham, and a long, driven pass was quickly dispatched to Giggs, coming off the touchline and touching inside Strunz for Cole to shoot. His effort was blocked by the horizontal barrier of Strunz and Babbel, Yorke wellying the rebound over the bar.

Then, on 15 minutes, Beckham advanced into space and released a dipping, spitting drive, Kahn bringing his fists in front of his face to divert it sideways. Next, Giggs picked up Kuffour's clearing header and indicated to Strunz that he was heading right before easily flexing left to cross for Yorke, who couldn't quite get over the ball, his header drifting wide.

Irwin then headed Zickler's crown, resulting in blood and temporary absence, after which United constructed the move of the half. Cole played the ball into Yorke, his back to goal, and he laid back to Scholes, he pushed square for Keane. Quickly, finding Giggs, side on to Strunz, he flicked inside and disappeared outside, Cole collecting and moving across Jeremies before cleverly dragging a Solskjær-style shot towards the near post, with Kahn already moving the other way – but the ball narrowly missed the corner.

Though Bayern improved, United almost took the lead on 33 minutes, Beckham bending a low ball into Cole who guided around

Kaffout with his first touch. Now close to the by-line, he wrapped his foot around a cross, hung up to the back post, where Giggs, underneath rather than coming onto it, headed wide.

Then, with only two minutes until half-time, Lizarazu's loose pass allowed Brown to head for Beckham, unchallenged, and he found Giggs, who in attempting to fool Strunz, allowed the ball to run too far across his body, forcing him wide. Dashing to retrieve it, he squared up his man parallel to the left edge of the box, sidewinding outside then inside and leaving him on his backside. Looking up as everyone prepared for a cross, he saw Keane approaching the edge of the box, and rolled a pass to its edge, the weight perfect; slow enough to mitigate a slice, fast enough to arrive with momentum, and even enough to allow for measurement of stride; if Keane hit it well, it was a goal. He hit it well! It was a goal! The usual business-like celebration followed, running back towards the centre-circle and stopping suddenly, arms flapping as they caught up – before pointing at Giggs as if to say see what happens when you do as I say.

But Ryan Giggs didn't need to do what anyone said; he had produced a mesmeric half of football doing whatever his instinct ordered from his technique. The smooth, hypnotic unpredictability was like watching water over rocks, guessing what was coming next as futile as predicting the stride pattern of a greyhound. Strunz, a midfielder playing at full-back, could consider himself fortunate to have pre-emptively bleached his hair Eurozany psychokiller blonde, because otherwise he'd have been made to look very silly.

During the interval, Markus Horwick, the Bayern secretary, showed Fergie the scores from around Europe, to his shock, displayed on a mobile. As it stood and was likely to stay, both teams would progress whatever happened in the game.

Irwin did not reappear for the second half, not only bloodied but concussed, and Johnsen replaced him, directly, with Gary Neville remaining in the centre of defence. "The Germans will have to come at you now," Gary Newbon told Fergie. "Well, that's OK," Fergie told him back.

United began in the ascendancy, Effenberg forced to back-head Beckham's cross away with Johnsen poised. From the resultant overhit corner, Keane pulled away to the back post and diverted it into the middle for former centre-forward Johnsen to tap in – only for him to miss his kick. But the chance for redemption arrived immediately, Kuffour chesting weakly away and into Cole's legs, but springing after it and pitching his body at the loose ball, he could only lift it over the bar.

Bayern were pushing now, Brown doing enough to take a cross away from Salihamidžić almost on the line. Then, they caught United attempting a break, Strunz sliding in on Cole, and poking the ball to Zickler from the ground. Allowing it to glance off his boot, Kuffour, still up from the previous corner, managed to drag it into his path, and whacked a shot from 20 yards as Brown came in to tackle and Schmeichel took the catch, high to his right.

After a first half that simmered without quite boiling, the second was now almost there, and on 56 minutes Bayern won a cheap corner on the right, Johnsen deflecting Elber's hopeful cross behind. Effenberg's delivery then went over Giggs' head, but Strunz, peeling backwards from the edge of the six-yard box, was able to divert it goalwards using the corner of his forehead. With Neville and Beckham moving out, Salihamidžić was left to scramble the ball over the line with Elber in close attendance, before running off to point at his name.

Back came United, Giggs' cross missed by Babbel but not by Lizarazu. Johnsen then won the ball back, but Beckham lost it to Effenberg who found Elber on the right. Moving infield, he stabbed a pass back outside to Zickler on the edge of the box, and when his shot clipped Stam's heel and reared up, launched a right leg that sent it just wide. "Sing ven you're vinning!" teased the away support – and given the scores in Spain and Italy, there wasn't even the excuse of nervousness.

But the players kept going, the increasingly influential Scholes driving a pass to Beckham that he nodded inside to Cole and got straight back, setting him up to cross. Again it was overhit but Johnsen managed to knock it back from the byline, forcing Kahn to punch clear. Waiting at the edge of the box, Scholes was first to measure the flight, racing into a jump and controlling it on his chest, post-bounce, on the run and on the rise, taking it away from Jeremies before shooting it as it bounced again, slicing high and wide.

Hitzfeld then brought on Linke for Matthäus, who spent most of the rest of the game chuntering on the bench as United rushed in pursuit of what he deemed to be an unnecessary winner. And

It almost came, Yorke's spinning volley saved by Kahn and Scholes screwing wide with Giggs well-placed after picking his way across the face of the box.

Next minute, Bayern had a corner, taken by Effenberg from the left and which Schmeichel palmed down to himself. Prevented by Linke from releasing the ball early, he instead booted it from his hands, Beckham flicking on to Cole, who controlled, turned Babbel and slunk quickly away from Jeremies, only for Babbel to come back at him. But Scholes picked up possession, finding Beckham, and from his cross, Cole glanced just wide of the far post.

As United got closer to a winner, both Zickler and Salihamidžić developed injuries, providing Atkinson and Tyldesley with an opportunity to bemoan the state of German football. "The general feeling is that there isn't a great amount of good, young players coming through in Germany," said the former – though the national team somehow achieved one more tournament final than England's Golden Generation™. "And as for the finance minister…" rejoindered Tyldesley, pausing to savour the titters of a nation affronted by Oskar Lafontaine's audacious suggestion that taxation be harmonised across the EU and no one country have the power to veto the will of the majority. "Europe's most dangerous man," reckoned the *Sun*, whose proprietor lived overseas.

Once all were present and correct, the next chance fell to Bayern, Brown again jumping well to deny a header, this time to Elber. And with the away supporters cheering each pass, Butt crunched Effenberg to remind Old Trafford of its responsibilities and the team responded too, forcing a pair of corners. Then, Schmeichel did well to save Effenberg's surprise shot from distance, and with the crowd urging them forward while the defenders knocked the ball across the back four, eventually it made its way into midfield where the urgency was greater, Beckham clipping a pass into Scholes' chest which he turned into space and away from Kuffour and Jeremies, shooting high and wide when off balance.

Then, with three minutes to go, United won a free-kick wide on the left, whipped in by Giggs, and when Kuffour and Strunz obstructed one another Kuffour schlepped back Cole, the referee uninterested in the hassle of awarding a penalty. And that was the last of the action, both teams through. "It's been probably the most exciting group, and we've been probably the most exciting team," said Gary Neville in the tunnel.

A made-up Fergie left the pitch with his arm around Hitzfeld, very clearly arranging a post-match slake. "Both teams have many strengths and perhaps we will meet again in the tournament," said Hitzfeld later.

It wasn't quite the great night Fergie had predicted after the Brondby game, but it had been enough, the performances of the midfield four and Andy Cole of particular thrust. "I thought we matched Bayern in open play," he said later, "and it was generally their superior delivery from set pieces that put us under pressure." Let's just leave that one to marinate.

Also that night, Arsenal won in Athens, Arsène Wenger commenting afterwards that his priority for the season was retaining the title. He also haughtily dismissed the group from which his team had failed to qualify as "very average", tautological churlishness in each of his five languages.

Meanwhile, another goal off the bench from Tore Andre Flo, this time in the last minute, had given Chelsea a win at Villa, meaning a point at Spurs on Saturday would send United top, with Villa not playing Arsenal until Sunday.

*

Ronny Johnsen was back for the visit to White Hart Lane, his first league start since September. To his left, Phil Neville came in for Irwin, it was Butt not Scholes, Giggs not Blomqvist, and up front, Yorke's overdue groin injury made it even harder for Fergie to resist the temptation of starting Sheringham, whom he partnered with Solskjær. Cole was left on the bench – but unlike previous occasions in which he'd been rotated out, there was no visible disappointment, borne of his new sense of security.

United started the game at quite a tempo, Keane and Butt controlling midfield and the wide players and strikers looking dangerous; "attacking extravagance", David Lacey surmised, which "threatened to reduce the strutting Tottenham cockerel to a feebly clucking capon". And within 16 minutes, they were two goals ahead.

First, Ferdinand beat Schmeichel to Sinton's free-kick, forcing him to paw away from Campbell, Johnsen picking up possession and rolling to Sheringham. Still in the box on its left-hand side, he took his time to nip back inside Anderton and stun a little ball the wrong side of Phil Neville that enabled Butt to flick forward for Giggs, first time with the outside of his boot. Suddenly, he was away, weaving into the Spurs half and moving left to right, quickly finding Beckham, who took a touch to control and measure before whipping a return cross onto his head inside the six-yard box and dead centre. The effort was parried by Walker, but only to where Solskjær was waiting at the far post and he knocked in from close range.

Second, just inside the Spurs half, Gary Neville found Keane square of him, who spotting Butt making ground from behind him, waited until he was a few yards ahead and wedged a pass into his path. He managed a touch before Campbell jolted into him, Sheringham nipping across to fire out wide to Beckham. Totally unmarked, he moved the ball out of his feet, set, and curved a low cross directly onto the laces of Solskjær, his run taking him ahead of Campbell at the near post. Using the pace and direction of the ball, he turned it into the far corner exactly as was necessary.

Then, it all changed. During the course of the first half, Uriah Rennie showed five yellow cards to United players, two of them to Gary Neville – one for a studs-up lunge at Alan Nielsen, the other a little more dubious.

"You could say it was a deserved sending off," he later wrote, "but some weeks I wouldn't have even got booked. Ginola put his arm across me, and I put my arm inside his arm and he fell down. If he'd stayed on his feet, I wouldn't have got sent off. Ginola is 6 foot tall, 13 stone of muscle and he's got amazing balance, so how does he fall over when someone puts an arm across him? I'm not saying he's wrong to dive, though, because he won his team a point."

Fergie was critical too, though replays showed Neville doing more pulling than putting. "Enter Uriah Rennie, a man who represents a new breed of referee," he wrote in his review of the season. "He features on billboard advertising and is believed to have his own agent. He is a high-profile guy and there was no way he was going to let the stars of Manchester United and Tottenham upstage him." And Neville agreed, mentioning Rennie's habit of waiting for the teams to gather in the tunnel before a game so that he could march out between them, as opposed to all the others, already there at the front, ready to go when they arrived.

And Ginola got it too: "There is no question, the French star dives," Fergie elegantly varied, "and although I have noticed he has made an effort to join in the spirit of the English game, he was going down too easily in this match… anyway, Uriah Rennie bought the ticket." Accordingly, at half-time, Fergie asked his players to take it in turns to tackle him, hoping Rennie would conclude that it was impossible for them all to be bad tacklers. He also withdrew Solskjær to bring on Berg, a third centre-back.

Though Spurs were on top thereafter, United were not unduly troubled for the majority, the highlight a hold-me-back between Beckham and Sinton. "The equivalent of Richmal Crompton's Violet Elizabeth taking on AA Milne's Mary Jane," smirked Lacey. Keane was quickly over to add some gravitas to proceedings, grabbing Sinton by the shirt, school bully-style.

But under George Graham, Spurs were a tougher proposition than before, and on 70 minutes they pulled a goal back after Johnsen fouled Sinton on the left. Anderton's free-kick was hard, flat and perfectly placed, allowing Campbell the couple of yards' momentum he needed to outjump Stam and smack a header into the net, his sloping forehead somehow able to defy the laws of physics. Minutes later, the scores were almost level, but Nielsen's finishing was every bit as poor in the League Cup game, his close-range header easily fielded by Schmeichel.

Just when it looked like United would hang onto the points, and with only the two allotted minutes of injury time remaining, Spurs won another free-kick, this time from the right. Again Anderton's delivery was exemplary, and again it found Campbell, this time pulling away from Johnsen. He stooped slightly to guide another header past Schmeichel, not directly at fault for either goal, but not commanding his box in the usual manner either.

Yet, once more, United could take comfort from results elsewhere. At Pride Park, Chelsea also conceded a last-minute equaliser, also drawing 2–2, with Derby. Then, the following day, Arsenal took a two-goal lead at Villa Park, Bergkamp scoring his first goals since the opening game of the season. But somehow, in just 21 second half minutes, Dublin scored twice and Villa thrice, to solidify their position at the top – even though few thought them legitimate contenders.

*

On the Wednesday, United played at home to Chelsea, catching up the game postponed for the Super Cup – but first, that afternoon, was the draw for the European Cup quarter-finals. Managerial confidence was such that Fergie's concerns were logistical rather than sporting – he wanted to avoid the trek to Kiev, rather than any particular opposition. In the event, United were paired with Inter, the bookies' fancied team, and would play the first leg at home – supposedly a disadvantage, but the disproportionate significance of second leg away goals, as evidenced during the previous two seasons, made a nonsense of any such supposition. "I'd have thought that Inter Milan would be favourites for this cup," said Fergie. "If we get through that one then you can call us favourites."

The excitement of the tie added to the buzz around Old Trafford, augmenting a needle that had been increasing over the previous couple of seasons. The 1997 Charity Shield was niggly, particularly between Butt and Dennis Wise. Then, when the teams met in the league the following month, a half-time tunnel scrap forced Johnsen to adjust Wise's facial features, with Keane and Poyet also altercating.

There was trouble, too, with Franck Leboeuf, whom United liked to target under the high ball. After the Cup game at Stamford Bridge the previous January, Beckham called him "a baby" in an interview, so he hung around afterwards seeking trouble, later telling a reporter that Beckham was a "spoilt child", Gary Neville "anonymous", Schmeichel guilty of "big blunders" and that Cole "made everyone laugh with his misses".

And clearly, the repulsive Ken Bates had joined in. Taking a break from running Chelsea into the ground, he'd bragged to the press about singing "Stand up if you hate Man U", and also called United "a club from the slum side of Manchester".

Though Yorke was fit to play, wary of the threat of Zola, Fergie shovelled three men into midfield, Blomqvist the only winger starting with Beckham and Giggs on the bench. At the back, Brown returned at right-back, Irwin at left-back, and Gary Neville moved into the middle.

Chelsea were without both Desailly, injured, and Leboeuf, suspended, forced to field Duberry and Lambourde in their stead. Perhaps because of that, Vialli picked four full-backs: Petrescu, Ferrer, Babayaro and Le Saux.

These relatively cautious selections meant that the game never really sparked, and the crowded midfield resulted in plenty of stoppages – in the final quarter-hour of the first half, Chelsea would have four players booked by Graham Barber. Of course, one of them was Wise.

In the opening 44 minutes United created only one notable opportunity, Blomqvist getting to the byline and clipping back a cross that Yorke nodded towards Cole, almost under the bar. For reasons known best to himself, he failed to respond, the ball hitting his leg and bouncing away. And it took 38 minutes for Chelsea to draw a serious save from Schmeichel, forcing him to push out Zola's shot.

Then, Brown fairly *wesleyed* and *fairly* wesleyed Le Saux into the Stretford End hoardings and down the tunnel, all within the rules of Association Football, before, in the last minute of the half, United took the lead. Irwin lifted a pass into Scholes, in space 45 yards from goal and left of centre. Turning to run at the Chelsea defence, as Ferrer came across to tackle, he nudged the ball outside him to Blomqvist, now unmarked. His cross was aimed towards the near post, where Duberry's touch took it into the path of Butt, on the edge of the box, dead centre – and his left-footer caught the boot of Cole, jumping to get out of the way. Brilliantly, he then landed and adjusted his feet while backing up, and with minimum backlift, drilled a shot off the post and into the bottom-left corner, De Goey too long to get down to it in the time available.

Soon after half-time, Lambourde brought down Yorke as he floated through the middle, somehow avoiding a second yellow card – much to Fergie's displeasure particularly after Butt's sending-off at Arsenal. Wise was also fortunate to avoid another booking, though the one already received turned an impending three-game suspension into four, his season's total reaching 15 – but this could not obscure the fact that Chelsea were clearly superior.

Nonetheless, United had the opportunities to win. Replacing Yorke just after the hour, Beckham's first touch was a cross that found Scholes unmarked, only for him to head straight at De Goey, and almost immediately afterwards Scholes found Blomqvist with a chip, only for him to drag miserably wide.

Then, with only seven minutes remaining, Petrescu pushed forward down the right and fed Wise, infield. He rolled a ball into the path of Zola as Flo's run took Stam away, leaving the substitute Poyet directly in front of him, his back to Brown and to goal. They played the gentlest of one-twos, neither pass longer than a yard, allowing Zola into the box, where a difficult finish still awaited – until Schmeichel careered out of his goal as far as the penalty spot, inviting Zola to lift the ball over his dive, which he did, easily. After which, United did well to avoid defeat, Petrescu missing a chance and Babayaro clipping the post in the time remaining.

"It was a good result for us because Chelsea were the better team," said Fergie afterwards. "They persevered with their football, which is the mark of a good team, and they have a consistency which will help them challenge for the league."

*

Following the death of his sister-in-law, Fergie was in Scotland when United played newly-promoted Middlesbrough, Jim Ryan taking charge. Boro hadn't won at Old Trafford in 68 years, and accordingly, Bernie Slaven promised on his radio show that in the event of a victory for the away side, he would present his backside in the window of the town's Binns department store, after the local maxim. And Boro, managed by Bryan Robson and featuring Gary Pallister – the only man to be involved in all nine trophies won under Fergie so far – were a decent side in decent form, undefeated in ten games and resolved to attack.

After 23 minutes, Brian Deane, back in the Premier League after a spell at Benfica, crossed from the left and Gary Neville dawdled underneath, waiting for a bus and missing it, allowing Hamilton Ricard to score. Then, just after the half-hour, Johnsen's soft header teed up Dean Gordon to smack a second past Schmeichel from 25 yards, one bounce.

Eric Harrison was not impressed. "Aside from the boss, Eric could make the most brutal comments of any coach I've come across," recalled Gary Neville in his autobiography. "At half-time he turned to the defence and said, 'We've had to stick three in midfield because, by fuck, don't you lot need protecting.'"

It didn't work. With 59 minutes gone, consecutive errors, first from Phil Neville and then Johnsen, presented a third goal, snaffled by Deane, which seemed to aggravate even the Stretford End stewards. Butt and Scholes pulled two back, but no equaliser was forthcoming. So while Bernie Slaven kept his promise, getting "one of the girls" to scrawl 3–2 on his bum cheeks, the United players were left to await the fury of Fergie's return.

"Watching a video of the Middlesbrough defeat stirred me to deliver some plain words," Ferguson recalled in his autobiography with chilling understatement. But Jaap Stam preferred metaphor to euphemism, his ghostwriter remembering that "He brought the roof down with his tongue lashing." Though the principal fault was with the defending – "as wobbly as a Weeble out on the piss", said *Red Issue*'s prescient December editorial – the ire was distributed evenly across the squad. "Lack of concentration, unforgivable sloppiness, had cost us 'joke' goals", it was informed, a manifestation of general laziness and lack of focus throughout the team, which also allowed Boro to dictate the pace of the game.

And the players knew that he was right, the potency of autumn fading into carelessness as the season assumed the hue of its predecessor, but without the excuse of injuries. "You always have a low point in a season, and certainly that Middlesbrough game was the low point," said Gary Neville. "I think you need, sometimes, you know, a big kick up the backside to get you going, and that certainly got us going. I think it was like a case of that's it, now, we're not accepting any more of that. I think the players even realised that coming off the pitch that day."

Those amongst them who had grown up at United had known only success. "Sometimes you use a phrase like 'it's a waste of time'," Gary Neville said of his international career, "but being someone who's grown up at a club team who's constantly won trophies year-in, year-out, whether it is the European Cup or whether it is the championship or FA Cups, League Cups, World Club Championships, reserve team leagues, Youth Cups, we never knew not winning, the group that came through. So the idea that you go away with England – I played in five tournaments – and we never got to a final and we never won a trophy – that's what I mean by a waste of time. It might be crude and crass, but it's the way I feel."

In a way, this obsession with winning was quite unUnited, in another it helped change the culture of the club for the better.

And even Paul Scholes, the purest playground player, felt that way. Interviewed by Neville on his retirement and asked what constituted 'Paul Scholes football', the answer prioritised ends over means. He'd like to be a manager, he explained, to "try and make a team play the way I like football to be played... to win games... scoring goals, not conceding a lot of goals – scoring more goals than the other team". Only when pushed to expand did he relent, admitting that "we all like intelligent footballers... football played the right way".

Add Keane and Schmeichel into that environment – men also unused to not winning – and it's unsurprising that the various issues were addressed, some of them at the club Christmas party, two days later. The players started with lunch, then moved on to The Old Grapes in town, where a guitarist came to lead a sing-song while the pub filled up with supporters. Eventually, they moved on to a private party, where they discovered that Yorke could balance a tray of 25 cocktails on his head and Keane made what Neville insists was "one of the all-time funniest speeches". And like all drunk folk, they had conversations they might never otherwise have had, understood one another better, and felt more comfortable swapping criticism afterwards.

At the end of the Middlesbrough game, United's league record was played 18, won eight, drawn seven and lost three, with 36 scored and 23 conceded. Following the Middlesbrough game, United played 20, won 14, drew six and lost none, scoring 44 and conceding 14. And its significance was not just in the defensive lessons learned, but as the first in a series of maniacal pursuits of lost causes. It would not be long before we saw the second.

That same afternoon, Chelsea went top of the league for the first time since 1989 with a 2–0 win at home to Spurs, becoming the bookies' favourites for the title. United were third, two points behind both them and Villa, though Villa had a game in hand – which they duly won, taking them top for Christmas.

*

In the absence of a local derby, a home game against the league's worst team is not the worst way of spending Boxing Day, in theory – and even for a team in that position, Forest were in some pretty poor nick. On a run of 15 games without a win, they would soon break their own Premier League record of 17, reaching 19 – a mark that would be demolished by Derby's 32 in 2007–08, cementing them as the undisputed pride of the east Midlands.

Promoted the previous season, in the summer, Forest had sold Kevin Campbell to Trabzonspor and Colin Cooper to Boro, who came up behind them, also announcing that Scotland Gemmill would be dropped from the first team for refusing to sign a new contract. Pierre van Hooijdonk had scored 34 times in Division 1, and, fortified by the glory of a World Cup goal for Holland, the fourth in a 5–0 win over South Korea, was angry that the team had not been strengthened in the way he said he had been promised, so went on strike, to much outrage. He had joined Forest from Celtic following a wage dispute, during which he argued that £7,000 a week was "good enough for the homeless, but not for an international striker".

Van Hooijdonk relented in November, by which time Forest were in trouble. His first goal back came against Derby, after which the majority of his team-mates ignored him, celebrating instead with the returned Gemmill, who'd supplied the cross. But he was suspended for the game at Old Trafford, arranging his Christmas break via wanton violence at Leicester, Denis Law-style, so Dave Bassett went for a Shipperley – Freedman striking axis. In defence, Jesper Mattsson was missing, suffering from a severely bruised spleen.

United, though, also had injury issues. Cole had caught Yorke's groin strain and both were absent, so Sheringham played up front, with Scholes behind him. In defence, Gary Neville was suspended and Stam ruled out with a troublesome ankle, so Phil Neville came in, while, by amazing coincidence, Berg and Johnsen were fit at the same time, so played together in the middle.

The first half was a fairly lame affair, both teams sure that United would win and simply waiting for confirmation, so it took almost half an hour for them to score, roused by a chorus of "Ferguson's Red and White Army" inspired by the exhortations of Schmeichel. Then, Beasant tipped Giggs' header behind, for United's first corner of the afternoon, taken by Beckham from the left. Floated to the edge of the six-yard box, right of centre, Johnsen's downward header was firm enough to find the far corner.

Goal aside, things didn't improve, United reverting to tedium as the rain got worse. But they came out after half-time like Hurricane Stephen, Keane foiled by a last-ditch tackle and Sheringham shooting too close to Beasant after excellent control had tamed Giggs' excellent cross. Then, on the hour, they scored again, Beckham chipping a free-kick from the left to the far post, Berg outjumping Bart-Williams to head back across goal, and Johnsen edging ahead of Chettle to sit down into a thumping volley. "Ronny's on a hat-trick, Ronny's on a hat-trick" chortled the Scoreboard End.

In the 16th century, there was a Turkish miniaturist who managed to gain entry to the Sultan's art collection, and before he left, deliberately blinded himself so that the last thing he saw was the work of the great masters. It's impossible to imagine what he might have done had he seen United's third goal.

Sheringham, in his own half, fizzed a ball into Giggs, coming towards him, which he touched back to Irwin. Stepping inside and twisting, he directed a majestic 40-yard reverse pass for Sheringham, now at outside-left. Waiting for it to arrive, he checked, looked up, and skidded square into the path of the onrushing Beckham, who, without breaking stride, a stride early, and without backlift, played in Giggs to his left, defenders and keeper readying themselves for the inevitable shot. When it didn't come, Beasant charged out while Giggs controlled, then dived while he flighted a chip into the far corner.

"The rhythm of it was so sweet, it had a harmony all of its own, which is why I say it reminded me of a song," said Fergie. "A nice piece of play from Denis Irwin, a touch from David Beckham, and Ryan scored without breaking stride, just as a melody flows along." Exactly.

Also that afternoon, Chelsea celebrated Gianluca Vialli's first anniversary as manager with a win at The Dell, a result that took them top of the table. And they stayed there overnight, because Villa lost at Blackburn later on, Michael Oakes controversially sent off for handling outside the area. But Chelsea's status was not achieved without cost; Gus Poyet sustained a nasty knee ligament injury, after Hassan Kachloul's two-footed tackle. He would miss several months.

And Chelsea, who had not lost a game since the opening day of the season, were United's next opponents, just two days later. Yorke was still unavailable, but Cole came in for Sheringham, Fergie again opting for three in midfield – partly to deny Chelsea space, partly to get the team used to not conceding goals again. At the back, Stam and Neville returned, in place of Berg and other Neville respectively.

For Chelsea, Desailly was fit enough to return after a knee injury, but left on the bench, while Le Saux returned after missing the Southampton game, and Di Matteo took Poyet's place, his injury presenting an opportunity to Jody Morris.

United were forced to absorb something of a kicking in the first half, thankful for the profligacy of Tore Andre Flo in particular, but the elusive Zola too. It was he who missed the first opportunity, sent through by Di Matteo, only to bash a shot over the top.

Then, he slithered in diagonally off the left touchline. Feinting to shoot and waiting for Stam to commit to the block, he cut back outside him and struck a shot across Schmeichel, whose strong hand could still only divert the ball into the path of Flo. Unmarked, eight yards out, dead centre, and with the keeper on the floor, somehow, he managed to send it wide.

Sitting too deep and missing a second striker, United created very little, though at the end of one break, Cole collected Scholes' through-ball to round De Goey. But forced wide, Duberry was able to scramble his shot off the line.

United were the better side in the second half, improving as the game wore on, particularly once Sheringham replaced Scholes just after the hour, his hold-up play allowing others to get forward. Then, Leboeuf was booked for fouling Cole, after which Sheringham's snap-shot went only just wide.

Eleven minutes from time, Leboeuf pulled down Beckham, and to the amazement of all, Mike Riley elected not to show a second yellow. "I think maybe I deserved a red card," said Leboeuf afterwards. "I touched his foot and grabbed him with my hand. I apologise for that, but I am very pleased not to be sent off."

Fergie, meanwhile, was equally vexed with Philip Don, the secretary of the Referees' Association. "Referees are so inconsistent," he wrote. "Don seems to have changed the aspect of refereeing, changed it to his vision of how it should be done, but it is not working. People are suffering from the decisions." It was like a song.

With eight minutes to go, Petrescu slid a pass in behind Stam for Zola, but his first touch took him a little close to the keeper, such that his only route to goal was between his legs. He aimed for it, but the ball clipped Schmeichel's undercarriage as he sat down trying to close the space, hard enough to deflect the effort wide.

After the game, there was an exhibition of magnanimity from Leboeuf: "A new year has begun, so it was probably as good a time as any for David Beckham and me to start afresh and bury the past. I shook hands with him in the tunnel to, hopefully, put an end to what has been built up into a feud. The whole point of seeing Beckham at the end of the game was to look forward to a happy future."

Vialli, just relieved to discover his man hadn't been after another row, also indicated his satisfaction with the result. But he couldn't possibly have meant it; this was a major missed opportunity, and cost Chelsea the league leadership, Villa's win over Wednesday the previous evening facilitating a two-point gap. United, pleased with another clean sheet, however spawnily obtained, were now third, with Arsenal behind them only on goal difference, following a narrow win at Charlton – a game in which Patrick Vieira was sent off for elbowing Neil Redfearn.

JANUARY

As the nations of Europe massacred their national identities by launching a single currency, so United launched their final FA Cup campaign before doing the same to the competition the following season. With the draw for the fourth round made before the Sunday afternoon tie against Middlesbrough, the winners already knew the prize was a home game against Liverpool.

With Beckham suspended and also feeling tired, he was sent off on holiday, as was Scholes, Fergie deciding that they needed a rest in order to be at their best later on. And Gary Neville was also unavailable, waiting for a hip injury to heal.

But the rest of the players were working hard. "We've done more on the training ground on defending this year than I can remember in my time here, and we're getting the organisation back," Fergie would later recount. "I set off with the intention of playing Johnsen alongside Stam. But he's had injuries, so Neville did a spell and then Berg. But I think eventually, and long term, it will be Brown."

Midweek breaks were also used to do the endurance work that would prime them for the run-in. Fergie, usually easier on them than Brian Kidd and more involved since he left, had them running more laps than ever before, while Jim Ryan and Robert Swire, the club physiotherapist, prepared a bespoke programme. And in the dressing room, Peter Schmeichel had started counting down the games, announcing how many remained after each one, to maintain momentum, focus and drive.

After missing all but an hour of United's previous five games, Yorke was back to take his place alongside Cole, Sheringham dropping down to the bench. "Teddy has done remarkably well, and I feel for him," said Fergie. "He has done nothing wrong – in fact he turned the course of the game against Chelsea last Tuesday."

Elsewhere, Brown made his first start in a few weeks, Berg partnered Stam, and Blomqvist played on the left wing, Giggs moving to the right.

Before kick-off, there'd been some controversy, newspapers reporting that Roy Keane would run down the last 18 months of his contract and leave for free, should the board refuse to pay him according to his status. Later in the month, Martin Edwards would describe this preposterous concern for his worth and security as a "disruption", while standing to make £88m from the Sky sale.

Since winning at Old Trafford, Boro had lost to Liverpool and Derby, and were without the injured Gianluca Festa. But Gary Pallister and Robbie Mustoe were both fit to play, as was Paul Gascoigne, back from a spell in rehab to make his first FA Cup appearance since the 1991 final.

For the first time since Spurs, United put it on an opponent from the first minute, Cole only just missing Keane's cross. But though they had Boro pinned, they were unable to pick their way through five midfielders in front of three centre-backs, and after 21 minutes, almost went behind, Gordon losing Giggs and crossing for Mustoe, his near-post diving header straight at Schmeichel, who still needed two goes to snatch it.

Keane and Irwin were then foiled by desperate bodies flung in front of them, and at half-time, the game was still goalless. Again, United came out like they meant it, almost scoring immediately when Cole stepped over Giggs' cross and collected Yorke's pass, Schwarzer fully extending to push his shot away. Then, three minutes later, Cole sent Yorke through only for Schwarzer to excel a second time, racing out and saving with his feet.

After which, Boro went ahead. Cooper took a free-kick wide on the right and well inside his own half, launched towards Deane, who outjumped Brown and flicked on. Already in pursuit along roughly the same line as the ball, Townsend was able to run past Stam and Berg to the far post, swivelling into a finish and celebrating with genuine belief that his team might win.

As United's tempo increased, Cole was again denied by Schwarzer, but it didn't look much like Boro could hold on, largely because they couldn't. Dropping ever deeper, they allowed Brown to pick up possession in the centre-circle, no one within 20 yards of him.

Sliding the ball right, Giggs received it on the move, feinting to go outside then easing inside, away from Cooper and into space. Espying Cole escaping Maddison on the edge of the box, he intimated a reverse pass; Cole paused, Giggs played the reverse pass, Cole pounced, and smashed the ball above Schwarzer into the roof of the net.

Unwilling to contemplate a replay, United swarmed Boro, Fergie bringing Solskjær on for Blomqvist after 73 minutes and moving Giggs to the left. But still United couldn't find a way through, until, with eight minutes remaining, Keane led another attack, first looking for Neville on the right before thinking better of it and dragging the ball back, turning the other way. Instead, he knocked off a short, square pass for Butt, from whom it went to Solskjær and then Cole. Inside the box on its left-hand side, he looped a cross for Keane at the far post, whose header back across was cleared, but only as far as Butt, pacing into the box to hurdle and then fall over Maddison's legs; "I haven't touched you. I can't believe you've gone down," were the words he claimed to have shared with him afterwards. "For Graham Barber to give us a penalty kick it must have been a penalty," said Fergie, with studied archness. From the spot, Irwin went left, Schwarzer right.

Then, in injury time, Giggs came off the touchline and poked the ball to Irwin, on his outside. As he took the return, the ever-alert Solskjær left his man and raced towards him, inviting a pass that was stabbed back into Giggs' path for him to slide under Schwarzer.

"We have come through this terribly tough period of nine games in 31 days," said Fergie afterwards. "We've had Bayern Munich, Barcelona, Leeds, Chelsea, Aston Villa. It makes me exhausted just talking about them. But we have had a bit of a breather now and we looked in good physical shape today. There was a freshness about them and it helps not having a replay to worry about… That's one of our best performances of the season… The intensity of the passing, the movement and the energy we spent on the game was brilliant."

And then there was the draw for the next round – "it's a belter, it's fantastic", he said.

*

Next up for United was West Ham the following Sunday, the game in doubt for a while following an Old Trafford power failure and eventually beginning after a 45-minute delay. During that time, those in the ground and with a programme had time to ponder the manager's notes, chastising the crowd for its apathy. "These days we get a lot of spectators coming from far and wide," he wrote, "to watch and admire rather than flinging themselves wholeheartedly into rooting for the team."

Returned after his mini-break, Beckham was back on the bench, and so too was Johnsen, his starting position lost to Henning Berg. Otherwise, Sheringham had a knee problem which would keep him out until March and Gary Neville the same hip issue, while Phil Neville was suspended, Scholes still on half-term and Schmeichel in Barbados, just starting his. This was not well received by Ian Wright, who'd been looking forward to parading his magnanimity by shaking hands with Schmeichel on the pitch, it being the last time they would face one another, and accordingly his last opportunity to score against him.

Though Paolo Di Canio would not arrive for a further three weeks, West Ham were doing well, having accumulated as many away points as United in the season so far. Victimised by the player shortage that has stalked his entire career, Harry Redknapp did, at least, have Neil Ruddock available, the centrepiece of a back three also containing Rio Ferdinand and Steve Potts – moved from wing-back to combat United's pace up front. That, of course, sorted it right aht.

Otherwise, 16-year-old Izzy Iriekpen was on the bench as was 17-year-old Joe Cole, following his debut the previous weekend in a cup tie at Swansea. Cole was the star of the team – also featuring Michael Carrick – that would beat Coventry 9–0 on aggregate to win the FA Youth Cup, the commentary box's desperation for him to amount to something, anything, was palpable.

From the very first whistle, United flew at West Ham with bad intentions, Andy Cole taking advantage of Ferdinand's hesitation to divest him of the ball and fire a shot at goal, Hislop shovelling it away. Then, from the corner, Berg did well to attack the near post, but with a free header available, was unable to bond brow and ball.

A minute later, Keane flattened Frank Lampard while the crowd goaded the away support with "there's only one United". Martin Tyler would later agree, stuttering to amend his half-time summary via the suffix "…of Manchester".

United's rhythm was already far too much for West Ham to handle, the twisting, turning, synchronised striking of Yorke and Cole pulling their back eight hither and thither – with the exception of Berkovic, quietly reclining into the game. On seven minutes, Blomqvist hared back to win the ball in the centre-circle and immediately switched right to Giggs, from where it moved back for Cole, on to Yorke, to Blomqvist again, touched off to Cole and dispatched to Giggs; perceptive, pacey, purposeful passes, all squashed into a confined space. Stepping inside onto his right foot, Giggs unwound a curler that was deflected wide by Ruddock's head, though the referee awarded a goalkick.

Soon after, more passing ended in a low shot from Yorke, his new fade dawning and his shot saved by Hislop, but only to delay the inevitable. On ten minutes, a Blomqvist drive was headed away to Stam, Keane immediately upon him to demand and collect, before sending a hard, low pass through the middle to be stepped over by Giggs, the condition clearly contagious. Coming back from an offside position and with his back to goal, Cole was ideally placed to receive it, taking a touch before feeding a pass out to Yorke, on the right of the box. His control appeared to have taken him too wide, with Hislop only a couple of yards from the far post, but after a stutter-step to wind up, he somehow caressed a bludgeon that hovered fast into the side netting, a better version of his Blackburn goal and first since the Nou Camp.

After a quarter of an hour, the ball had spent 41 per cent of its time in West Ham's defensive third, and there were no signs of imminent change. So, the crowd took matters up with Ruddock, "just a fat Scouse bastard", as Butt had a shot and Stam dispossessed Hartson with degrading ease.

With no on-pitch activity to divert them, the away supporters busied themselves with making some reasonable noise. "Rio, you'll never get Rio", they cried, met by "we've got Wesley Brown". Then, United scored again.

First, Cole won a tackle with Lomas, on the right and just inside the West Ham half, before Keane took over, moving into the centre and ushering Blomqvist outside him to receive a pass. With two men blocking his route around the back, he moved inside and waited for Butt, rolling into his path. Sacrificing power for control, he hit it with his laces and watched it rebound off the post, one bounce – and fall straight to Cole, who adjusted his feet and resisted the temptation to snatch, allowing the ball to come to him and hooking a half-volley into the net, a trickier version of the chance he missed against Blackburn.

Down 2–0 at half-time, it was hard to see how West Ham might alter the flow of the game – "There's a limited capacity for change for Harry Redknapp," said Martin Tyler. Indeed.

But United couldn't maintain their intensity after the break, allowing West Ham a go of the ball, and even to create an opportunity. Cole was involved, on for Sinclair and banging a cross-field pass left to right for Lazaridis, who centred to find Berkovic in the middle and unmarked, only for him to direct a header well wide. And that was pretty much as good as it got for them, Keane spurred into action and shooting low, hard and bending away after a one-two with Blomqvist. A surprised Hislop was happy just to push it around the post.

And United kept coming, Yorke moseying down the left and teeing up Butt, Irwin making a mess of the heading opportunity created by Hislop's parry. Then, on 66 minutes, Butt broke and found Blomqvist, whose chip towards Irwin drew a challenge from Pearce, his header falling to Yorke, outside the box and left of centre. Opening his body to spread play right, Yorke again used the angle and momentum to drag himself left, into a reverse pass to Cole, sneaking in behind the defence, which was rolled precisely into the far corner. "Talk about being on the same wavelength," marvelled Martin, "these two are in perfect harmony!" Old Trafford was less loquacious but equally pointed, hollering "So fucking easy".

The points secure, Butt and Brown departed, replaced by Solskjær, his face beaming pleasure, and Johnsen. Their arrival heralded more delicious football, Stam's lofted pass headed square by Irwin, before both Yorke and Cole failed to get hold of their shots.

But another goal soon arrived, Yorke sliding a pass between two defenders and finding Giggs in the inside-right position, where he insisted on shooting with his left foot, allowing Hislop to save. The ball ballooned to where Solskjær was waiting, and he made a difficult finish look easy, nodding in from 15 yards as Ferdinand chased into the net.

With a minute to go, West Ham sneaked a goal, Lampard, its scorer, unable to resist waving his splendour to the crowd in celebration of the 1–4. Otherwise, that was pretty much it.

*

The following day was January the 11th, which is Bryan Robson's birthday.

*

After two relatively easy wins, the following Saturday promised a trickier fixture. Leicester were tenth in the league but only four points off Leeds in fifth, in the semi-final of the League Cup, and had lost only twice at home in all competitions. They also had an excellent recent record against United.

However, missing were the unwell Emile Heskey and the suspended Elliott and Sinclair, while Schmeichel returned for United. And so too did Beckham, ahead of schedule after Butt failed a late fitness test, he would play on the right, Giggs in Butt's midfield role.

From the first whistle, United were lively, particularly down the left, and though Guppy managed a shot from 30 yards that had Schmeichel scrambling, it was no surprise when they took the lead on ten minutes. Giggs found Blomqvist just outside the corner of the box, Lennon and Guppy colliding as they tried to stop him, the ball transferred wide to Irwin. His low cross arrived at Cole who performed a step over to leave it for Yorke, in splendid isolation at the back post. He took a touch, righted himself, took another touch, and then rammed a finish into the far corner.

But United could not add to their advantage with Giggs particularly culpable, heading weakly at Keller after Beckham's cross, and gradually, Leicester struggled into the game, without ever suggesting much in the way of a threat. So the arrival of their equaliser was unexpected and the man responsible for it equally so, but after 30 minutes, the teams were level. "Theodoros Zagorakis scores for Leicester City against Manchester United on 16 January 1999 a wonderful goal," recalls Wikipedia.

And then, just before half-time, came an opportunity to take the lead, Guppy's deep cross finding Kaamark alone at the back post.

But as the ball kicked off the turf, he wasted it on the rise and over the bar, by an impressive amount given the closeness of the range.

During the break, stern words were dispensed in the United dressing room, they re-emerged with blood in their eyes. On 49 minutes, a long ball from Giggs found Cole in the inside-left position, who, nodding down to himself, left Walsh, then took as many touches and as much time as necessary, before gliding a finish across Keller, into the corner.

But no one was celebrating just yet – there was work to be done – and Keane and Cole both missed chances, Cole's of particular excellence, before, just after the hour, United scored again. Inside the centre-circle, Keane turned a pass in to Yorke, his back to goal, and he cushioned and followed it right, spinning his man and sliding a pass outside the next one for Cole to stride onto and slot home, under and off Keller's hands. His 15th goal of the season, it took him ahead of Yorke for the first time.

Then two minutes later, Irwin hit a hopeful long ball that bounced into the space behind the Leicester defence, stepping up, and Keller came out, to the left edge of the box. Under pressure from Yorke, he allowed it to bounce past him, to make its gathering easier. But then he slipped, Yorke slipped past him, and slipped the ball into the far corner from an acute angle, while slipping.

Unexpectedly, it was Leicester who scored next. Schmeichel, confidence but not competence restored, came for Campbell's right-wing cross and missed his punch, the ball falling for Guppy. His shot was flying comically wide until it hit Walsh on the thigh, which diverted it into the net.

This did not precipitate even the hint of a fightback. Instead, Cole, free on the right, lofted a pass to Blomqvist, finding him at the second attempt. Taking it down on his chest, he lifted a dainty one over the defender and back inside for Yorke to take down with his own leaping chest control, before banging straight at Keller from in front of goal.

But United's dominance was such that another opportunity soon arrived, Irwin clearing and Taggart's attempted header back to Keller trickling into the path of Cole, facing him and waiting for it. Chasing away from the defence at inside-left and in search of his hat-trick, he hit a rising shot close to the near post that battered against the bar and fell onto the foot of Yorke, who completed his instead.

"We thought we'd score every week," Cole later recalled. "If one of us didn't score, the other would. We could alter our play depending on the opposition: I'd go long, he'd go short. Nobody knew how to mark us. At times, we had so much space that we took liberties."

And there was still time for another, Beckham taking a corner short to Blomqvist and curling the return to the back post, where Stam was waiting to steer home a well-controlled volley – the only goal he would score for United. His celebration was not so good.

"All things considered we did very well," said Martin O'Neill afterwards, reflecting either his own lunacy or the lunacy of United's standard. Whichever it was, with two decent Premier League teams wiped off the pitch on consecutive weekends, abused to the tune of ten goals, appreciation and trepidation were growing.

"It could just be," wrote Ian Ross in the *Guardian*, "that the nation is now finally ready to dispense with its crass and petty prejudices and draw heartily to its bosom a truly marvellous team. The accepted etiquette of your average English fan, the vindaloo and lager children of the late Seventies and Eighties, unashamedly decrees that, irrespective of United's feats, they must be derided and despised at all times; it is almost a mantra for the Millennium."

*

"Ah told ye, ah told ye hauf an oorago, this is Liverpool's day," chuckled Andy Gray when Roy Keane lasered a shot against the post. Except he hadn't, he'd hedged that it might be – but it didn't matter because it wasn't.

Both teams came into the tie in handy form; United had taken 13 goals in their three preceding games, persuading Keane to make the first public acknowledgement that the Treble was possible. And for their part, Liverpool Football Club had won five of their last six, the only blemish a creditable goalless draw at Highbury, and the previous Saturday, they'd dispatched Southampton 7–1. But they'd not beaten United in the FA Cup since 1921, at Old Trafford since 1990, and at all since 1995.

The league meeting between the clubs had prompted spirited pre-match discussions, which, along with a Cup allocation, made Old Trafford and its environs an even livelier place that morning. Brad Friedel had been in goal for Liverpool Football Club then, and, dropped immediately afterwards, would spend the rest of his career wreaking a terrible revenge. His place was taken by old friend David James.

United were glad to have Gary Neville back, though not as glad as he was to be back, having spent a miserable week alone in the treatment room, watching the others laughing and joking. Then, on the Saturday, he used his newspaper column to explain his relationship with the United – Liverpool rivalry: "You might think the intense dislike that the vast majority of Manchester United fans feel towards Liverpool would grow less when you become a professional footballer," he wrote. "Well, it doesn't. The feeling of the fans has got to be mirrored by the attitude of the players as we represent them. I'm not just saying that. It would go against everything I have ever believed in… I just don't like the club. I never have done and I never will."

Also returning for his first game of the year was Paul Scholes, though he was left on the bench, Butt joining Keane in midfield. Behind them, the centre-backs were Stam and Berg.

Within seconds of the kick-off, James flew out of his goal searching for a corner many levels out of his reach. But he escaped, and after not many more Liverpool took the lead, Michael Owen somehow left alone in the six-yard box. "God almighty, you wouldn't think a 5 foot 6 striker would score with a header in the first minutes at Old Trafford," said Fergie. "I wasn't too pleased with that."

Though they spent the remainder of the game on the attack, United weren't quite there – "a vacant possession that lacked the normal imagination", wrote David Lacey. So, a post-hit from Keane aside, they didn't come all that close in the first half, with both Fowler – whose amazing right-footed curve from distance whistled wide, and Berger, who forced a smart stop from Schmeichel at his near post – almost doubling Liverpool's advantage just before the interval.

Driven on by Stam, United turned it up in the second 45, Liverpool's formation one more frequently seen on a chess board than a football pitch. Giggs somehow evaded a Beckham cross, Keane's deflected shot passed just wide of the post, and after Matteo whacked an attempted clearance straight at James, he valiantly avoided bungling it into the net.

Liverpool were, though, still a threat on the break. On 55 minutes, Owen screeched away from Irwin and Keane, tapping back for Fowler to swing a right foot and shoot narrowly wide of the post. Then, just after the hour and following rare coherence from United down the left, Irwin, Yorke and Giggs linked to arrange a shooting opportunity for Keane. When it was deflected wide, Andy Gray *wondered* whether it *might* just be Liverpool's day.

On 68 minutes, Scholes replaced Butt, and then Matteo deflected Beckham's cross, hard – but straight into the arms of James. "Well that's it for me, I think we can all go home now," said Andy Gray, and immediately afterwards Houllier brought on McAteer, instantly thickening his midfield – for the injured Ince, who departed to ridicule.

As United's frenzy increased, Fowler almost settled the tie, shooting wide after an Owen whoosh down the left, and then again a few minutes later, Schmeichel and Stam combining to deny him. When, after 79 minutes, Yorke flicked to Cole, and Keane hit the post, it was becoming trickier to see a way.

Fergie sent Johnsen and Solskjær on for Berg and Irwin, the pitch now resembling a World Cup Doubles world record attempt, but within two minutes, Fowler sent Owen away, who tripped over the ball. Shortly afterwards, he was booked for fouling Neville, and when Schmeichel took the free-kick from inside the Liverpool half, hoicking it into touch, Gerard's army was on the march. And they ought to have sealed the win when McAteer broke down the right and crossed for Fowler, who arrived before Stam but missed his kick, the ball rebounding to Schmeichel.

Then, with two minutes remaining, Redknapp was adjudged to have fouled Johnsen. "Maybe we showed a bit of inexperience by worrying about the decision instead of getting into position," Houllier excused later, hoping no one would notice that his was not remotely an inexperienced team.

So 25 yards from goal and level with the right edge of the box, Beckham caressed the ball towards the back post and Cole stooped to cushion while Heggem dreamt of fishes, with heads like combine harvesters, and fibreglass flowers, and cakes made of otters, and otters made of cakes, purple cakes, and Yorke tapped in from a yard. Just when it looked like it wasn't coming, there it was.

"Liverpool's resistance finally broken, and there's still time... for more to come," said Martin Tyler.

No sooner were minds cast towards a night game at Anfield with a Cup allocation, than United had won. Stam clipped long from close to the right touchline, just inside the Liverpool half, and Cole and Matteo both missed their headers, Scholes coming onto the ball and smothering the bounce with his chest, bumping and staggering Carragher out of the way. But before he could shoot, Solskjær assumed responsibility. The circumstance demanded one touch to control and another to set himself, so he took those at speed, exuded some composure, then expelled Liverpool from the FA Cup, pulling a left-footed finish through some legs and inside the near post as James heaved towards the opposite corner. Mayhem.

Fergie, of course, was all over it, his love of a celebration an enduringly endearing aspect. During the previous season's run-in, he'd gone as far as ordering his players to perform theirs together and in riotous style to send a message of unity to Arsenal, which resulted in a particular display at home to Wimbledon – but this one required no such arrangement. While Phil Neville booted the hoardings, Gary Neville alerted the away fans to this new development in the match, racing towards K Stand in order to share his goon, Schmeichel doing the same. Then, after Berger sliced a free-kick wide just before time, Beckham made it his business to retrieve the ball, punching the air at the same time and attempting to catch every last pair of Scouse eyes. This instigated disress, expressed via a shower of coins and then a seat, but he remained for a few seconds longer, before turning, saluting the crowd and getting on.

At the final whistle, an eggy Phil Thompson made straight for Graham Poll to share his outrage at the free-kick that precipitated the equaliser, while in the tunnel, Houllier attempted rousing and achieved impotent. "We'll beat Manchester United one day, I'll tell you," he pleaded, like an infant Dr Claw. It was no, "We'll get there, believe me, and when it happens, life will change for Liverpool and everyone else – dramatically," that was for sure.

By the press conference, Houllier had calmed down. "The game was five minutes too long for us," he rationalised. "It's a shame because the players could have written a page in the club's history in capital letters. I feel very proud of what we did." He did not specify precisely what what was.

Paul Scholes would later call it "one of the most one-sided FA Cup encounters I can remember," and as a man not given to exaggeration, his hyperbole is to be respected – but United had arguably the worse of the chances. On the other hand, describing it as "the most exciting and ultimately satisfying finish to any game I ever played in" seems fair enough, his schadenfreude too. "To beat Liverpool at any time is wonderful; to do it in this manner defied description," he wrote. "Devastating for them? Yup, and the more devastating the better, as far as we were concerned… I don't think they liked us really. Maybe there was a lot of jealously because we were winning things all the time."

In particular, the win was fitting reward for Ole Gunnar Solskjær, who now had more goals, 11; than starts, nine. No finish was ever rushed unless it was the optimal way of effecting it and almost all of his shots hit the target, so many apparently saveable but eminently not, directed precisely at where it was hardest for the keeper to reach them. It just all looked so simple, and it was. "There's a goalkeeper left, just put it past him," he explained, the ability to see simplicity and clarity where others saw options and obfuscations a rare quality that he shared with Scholes.

And his imperviousness to panic was as crucial off the pitch as on it, allowing him to hold his nerve in the summer, and his role in the squad – a specialist one – was high on importance, if relatively low on game time. So rather than sulk, he watched carefully in order to take advantage whenever a chance came, applying the patience, angles and body position learnt wrestling in his youth.

"If I ever feel guilty about the teams I pick and the players I leave out, it invariably centres around him," wrote Ferguson. "He really deserves better than the number of games I give him, but the other factor that influences me is that he is better than everyone else as a substitute."

Both were vindicated with more goals off the bench than any player in the history of the Premier League and probably before, and though his total has been overtaken by Jermain Defoe since he retired his ratio has not. "Everything he did was for the team," said Gary Neville.

And now, it was a team in the most genuine sense of the word, disparate personalities melded into a coherent whole, with someone for everyone: the unhinged mind-speaker, the stylish metrosexual, the Gary Cooper, the party boy, the flash one from that there London, the unassuming genius, the quiet nerdish one, the moaning workaholic, the sensitive brooder, the flighty aesthete, the Manchester boys. Try that game with the current collection and see if you don't come up with a whole lot of cuss words and nothing.

The last cohort before the ftbllr generation, these were the last to genuinely represent Manchester, Manchester United and the support; a team to connect with actually as well as conceptually, love justified intellectually as well as emotionally. They might not have beaten the 93–94 team in a ruck, but Cantona aside, they were someway more interesting.

"We all had that common work ethic, and that is what made that team special," Beckham said later, the drive and consequent refusal to lose coming straight from The Top. And Scholes agreed, commenting that the most significant lesson he learnt from the manager was "to work as hard as you possibly can", while Gary Neville was convinced too. Asked to reflect on how Fergie shaped him, he was unequivocal: "Keep going, hard work, the relentless nature of his personality... he would win a trophy, but then really it wouldn't affect him, we'd lose a game and he would make sure we responded, he responded... relentless, it's my favourite word. It's my favourite word because I've been surrounded by relentless people... Sir Alex Ferguson is just *relentless*, constantly, every minute of every day, every match, every year, every season."

And it is this aspect that enabled him to demand such high standards of everyone else. "He's moulded me into the professional footballer and person that I am," Solskjær said. "He taught me the difference between going through the motions, as you say, and be happy – or get everything out of your talent." Neville recalls a dressing room dressing down after United lost the 1993 Youth Cup final to Leeds: "He had a little bit of a go at us... a lot of a go at us. 'You've no chance of playing at this club if you're gonna perform like that.'"

But ire of this ilk was more about securing requisite reaction than wanton unburdening, usually delivered to men he knew could take it. "To play for him, you have to have, and be, a certain type," reckoned Steve Bruce, "and if you can't stand up to him then he knows that you're not strong enough to play for Man U."

Though this did change somewhat – "I'm dealing with more fragile human beings than I used to be," he told the BBC years later. "They are cocooned by modern parents, agents, even their own image at times."

But the basis of Fergie's values remained constant. "I hammer it into them that the work ethic is what got them through the door here in the first place, and they must never lose it. I say to them, 'When you're going home to your mother, you make sure she's seeing the same person she sent to me, but if you take all this fame and money the wrong way, your mother will be disappointed with you.'"

And even in the earlier, angrier days, he was rarely indiscriminate, picking only on those he felt could handle it, often to establish a point for the benefit of those who couldn't. "I think he deliberately tried to provoke a temper in the team that would make us naturally aggressive during games," wrote Peter Schmeichel in his autobiography – and rage was certainly used as a device. "There's nothing wrong with losing your temper, as long as you do it for the right reasons," Fergie said in 2010. "My reasons were always about not reaching a certain standard. Then I would let them know. I never leave it until the next day. I don't believe in that. Some managers wait until Monday when things are calmer, but I want to let it go after the game because I am already planning for the next game. Once I let it go, it's finished and I don't bring it up again."

Yet, despite all the hairdryer hilarity that permeated the media, the players knew he was making serious points; his lessons, says Gary Neville, "stand you in good stead in life, not just football". He would not, for example, allow them to begin or finish a journey in anything but club blazers: "You're walking through an airport representing Manchester United," was the argument, implicit its qualitative distinction from any other club, a detail that manifested not just in pride, but performance.

"At Manchester United we have to be better than everyone else," Fergie explained. "That's why we have worked so hard on discipline. Somebody wrote… that every great team needs bad behaviour at times. But I disagree. I had one terrible patch back in 1994 lasting about three months when everyone was being sent off. It got to the point where I had to step in and do something about that. Now the discipline on the pitch at this club is bloody good. We play the right way."

Partly because his standards were intended to develop characters, he enjoyed the achievements even of those who left United, many of whom he helped find new clubs. "You're in his hands, he's the boss," says Neville simply.

And this ability to influence others, the charisma that inspired, didn't simply follow fame. Brian McClair once told David Meek of their first meeting in Monaco – he was a Celtic player then, receiving an award as Europe's top goalscorer. "He was there representing Aberdeen and after the dinner and presentations he asked me what I was going to do. I told him that I wanted to take the opportunity of being in Monte Carlo by going to the famous casino, to which he said, 'Oh no you're not, son, you are going to your bed.'

"The funny thing was that even though I didn't play for his club and he wasn't my manager, that's exactly what I did. There was just something about the man that I didn't want to argue with. He has a natural authority. Somehow you just accept that what he says is right. I was young, but even so, that first experience of meeting him has never left me."

Finding an ex-player willing to criticise him is close to impossible, and even those with whom he falls out generally initiate rapprochement. And because he provided genuine pastoral care, his influence extended beyond the confines of the dressing room, a man always there for his players.

Accordingly, his trust was coveted and respected, the theme a recurrent one. Gary Neville has spoken of wanting to maintain it by behaving properly, Solskjær by performing properly, "because he deserves it", and even Roy Keane felt the responsibility. "Sometimes after big games it wasn't the hairdryer that worried me," he wrote, "it was when he was quiet. We worried we'd let the man down."

Of course this was deliberate; "I trust my players" was a Fergie cliché, used not just before big games but after big defeats – the successive hammerings at Newcastle and Southampton in 1996, for example. It was on those occasions that he was most vocal, rebuilding and reassuring.

And it worked, each of his teams renowned for its late goals, these perhaps the most spectacular yet. "From there you just felt they were never gonna be beaten," he said. "Such was the will to win and determination in that game, and that's carried itself, and the momentum's carried on with it. You hope your personality and character eventually seeps into their pores and I think we've got a few players who in their own way have developed the character in the shape and form I thought I was like and I think I'm like as a person."

"*In their own way*": the four words that reveal the genius of the master man-manager.

*

And then there's Glenn Hoddle. Keen to debunk his image as a hocus-pocus crackpot, he told *The Times* about his various spiritual beliefs, in particular, that disabled people were being punished for bad karma attracted in a former life.

Obviously the FA supported him. Obviously there was a shitstorm. Obviously the FA then bottled it, and sacked him three days later. He never did speculate as to the horrors he had previously perpetrated in order to merit such public humiliation.

*

United hadn't visited The Valley since February 1957, when a Charlton hat-trick and Taylor brace helped them to a 5–1 win, en route to a second consecutive title. This time, there was the possibility that they might go top if they won – United's game at Charlton kicked off at the same time as Chelsea's trip to Arsenal, where a home win or a draw would complete the job.

Before the game, Ferguson had the difficult job of deciding whether or not to select Solskjær. But unwilling to field three up front – "you could do that if you wanted to but we have a system of play here that we don't want to tinker with" – in the end, he stuck with Cole and Yorke. Otherwise, Blomqvist was back, and Berg partnered Stam in defence.

Charlton were not in a good way, second from bottom and only a point ahead of Forest – and missing first-choice defenders, Danny Mills and Eddie Youds. Though they'd drawn their previous game with Newcastle, they'd lost the seven prior, equalling what was then a Premier League record for straight defeats, until Sunderland took it apart in 2002–03, recording 15.

But, against United, they played with confidence and fortitude, withstanding almost 90 minutes of pressure, and without much undue alarm. The game was, wrote Martin Thorpe in the *Guardian*, "on a par with a mimed production of *Waiting for Godot*."

In the first half, Charlton's three centre-backs stifled Cole and Yorke, while their wing-backs stayed deep enough to restrict the wide players. It was not until the 24th minute that Simon Royce had a shot to save, and even that was a right-footed volley from Giggs.

Probably United's best chance of the half came after 36 minutes, when Keane picked his way into space and teed up Butt, whose shot flashed wide, and shortly afterwards, Giggs forced Royce to dirty his knees when he volleyed Beckham's cross at goal. Then, in the final minute of the half, Schmeichel was induced to dive at Kinsella's feet, causing the crowd to appeal for a penalty – but the referee was having none of it.

United increased the pressure after the break, Robinson's desperate block diverting Giggs' goalbound shot behind, and Brown's back intercepting a Keane volley headed in the same direction. For the final quarter, Fergie replaced Beckham with Solskjær, the extra striker taxing Charlton's centre-backs, no longer able to have two marking and one spare. With 12 minutes left, Butt played a one-two with Yorke and shot wide, departing shortly afterwards to allow Scholes to come on, but the difference was marginal – another desperate tackle, this time from Tiler, deflected a Yorke effort over the bar, but there was little else.

Then, in the 89th minute, Neville thwhacked a diagonal ball towards Keane, and he nodded down for Cole, his back to goal. Trying to tip the ball behind him and turn, Rufus was wise to it, lumping away, but only as far as Neville, who was now only 40 or so yards out. With Robinson coming in to challenge, he volleyed first time, short and inside to Scholes, left unmarked while Charlton defended the box. As two men approached, he shuffled, feinted and went right, taking the ball around the first and away from goal, then pivoting when he reached the edge of the box to clip a curling, blind chip to the far post. "He's not the quickest, he doesn't run the most, he never wins a header, he can't tackle," Solskjær once said of him, "but he's the best player" – and this was why. Because waiting, hovering, was Yorke, up well before Brown and there until the ball had been headed in off the woodwork, for a goal that even Fergie hadn't seen coming.

"Late goals, 1–0s, away from home, 2–1, 3–2, doesn't matter," he said. "If you get there – it's the getting there – and we're prepared to risk to get there."

Meanwhile, at Highbury, Dennis Bergkamp's strike was enough to give Arsenal the win, Chelsea's first defeat in 22 games. This meant that for the first time all season, United were top at the end of a weekend, and Fergie was pleased.

"That tells you you're doing something right. We're doing a lot right at the moment. We've been playing very well, working hard everywhere on the pitch. They're working hard to get the ball back when they haven't got it. The movement is very good and you get rewards from that." He also said that "staying at the top may be slightly easier than getting there". It was not.

FEBRUARY

After Hoddle's sacking, Howard Wilkinson somehow managed to insinuate himself as England's caretaker manager – not quite as astounding an effort as when he did the same at Sunderland, but notable nonetheless. Immediately, he recalled Andy Cole for the forthcoming defeat against France.

But that same day, Cole found himself on the bench for United's game at home to Derby, one it was felt could be won without him, Solskjær coming in. Beckham was also rested, his place in the team and more nominally on the pitch taken by Scholes, while Johnsen replaced the injured Berg. At left-back, as usual, was Irwin, who earlier had signed on for another year after delaying the start of negotiations until November, to check that he was still getting picked.

The fixture had originally been scheduled for Easter Monday, but, with United definitely playing on the Saturday and with a potential European semi-final on the Wednesday, Derby agreed to the move. They were on a decent run, beaten only once in nine games and drawing with both Arsenal and Chelsea – and in particular, were defending well, conceeding just six goals in the same period and boasting the third best overall record in the divison.

In the opening bit, it was Jaap Stam who came closest for United, bashing the kind of 30-yarder he'd have let go at free-kicks if ever allowed, at the end of a surging run. Hoult did well to parry.

He then clobbered another shot just wide, before, on ten minutes, Giggs was forced off and possibly out of the Inter game, with another hamstring strain. "There's not a lot of fat on his muscle, and it's one of those characteristics that you have to accept," wrote Fergie later. The previous season, his injury in the same fixture and around the same time had precipitated a disintegration – now, he was just replaced by Blomqvist.

Then, ten minutes before half-time and showing the skills that would earn him a shock deadline-day move to Manchester City the following year, Spencer Prior slid in to dispossess Yorke as he prepared to shoot at the end of a sprint into the box. Next, Keane hurried a shot wide, before another counter led to Kevin Harper being incorrectly adjudged offside, when clean through.

The second half offered little more, United limited to punts from distance, Keane and Neville thrashing wildly into the stands, and just past the hour, Cole was told to prepare himself. Moments later, he was sitting down again.

After some nondescript head-tennis on the United left, a clearance found Johnsen close to halfway, and unchallenged, he rode the bounce and nodded to Butt. In space, 40 yards from goal, he used the next bounce to skip into a lovely lofted pass for Yorke – "his one contribution to the match," snarked the *Guardian*'s Michael Walker. With the Derby defence square, Yorke was through, and though there was still work to do – catching the ball precisely as it dropped to bring it under control, opening his body while waiting for it to drop again, then tenderly curving a finish past Hoult – it was done in a flowing, easy manner. He had now scored in five consecutive games.

Everyone relaxed after that, Keane belting one wide and Hoult making two more excellent stops, Derby never really permitted to threaten. At full-time, United had a four-point lead at the top, having played once more than the other challengers, who would catch up in March: Arsenal and Villa in the gap between the two Inter ties, Chelsea on the night of the second leg.

After the game, Fergie hung around for Jim Smith in the corridor connecting the press conference room to the dressing rooms – his office was full of people, and he wanted Smith's assistant, Steve McClaren, to replace Brian Kidd. Next day, the two men met, and a deal was then concluded.

*

United's Saturday opponents were Forest, who had finally ended their winless run at Goodison Park the previous week. The clinching goal had been scored by the charming van Hooijdonk, but his return had come too late to save Dave Bassett, sacked after a home Cup defeat to Portsmouth.

Bassett's replacement was Ron Atkinson, specially returned from the Caribbean, and who, before his first game in charge, sat himself in the wrong dugout, to the intense mirth of all. The previous season, he had rescued Sheffield Wednesday from a poor start under David Pleat, but was not rewarded with a permanent contract – believed by some to be revenge for his leaving the club in 1991, joining Aston Villa only days after promising to stay.

He made his mark immediately. In every rubbish Sunday league team there is found a player with no discernible ability, who plays centre-back and barks orders "because he reads it". Well, now Forest had Carlton Palmer. And they also had John Harkes, fresh from his removal from the US World Cup squad – according to team-mate Eric Wynalda, on account of pursuing "an inappropriate relationship" with team-mate Eric Wynalda's wife.

As for United, Giggs was still out, and Phil Neville and Beckham came in, for Irwin and Solskjær respectively. The game took place on the anniversary of Munich, and though there was neither silence, nor armbands, no one suggested that the losses were not keenly felt.

The pre-match warm-up was led, for the first time, by Steve McClaren, not that anyone participating knew who he was. Meanwhile, a rowdy away end spent the period before the game first joining in with 'Sit Down', played over the Tannoy, then serenading Solskjær, while in commentary, Martin Tyler bemoaned the state of the pitch just as United began "the type of passing that might just be a bit difficult on this surface".

Within two minutes, they won a corner, Beckham's in-swinger somehow avoiding everyone, bouncing in the box and falling to Keane, just outside it and close to the byline. He laid the ball back to the edge, where Scholes arced over a first-time cross directly onto Yorke's instep, which tucked a tidy finish underneath Beasant. Behind the goal, there was not the slightest pretence that the stand was not full of United.

But Forest didn't crumble. When Johnsen came to halfway and lost out to Darcheville, the ball was knocked left to Rogers, then back and back again, Gary Neville caught in between the two, and Rogers arriving inside the box to crack a low, equalising drive into the far corner.

This effrontery roused United once more and immediately following kick-off Stam aimed a long ball towards Cole. Outstripping defenders not paying attention, Beasant was forced out of his goal and Cole had to do very little to get around him to the right, sliding the ball in from a narrow angle despite Hjelde's slide.

After more United pressure, Van Hooijdonk led a rare Forest break, finishing the victim of a signature vignette of Stam. Thinking he could tempt his man wide and use the space to outpace him, he was helpless as Stam effortlessly sailed alongside, relieved him of the ball, and moved off.

United attacked next, Beckham's searching pass from halfway finding Cole, Palmer so busy organising that he clean forgot to mark. Cole took the ball down on his chest and fired across Beasant who dived the other way, the shot just narrowly wide of the post.

Keane then fixed himself a booking, handling to abort a Forest attack, which came about after a loose Schmeichel kick. But the root cause was Stam's bouncing back-pass, and for this he received a lengthy coating, along with an indication that this was not his first offence.

Just before half-time, Scholes jumped to control a Beasant clearance on his chest – the genius not solely in the technique but the predetermined angle he knew would take it away from the nearest potential challengers. Tapping left, Keane then found Yorke with his back to goal, who returned for Scholes to seek Cole running through the middle – but Beasant was out sharply to smother.

Though it didn't result in a goal, the move again revealed United's attacking crux. At almost all times, at least one striker faced the play, and when the ball was fed in, with pace if possible, the aim was not to hold, but to set it up – with a quick touch, before making a move. Consequently, possession was retained, but higher up the pitch, the passer able to see the complete picture and defenders forced to guess where the ball and various bodies in the vicinity might go next – a method workable only with two such mobile all-rounders up front.

United began the second half on the attack, a Phil Neville cross headed away as far as Scholes. Again, the angle of his control was too much, taking the ball left and then right, the kind of scripted improvisation – deciding what to do, based on what he knew his opponent would do, often at his inducement – more commonly found in boxers, bowlers and tennis players. He then clumped a shot that swerved away from Beasant and against the post, earning the rich, rare reward of a push on the back from Roy Keane.

And it wasn't long before the lead was extended, Palmer heading Neville's long ball clear, but straight to Beckham – "again, United picking up all the pieces", marvelled Barry Davies. Swapping passes with Yorke, Beckham then crossed, the ball headed more up than away by Hjelde. Jumping with Gemmill, his back to goal, Yorke hooked behind him, and with Palmer organising he and Hjelde to collide, there was no clearance – instead, Yorke was able to shoot from the right edge of the box, low and hardish. Frazzled with overwork, Beasant could only push it onto his body, and with no one but Cole paying attention, he arrived to slot home.

Almost immediately, United created another opportunity, Yorke turning Blomqvist's cross around the near post. Atkinson had seen enough, and brought on Mattsson for Gemmill and moving Palmer into midfield. This, of course, sorted everything; within minutes, he was marauding forward to geoffthomas a shot in tribute to his out-of-favour team-mate. And next, Stone set up Johnson for a shot from outside the box on the right which he blasted against the bar, to elicit alternate shouting and muttering from Keane.

The chances were coming at quite some lick now, Beckham and Yorke exchanging flicks along the right touchline before a cross located Cole at the far post, but he could only plop a header into Beasant's arms. Then, Keane moved possession onto Gary Neville, who gave it back so it could go down the line to Beckham. Feeding infield to Yorke, his back to goal, he picked up the immediate return and cutting a crossfield ball into the path of Blomqvist. Swaying inside and then outside Harkes, he strolled past, evaded the comeback on the byline and crossed, Kjelde extending a matter of principle leg that deflected the ball against the post that deflected it to the feet of Yorke, inside the six-yard box. He couldn't miss and the hat-trick race was on again.

The hat-trick race was off, Fergie withdrawing Yorke for Solskjær, and Keane for Curtis. Beckham immediately tried his luck moving into the middle, but was sent back, Phil Neville slotting in and Curtis taking his spot. Meanwhile, United's support, as remorseless as its team, set about Atkinson with alacrity – "Big Fat Ron has fucked it up again", followed by "Big Ron for England", and eventually, "Big Fat Ron, what a difference you have made".

Then, after Rogers had missed his kick when in front of goal, spooked by the onrushing Schmeichel, with ten minutes left, United scored a fifth. Butt, on for Blomqvist, gathered a loose ball in centre-field and spread it wide to Beckham as Porfirio charged him from behind – he was booked after the fact – and the two scuffled on the ground. Meanwhile, Beckham drifted inside and waited for Gary Neville to speedscurry by on the outside, pushing him in and watching as his low cross was tapped in by Solskjær at the back post.

The next eight minutes passed fairly uneventfully, Phil Neville cautioned for a late tackle on van Hooijdonk and Porfirio avoiding a second yellow for a hard and potentially fair one on Gary Neville. Johnsen then won the ball from Freedman by the corner flag on the Forest right and Curtis took over, finding Beckham, who hit a long ball for Solskjær, at inside-right and through. Looking up to see Beasant off his line and narrowing the angle on the edge of his box, he attempted a chip that was blocked, and when the ball came back, made to go left, shimmied away right, and drilled a perfectly straight finish high into the net. Method and technique similar to that used by Mark Hughes against Barcelona in 1991, it was celebrated in the grand style with a Barry Davies "Oh, that's brilliant!" 6–1, and the hat-trick race was on again.

Just after van Hooijdonk was caught on his heels when Johnsen unexpectedly missed a header, the referee indicated three minutes of stoppage time – in a half that had seen five changes and four goals. To gunfire grunts of "attack-attack-attack", United swept forward again, Butt moving possession wide to Curtis, who found Scholes infield. With van Hooijdonk approaching, he sent the ball one side of him and bounced around the other, before intimating a shot, and instead clipping the ball left to "Solsharrer", who brought it down with his left foot and slammed it home with his right, close to Beasant but precisely where he would never think to position his hands. The hat-trick race was done.

Moments earlier, Solskjær resigned to an afternoon of inactivity, had been surprised when he was ordered to get ready: "Jim Ryan had few famous words," he recalled, "like 'we don't need any more goals, just keep the ball, pass it, just play nice and simple', and… err… of course I don't like to do it that way, do I?"

And therein lies the beauty of a squad with genuine options, teams picked according to form not tombola. Each time players played, and regardless of circumstance, they had a purpose – fortified, on this occasion, by the need to impress Steve McClaren, of all things.

"If I got 20 minutes, I'll prove him wrong, make him think maybe I should have started," Solskjær explained. "When you're young you don't really see the broader picture. I realise now I was a fantastic sub for him, I reacted exactly how he wanted me to... I had 20 minutes to put 90 minutes' work in. I'd seen loads of subs because I'd seen quite a few of them come and go, and sulking this, unhappy that, the manager this, the manager that, but it was just in me to do my best whenever I could."

His ascent into the pantheon, confirmed by the Liverpool game, began the previous April when he tripped Robert Lee, who was through on goal, and accepted the inevitable red card. This did not, though, go down well with everyone – Fergie considered it the basest form of cheating and against the ethos of the club, and told him so. But, on the other hand, Wayne Rooney has never spoken of managerial condemnation following his dive against Arsenal in October 2004, and Phil Neville commented that though he didn't handle David Platt's winning header off the line in 1997, he'd have done exactly as Solskjær did against Newcastle, because that came at the season's climax. He was congratulated for his selflessness, but that wasn't right – it was just that his needs coalesced with those of the team, as they always did.

And he wasn't finished here. Butt hopped to lift a bouncing ball to Beckham, who drifted it in to Cole, again with his back to goal – and he returned to Butt. Dragging back a cross that was missed entirely by Scholes, the ball then deflected off his standing foot and arrived perfectly for Solskjær, the roar from the away end pre-empting the finish, dispatched almost apologetically. He now had four goals in the final ten minutes of the game, and United were up to eight.

"It was one of those days you felt you were on the playground," Solskjær said. "The ball just landed in my feet, if I missed it the first time it just landed back in my feet and you score again." This self-effacement was also reflected through the absence of celebration, simply a man doing what he was meant to do. And it later transpired that he was wearing dinky new boots, bought for him and by him the previous day in the Trafford Centre. "We couldn't believe it when I saw Ole was wearing the size 7s that we had sold him," Sports Soccer manager Colin Broadhurst told the obligatory *Sun* reporter. "It was incredible." What he expected to be done with them remained a mystery.

Meanwhile, Atkinson endeared himself further to Forest fans by telling them he'd provided "a nine-goal thriller" – if only he'd known, he might also have advised them to take pride in a new Premier League record, the ten shots on target to nine goals scored a new leading ratio. Elsewhere, Arsenal came off the pitch at West Ham, no doubt revelling in a notable 4–0 victory, only to discover that their efforts had been entirely overshadowed, while Villa were beaten at home by Blackburn, their second defeat in a row.

In any other season, away slobberknockers of 6–2, 6–2 and 8–1 would constitute substance and highlights, and yet, in this one, they are mere details; ornate details, but details nonetheless. After United beat Anderlecht 10–0 in 1953, Matt Busby observed that, "I can still see young Colman running to collect the ball for a throw-in with only two or three minutes left, as if we were losing and his whole life depended on it", the motivation not cruelty, but pride and joy. This was how football was meant to be played.

*

The following weekend, Arsenal had the headlines all to themselves. Nwankwo Kanu, recently signed from Inter – compared by Arsène Wenger to Alan Smith, presumably as a form of misdirection – made his debut against Sheffield United in the FA Cup, a game that Arsenal won. But their clinching goal came after the ball was kicked out of play to allow an opposing player to receive treatment, and, Kanu, unaware of the etiquette stipulating that possession be returned, instead broke away down the right and squared for Overmars to score. Following much outrage, Wenger magnanimously offered to replay the tie, safe in the knowledge that no way would such a carry-on be permitted, before in a tremendous piece of bluff-calling, permitted it was – which turned out to be just as well, as otherwise we would've been deprived of yet another Dennis Bergkamp masterpiece.

United didn't play until the following day, at home to Fulham, miles ahead at the top of Division 2; Mohamed Al-Fayed's millions had presented a net so gaping that not even Kevin Keegan could contrive to miss it. Luckily, Keegan's position as the favourite to succeed Glenn Hoddle restricted the "I will love it" narrative in the lead-up to the game, though this brought with it fresh tedium.

"I'm not gonna give up what we've started at Fulham," he told ITV, before discussing how his sentiments hadn't altered since they'd last asked him, the previous day. Usually, the constant harassment would indicate a lack of effort or imagination on the part of the interviewer or simply that there was nothing else to say, but, here it was simply because no one believed him. So he reiterated: "I'm not gonna walk out on Fulham." That was 14 February. Three days later, he was appointed part-time England manager, and on 6 May, left Fulham to take the job permanently.

Fulham had got rid of Southampton and Aston Villa in the two previous rounds, but were weakened by injuries and suspension for this one. Bracewell, Morgan, Peschisolido and Horsfield – whom Robbie Savage rated the hardest player he ever encountered, just ahead of Keane – were absent.

United were without Scholes and Keane, both suspended, but Gary Neville passed a late fitness test, and his brother came in for his first start since Boxing Day to join Beckham and Butt in a narrow midfield three. Ahead of them, Solskjær's goals at Forest earned him a start, on the left, with Yorke on the other side and Cole in the middle.

Cole also spoke to ITV before the game, making it clear that despite the new him, there remained plenty of the old pissed-off one: "The stigma was there, when I scored 25 goals last season," he said, "and everyone was saying like oh, he's playing with Teddy and Teddy's made him a better player, and now Dwight's come, it's the same kind of thing. I like to think I've done as much for Dwight as Dwight's done for me."

Fulham started as well as United started lethargically, and the closest either side came to a goal in the opening minutes was Salako's header from the edge of the box after Finnan's cross, which went only just wide. United's various promptings were not quite up to standard, an early warning as to the stodginess of a midfield without Keane and Scholes. This could, though, be blamed on a lack of natural width, with Blomqvist, suddenly essential against Arsenal in the absence of Giggs, left on the bench, and Solskjær not yet comfortable out wide.

Then, after 26 minutes, Butt injected some pace into proceedings with two quick passes, the first going through Yorke, Phil Neville and Stam before returning, and the second finding Beckham in centre-field, whose reverse pass located Yorke again. From him the play moved out to Irwin, and Taylor did well to cut out his cross, but when Brevett's clearance hit Cole, Fulham struggled to clear.

And when they did, United came straight back, Butt sending the ball wide to Gary Neville, who exchanged passes with Beckham and fed Yorke, who tapped back to Butt. Out of nowhere, he hit a long pass with minimum backlift over Finnan's head for Solskjær, and his dribbled cut-back allowed Cole to open up his body and direct a side-footed finish into the far corner, via Symons' thigh.

Immediately afterwards, a long ball found Lehmann alone in the United box, but as he shilly-shallied, Gary Neville took the opportunity to slide in from behind and curl right foot around right foot to avert the danger. And Neville was involved in United's next attacking threat, taking Butt's pass and crossing, Coleman's deflection giving Yorke the opportunity to shoot over the top.

Greening replaced the injured Irwin for the second period, Phil Neville moving to left-back to accommodate him in midfield. And United went on the attack from the off, Solskjær the next to contract the contagious stepover and leaving a pass intended for him to Cole, only a desperate intervention preventing him from reaching the return.

Then, on 67 minutes and down in the left corner of the United half, Greening clattered off the pitch, down the ramp and into the hoardings while keeping the ball in play, and Phil Neville's subsequent clearance was returned to Finnan, 25 yards from goal on that same side. Taking a stride to prepare himself, he hit a low dipper that bounced in front of Schmeichel, able to do nothing better than press it into the path of the onrushing Salako, able to do nothing better than side-foot it into the path of the recovery dive.

With only four minutes left, Cole was chased backwards away from goal and found Stam, who swapped passes with Berg, the ball making its way back to him then out to Blomqvist and down the line for Phil Neville. He produced another great left-footed cross on the run, picking out Yorke, who chested down diagonally away from Brevett and onto his right foot, walloping a shot at goal that was brilliantly tipped over by Taylor.

Still unable to make the game safe, United endured the ignominy, first of bringing on a defender for a striker, and then of holding the ball by the Fulham corner flag. In between times, Beckham could only jab Gary Neville's low cross at Taylor's foot, before Neville drove straight at him from an acute angle.

Otherwise, it took until injury time for anyone to comment on how Keegan "wears his heart on his sleeve" – imagine if he did – and then it was full-time, after which he talked of the "fantastic reception" he'd had from the home crowd, without a hint of irony. "Perhaps they want you as England manager," surmised the interviewer, without a hint of irony.

*

If apprehension were excusable, you could almost excuse it in United's players before the home encounter with Arsenal, beaten by them on four successive occassions and badly so in three of them. Certainly, most neutrals certainly believed Arsenal to be the better, and, even worse, more stylish team, and with good reason; they were double champions, and though out of the Champions League, their exit could be blamed on a Wembley hoodoo similar to that which affected Melchester Rovers in the aftermath of the 1988 Mel Park earthquake.

But to their credit, "the real United" promised by Roy Keane just went out and played. That morning, an interview with Fergie had appeared in the *Guardian*, where he had pointedly declared his own ambition. "It pisses me off when everyone says: 'He'll be retiring if he wins this, he'll retire if he doesn't win that,'" he informed. "I don't think achievement decides when you go. Or age. The important thing is when your energy levels go down, and mine are the same as they were eight years ago. I still feel fit, I still feel healthy, why should I retire? I don't think the time even to assess it will be until I'm in my sixties."

Apart from Irwin and Giggs, surprisingly on the bench despite only three days of training, United were all present and correct, Butt chosen alongside Keane. Arsenal were missing three regulars: Keown had picked up a hamstring injury in England's defeat to France – for whom Anelka had scored his country's first goals at Wembley – and was replaced by Bould, while Petit and Bergkamp were suspended, so Hughes and Kanu came into the starting line-up. There were doubts, though, regarding the fitness of both. Hughes had been injured and not started a game in four months, whilst Kanu had hung around for three weeks waiting for a work permit, not even allowed into the country to train with his new team.

Preparing to kick off in proper United weather and on a typical Old Trafford pitch, the players were visibly more hyped than usual, Cole, Yorke and Keane bouncing in the centre-circle – and they looked sharp from the start. But so did Arsenal, who created the first shooting opportunity, Parlour hooking a bouncing ball from the right corner of the box to force Schmeichel to dive low at his near post.

United attacked next, Cole and Yorke trying to pick their way through, before Gary Neville's cross was headed clear, and then when Arsenal came forward, Parlour swerved away from Johnsen and Keane slid in. He fell, but no foul was given.

But on six minutes, a free-kick was forthcoming, Blomqvist felling Anelka, 40 yards from goal towards the right touchline. While United organised, Dixon homed in on the ball and surprised Schmeichel with a chip that went narrowly over the bar.

The game wasn't quite flowing yet but the pace was proper, the players operating according to a refined charge. There were muted appeals for a penalty when Yorke, pursuing a bouncing ball along the right side of the Arsenal box, forced Vieira to step in front of him and chest away, but United made do with a corner. And Beckham's cross was a good one, reaching Yorke's head, but he'd seen it late and couldn't find the necessary purchase to trouble Seaman.

Next, Beckham caught Vieira in possession and Butt took over, breaking through the centre-circle. Finding Yorke ahead of him on his outside, the danger was averted only on account of Winterburn's excellent tackle, justifying a selection that was in doubt due to injury.

Quiet in the opening passage, on ten minutes Kanu gave an insight into his unique brilliance, forced back by Stam and facing his own goal with no danger apparent, he suddenly turned into a through-ball that almost found Anelka, but Schmeichel, initially reticent, managed to reach it first.

United gained the ascendency after that, Cole shooting wide from 25 yards after being found by Keane, who then crunched Vieira without punishment. But, minutes later, Vieira devised the best opportunity yet, the ball touched back to him by Parlour on the Arsenal right. First time, he bent in a cross behind the United defence that appeared aimless, only for Overmars to appear in its path, away from Gary Neville. Jumping to get over it and ride an unkind bounce that rushed him, his effort went wide of the near post.

There followed a frantic passage of play, ending when Keane and Hughes shared a slide tackle, Keane's trailing leg catching Hughes clean in the countenance. Kanu then tricked Stam and Johnsen with more serpentine deception, but Parlour couldn't go on, before United made another chance. Phil Neville flighted a ball down the flank, putting Cole in a race with Bould as they chased over from the middle. Arriving first, Cole squared him up along the edge of the box, stepping over right, shifting weight left then moving off right, cutting in and shooting early. Seaman spilled the effort, but with no one around to profit, Adams could kick clear.

Then, just before the half-hour, Keane pounced on a stray pass just inside the Arsenal half and set off, exchanging passes with Yorke to his right. As Bould came in also from that side, he jumped into a sidestep as one would a stamp, ball passing through legs, and marched into the box. Delaying his finish just a moment to place rather than drive, just as he had in scoring on his Old Trafford debut, he went for the near corner, anticipating a dive towards the far – but Seaman waited, a strong arm diverting the ball behind superbly.

Vieira then headed the corner away from Johnsen, but United kept pushing. Beckham crossed again, for Stam, not quite there in time, the ball running past Blomqvist who fetched it and pinched a yard outside Overmars, overhitting a cross. Again Vieira headed clear, and this time Johnsen picked up possession, just outside the right point of the box. Controlling as the ball skipped up, he switched feet to keep it away from Parlour coming in on his left, their bodies perpendicular as his turned. Hip then contacted hip, Johnsen fell, and a penalty was awarded, its unnecessary nature fuelling spirited protests that belied its clarity – Parlour was booked for complaining even once it had been taken.

With Irwin injured, Dwight Yorke quickly took responsibility, his straight run-up – something he'd been warned about at Villa – making it harder to open his body and find the bottom-right corner.

Accordingly, the kick went past the post, prompting first a Pob face and then a grin.

As you might expect of someone with a self-awarded nickname, of complimentary nature, that he used as a signature, Safe-hands Seaman claimed credit for the miss. "The last time Dwight took a penalty against me, he chipped it over me, and that was going through my mind," he explained after the game. "I tried to stand up, and in the end, it forced him wide."

But still, United pressed, Blomqvist purloining possession from Vieira. Sending it inside, Cole then moved onto Beckham and anticipated the low, early return cross, meeting and deflecting it behind him as he turned, leaving Bould kicking fresh air. He shot low and hard, and again Seaman stood up well, barely moving as the ball struck his left boot and flew away.

United were much the better team, their play confident and incisive, with Keane easily the game's most influential player. Then, just before the break, Parlour knocked him over, running shin into shin with the ball gone, but Gary Willard saw no need to flourish a second card – and no one minded.

In the second half, United again took the upper hand, until, on 49 minutes, Adams won possession in his own half. Where once he would have wellied forward in the general direction of a head, now, he stabbed a short pass to Parlour, who found Kanu. Thirty yards from goal, he paused, and then, as Johnsen came in from behind and with Stam in front, feinted to spread right and poured himself left, a deluxe, slow-motion Yorke-trick that took him into the box. Again, he paused, which this time allowed Phil Neville to slide into his path, making a brilliant block – but the ball squirted off behind him to Anelka, and with Schmeichel already out to meet the initial danger, he easily lifted a side-footer high into the net. Later, Fergie called it "the flukiest of goals", but that was nonsense – not many players could account for Stam as Kanu had. Turned out he wasn't so much like Alan Smith after all, though the man himself, in the studio for Sky, had wanted him off at half-time to get Garde or Vivas on, in true George Graham style.

But United kept at it. Yorke pursued a long ball almost to the right byline turning back towards his own goal before swaying inside past Adams and Winterburn. Shooting low and hard, the ball was headed towards the far corner before Adams slid in to deflect it by the post.

A stray Keane pass was then intercepted by Hughes, who knocked forward to Vieira. But just as his legs began to extend, Keane pulled him back, first by the shirt and then by the shorts, finishing with a swinging kick. Accordingly, Vieira spun to insert forearm into neck, the momentum taking him to the ground and Keane's face following, to bestow the obligatory invective. Butt was first on the scene to intervene, followed by various others, the referee allowing the swedge to recede before booking both protagonists.

Next, the ball stuck under Cole's feet, allowing Adams to clear and Hughes moved it on to Kanu. Across came Gary Neville, sliding square to his brother, who found Blomqvist on the touchline, just inside the Arsenal half. Meandering infield, he slid to Beckham, able to stun a pass back wide to Phil, who'd continued his run. Shown outside by Dixon, who wasn't then close enough to intervene, he feinted in that direction then took a step the other way and flighted a cross into the middle where Cole had lost Bould. Bowing delicately while doing a Gladstone Small, he nodded into the bottom left corner with his surprisingly bushy eyebrows. It was the first goal Arsenal had conceded in the league since 20 December.

The moment was an important one for Phil Neville. Oddly for someone who won so many medals, his career was in some small sense a disappointment, never quite fulfilling its early promise. A natural sportsman – Andrew Flintoff would later assert that the most important day of his cricketing career was when Phil chose football, freeing up the all-rounder's spot in the Lancashire team for their age group – in 1996, he'd ousted Gary from United's starting XI. Then, he was picked ahead of him for the FA Cup final, and also in the Dream Team that Fergie selected for a video in 1997–98, but within months had lost his spot for good.

Finding someone with a remotely bad word to say about him is close to impossible, and perhaps this lack of unpleasant edge compromised his talent, also manifesting in a lack of competitive confidence, particularly under pressure. At two of the most significant moments of his career, he conceded entirely unnecessary penalties and arguably never quite rebounded from the second, when the keeper couldn't rescue him.

Immediately following the goal, Scholes replaced Blomqvist, United pursuing the win that would extend the gap between the sides to seven points. Arsenal, keen to preserve what they had, took off Kanu and brought on Garde. This meant that Hughes moved to the left and upfront went Overmars who isolated Gary Neville for the first time shortly afterwards, cutting inside and shooting low, well wide of the near post.

But United were still the more dangerous side, Adams raising a shin to keep Gary Neville's cross from Cole, then Yorke allowing Keane's pass through his legs, again for Cole. But this time Bould was there, forcing an early, weak shot that a sprawling Seaman saved.

Seeking a winner, a cold-looking, collar-up Giggs was sent on for Butt. And after Hughes' cross from the left evaded everyone, Giggs led a break, pushing a pass in low to Yorke, who back-heeled to Cole. He might have played a return but instead moved into the middle, getting rid of Adams and sneaking a yard from Bould, before shooting too close to Seaman.

With five minutes left, Phil Neville found Giggs, who flicked inside and spun with it, leaving Dixon. His low cross towards Cole was too strong, but ran on for Yorke, unmarked and near the penalty spot. Allowing it across his body to finish with his right foot, Seaman used the delay to close the distance, blocking with his knee.

Then, finally, a Parlour handball gave Beckham a free-kick in a great position, central and 30 yards from goal. His shot went into the wall, but somehow squeezed between Bould and Vivas to Keane, inside the box on the right. But Keane slashed wide of the near post, and shortly afterwards, the final whistle went.

In the context of both the season and the rivalry the game was a forgotten classic, due in part to the quality of the officiating – even though Gary Willard had been in the middle for a League Cup semi-final the night before. "An example to all referees," said Gary Neville. "Tensions were high, the tackles were flying in and there were probably far worse situations than Sunday. Willard booked some players but we came off at the end saying 'Well done, ref'. He could have sent two or three off but he didn't. He applied some common sense and let the game flow."

Both sides were also happy with aspects of the game: Arsenal were keen on the result – "We just enjoy the draw tonight," said

Vieira afterwards – and United with the performance. "We were the better team," reckoned Fergie also observing that Cole and Yorke had drawn the shakiest performance from Adams that he had ever seen.

There was other good news, too. Though Jody Morris gave Chelsea the lead against Blackburn – their first league goal of the season scored by an Englishman – Ashley Ward's late equaliser cost them two points. And in the remaining seconds, Vialli managed to get himself sent off as he pretended to limp off, following a scuffle with Marlon Broomes. Elsewhere, Villa lost again, at home to Leeds.

*

After a creditable mid-table finish the previous season, Coventry were struggling, only four places off the bottom. But in recent weeks, they'd lost to Chelsea only because of a last-minute wonder goal, beaten Liverpool, thanks mainly to a dominant midfield effort from Gary McAllister, and drawn at Spurs. They had also, however, just been clattered 4–1 at Newcastle, and did also, however, have a problem scoring goals – though they were already doing badly when Dion Dublin left, replacing him with John Aloisi was never likely to compensate. McAllister's rationale that "Snowy (Whelan) was the star of our juniors at Leeds when they beat Manchester United in the Youth Cup final and he stood out above the Beckhams and Scholes," was neither here nor there.

Their manager Gordon Strachan was typically gnomic. "I thought about going to watch United on Sunday, but then I scrapped the idea," he said. "What do you learn except what you already know: that there are 11 world-class players working their socks off for each other. I stayed at home and watched on television. There are no weaknesses. You can screw yourself to the wall trying to find weaknesses. You have to come up with a plan so that everyone knows what they have to do. We have players who can turn games however. People like Boateng, Huckerby and Whelan."

United made two changes from the Arsenal game – Scholes came in for Butt, and Giggs returned ahead of schedule, Fergie satisfied that the pitch was in decent enough nick for him to start. "There was no point in going easy with him for two weeks and then finding he hasn't got the stamina for the quarter-final. He is the type of player who needs games, anyway," he explained.

Perhaps United were tired following the intensity of their effort in midweek, because they were not at their sharpest. Beckham, though, found his range quickly, and one 40-yard pass to Cole allowed him to set Giggs for a shot, which he crashed over the bar. Not much happened for the next 20 minutes, save "United, United rah, rah rah", emanating from the away end and a police helmet flying from the back to the front.

Then, on the half-hour, Boateng capitalised on good play from McAllister and Telfer, turning cleverly and unleashing a swerver from 20 yards that forced Schmeichel into a flying save. Moments later, Telfer crossed from the right, but Whelan, under pressure from Stam, hooked too high – but only just. And the next effort on goal also came from Coventry, McAllister shooting straight at Schmeichel, hard enough so that he couldn't hold it.

The home side would have been pleased with their efforts as the dancing girls arrived to mark half-time, joined by a member of the travelling support until stewards intervened, six or seven required to catch him as he jiggled in front of them. Meanwhile, in the away dressing room Jaap Stam was taking his clothes off, a minor hamstring twinge causing his precautionary substitution.

From the restart, United were mithered into action. First, Cole prodded in a Giggs cross only to be ruled offside, before he stretched down the right and squared for Giggs to slice wide his second opportunity of the afternoon. But otherwise, Shaw and Williams defended well, so on 73 minutes, Solskjær was sent on for Cole.

Five minutes later, Boateng's shot deflected behind off Irwin, and Schmeichel, confidence restored, came and punched the corner, straight back to McAllister. So he crossed again, and this time Schmeichel caught it, stepping into a hurl that found Yorke alone and accelerating over halfway, cutting in off the right. Waiting for support, he allowed Giggs to whip the ball from his toe and it went immediately wide to Beckham, who took a touch and crossed towards Solskjær in the middle. Too high to head for goal, his flick arrived at the foot of Giggs, and he bumped a mishit into the ground and past Hedman, Shaw desperately flinging himself after it and slamming into the roof of the net to embroider an already finely crafted goal. "The one time we are not focused, they score," lamented Strachan.

As against Derby, United were relatively untroubled in the closing stages, with Fergie, mindful of the previous season's subsidence, replacing Yorke with Phil Neville. The winning goal in that game came from Huckerby's slalom and finish, and again, he had an opportunity to score when the ball fell to him in the box. But Schmeichel was out quickly to absorb the effort – "he is back to his very, very best," said Fergie afterwards – and Berg tidied up behind him to secure the points. Then, at full-time, the players came over to the away end where Beckham, after punching the air, clasped his hands in supplication and bowed to the Coventry fans wearing a big, daft grin.

"With the pitch being so difficult as well we never got the forward game going like we normally do," said Ferg, "but I'm fed up with entertaining everyone! It was a day where we ground out a result and they are just as significant. I would think that Arsenal and Chelsea would have looked at this fixture and expected us to drop points. That shows how important this win was."

Also that afternoon, Arsenal thumped Leicester 5–0, the brilliance of Bergkamp overshadowing Anelka's hat-trick, and Chelsea won at Forest. Meanwhile, at Anfield, Steve McManaman was substituted during Liverpool's draw with West Ham, prompting the crowd to cheer the decision and then jeer the player, who had recently announced his incomprehensible intention to abandon the famous red cassock and move to Real Madrid on a free transfer at the end of the season.

The following afternoon, Inter were beaten 1–0 by Serie A leaders Lazio, their fourth away defeat from five since the turn of the year, games in which they had not scored a single goal from open play. Their coach, Luigi Simoni, had been sacked in November, with Mircea Lucescu taking charge, but things were not going well. Described by Brian Glanville as "hapless" and "no more than a bird of passage", everyone knew that Marcello Lippi, fired by Juventus earlier in the season, would take over in the summer, and there were even rumours that he might do so before European competition resumed.

*

Like Coventry, Southampton had finished comfortably in mid-table the previous season, only to struggle afterwards, and they came to Old Trafford second-bottom. They were again without the suspended Mark Hughes, while Hassan Kachloul was away on international duty and Stuart Ripley injured. Matt Le Tissier was fit enough only for the bench, where he was joined by Francis Benali, back after nine weeks out, caught in a landslide.

United rested Roy Keane, who had generally played a lot and was feeling a tight hamstring, Butt and Scholes playing in central midfield. Also rusticated to the bench were Irwin and Cole, while Stam was left out altogether.

And the teams would play on yet another new pitch. The groundsmen hadn't expected the one laid before Leeds to last until the end of the season, planning to start replacing bits of it in January. But deciding to let it be when the going looked good, the Fulham game and seven straight hours of rain followed by the Arsenal game and nine straight hours of rain left them with no choice, this time the relevant sods arriving from Lincolnshire.

Southampton had lost ten straight at Old Trafford, but started well and created the first chance of the game, Beattie unable to quite get over Østenstad's cross, putting it wide. Then, on 13 minutes, Monkou headed Giggs' centre behind, and from the corner, Colletter was forced to clear Yorke's header off the line.

Just before the break, United injected some energy, Beckham snatching space down the right guiding over his usual measured delivery. Giggs was free at the back post but Dodd blocked his header on the line.

On the basis that there was no point wasting any further time, Keane was chucked on from the start of the second half and made an immediate difference, the purpose in his passing giving direction and authority. His creative ability was forever underplayed by those unable or unwilling to see beyond the tackling and intimidation, but he was playmaker as much as enforcer and perhaps the last truly great midfield general, before the obligatory "attacking" and "defensive" prefixes and caveats.

Even so, United did not begin creating chances immediately, nor when Monkou was forced off with injury. Instead, Le Tissier, on for Østenstad, crossed for Beattie to head against the bar.

But in the 78th minute, United made the breakthrough. Confusion between Jones and Marsden resulted in a corner, taken by Beckham from the right. Sent deep to the far post, Berg did superbly to chase, leap and head back into the middle where Yorke reacted first, stretching to stroke the ball back into the path of Keane, who frightened it into the net, off Colleter on the line – and actually celebrated – though, as ever, whilst offering words of guidance.

Because so many goals came from so many others, the scorer's instinct he had shown at Forest was becalmed at United, but it never left him. The following season, when those around him slowed down, he would contribute 12 goals, including two at Arsenal, that which secured the championship of Planet Earth, and also against Valencia and Fiorentina. Though he didn't have quite the knack of Bryan Robson, he knew exactly what he was doing.

Four minutes later, Irwin intercepted Colleter's cross from the left, his long, high clearance beautifully killed by Beckham, as it dropped and on the run. Advancing and assessing, he crossed for Yorke, behind the defence, inside the box, left of centre – and, it turned out later, also offside. Controlling with the outside of his foot to manoeuvre the ball back towards goal, Jones came out and narrowly missed with his dive as Yorke continued past him, then turned a shot into the empty net at the near post.

In injury time, a Le Tissier effort drew a parry from Schmeichel, Beattie somehow hitting the rebound against the post, and then, even deeper into injury time, Southampton won a free-kick 35 yards from goal and right of centre. Dodd curled into the middle, no one did anything, and Le Tissier headed in as Schmeichel came out, before turning to the K Stand and letting them know precisely what he thought of his "fucking shite" defence.

At full-time it was still 11 wins from 12 games in the calendar year – five of them thanks to goals in the closing stages, the drive of Keane a major contributory factor. After defeat at Chelsea in the 2013 FA Cup, he uncharacteristically affected ignorance, surmising that "this United team is lacking something; I can't quite put my finger on what it is." But the answer was obvious: the same thing it lacked for most of 1997–98. He may not have been the main man earlier in the season, but it was clear who was running things now, the real Roy Keane standing up for all to see.

Elsewhere that afternoon, Chelsea beat Liverpool in a game infamous for Le Saux elbowing Fowler's head, in retaliation for homophobic abuse. Then, the following day, Newcastle earned a point against Arsenal, their equaliser scored by Hamann, in the week of Purim. But afterwards, Wenger remained confident – smug, even – in predicting that 75 points would be enough for the title, by which rationale his team needed 25 more from the 11 games they had left. For now, though, United were seven ahead of them, four ahead of Chelsea, having played once more – but had away trips to Leeds and Liverpool still to come.

MARCH

You can always rely on Roy Keane to ensure that you're sure that you aren't any good, and in the tunnel after the Munich home game, he made sure to point out that United had qualified for the knockouts "without playing particularly well". Not remotely fair, but it was fair to point out that Brondby were the only team to be beaten so far, and Inter, their quarter-final opponents, had finished the group stage with more points than any other team and the fewest goals conceded. United, though, had scored the most.

The first leg marked the start of a run that looked daunting; it wasn't, because this lot were dauntproof; but next was Chelsea in the FA Cup, then Newcastle away, Inter away, Everton at home, Wimbledon away, then a potential European semi-final. Life: what happens to you while United are busy making other plans.

Though still without Lippi and Ronaldo, Inter were with Djorkaeff, Baggio and Zamorano, and were widely considered to be the continent's best side. But Taribo West was unavailable, excluded by coach Lucescu after throwing down his jersey in response to being subbed against Vicenza, a row that was never resolved. "He was so uncoordinated he'd fall over and we all laughed," sneered Lucescu a full 14 years later. But against Yorke and Cole, would Inter miss West's aerial presence, and would Aron Winter, filling in at left-back, be able to subdue David Beckham?

United were close to full strength – unlike at the same stage the previous season, when Schmeichel, Pallister, Keane and Giggs were all missing. In addition, thanks to what can now be diagnosed as a value epidemic, they had strengthened properly; Fergie would later assert the Treble as "a plain impossibility" had the board "not shaken off commercial caution and bought Stam, Yorke and Blomqvist", breaking the club's transfer record twice in the process.

Left: Everyone knew what was coming, everyone thought that it wasn't coming, and then it came. David Beckham celebrates after equalising against Leicester City in injury time, on the opening day of the season. *Getty Images*

Below: Ryan Giggs celebrates opening the scoring against Barcelona, after hovering for no short time before easing a difficult header past Ruud Hesp. *Getty Images*

Right: After moseying through the Bayern Munich defence to put United ahead – "like a man cutting corn", according to the *Guardian*'s David Lacey – Paul Scholes celebrates. *Getty Images*

Below: Ole Gunnar Solskjær pulls a left-footed shot through some legs and inside the near post as David James dives towards the far, expelling Liverpool from the FA Cup. *Mirrorpix*

Above: After United take the lead against Liverpool, Gary Neville races towards K Stand to share his happiness with the away fans. *Mirrorpix*

Below: After David Beckham flips over a perfect cross, Dwight Yorke sends a diving header spinning into the far corner to give United the lead against Internazionale. *Getty Images*

Above: "Welcome to bedlam." The players of Inter and United take to the field at San Siro. *Getty Images*

Above: "It's Paul Scholes! He's done it! Matchpoint Manchester United!" *Getty Images*

Below: United celebrate after Ryan Giggs dematerialises a deceptively difficult finish into the roof of the Juventus net, prompting a primal Old Trafford roar and earning a draw in the second minute of injury time. *Getty Images*

Above: Giggs, the world expert in ruining brilliant goals via the careless application of easy finishes, sends a deceptively difficult one spitting, roasting, hissing and burning into the roof of the net as Tony Adams plunges in, and United have knocked Arsenal out of the FA Cup. *Getty Images*

Below: Roy Keane celebrates after willpowering in a glancing header against Juventus, symbolically leaving Zinedine Zidane on his back. *Getty Images*

Above: Receiving the booking that will keep him out of the European Cup final, Roy Keane distributes viscous chunks of his mind in the direction of Jesper Blomqvist, whose loose pass preceded the incident. *Getty Images*

Below: Andy Cole runs off in the direction of Jaap Stam, after his brilliantly improvised control and chip results in the goal that ultimately clinches the league title. *Getty Images*

Above: United's players celebrate regaining the league title. *Mirrorpix*

Below: Paul Scholes thuds the ball across Steve Harper with his left laces, putting United 2-0 up over Newcastle in the FA Cup final. *Mirrorpix*

Above: Roy Keane raises the FA Cup, away from Peter Schmeichel, the royals, or both. *Mirrorpix*

Below: United are in the European Cup final! *Getty Images*

Above: The largest airlift out of Britain since D-Day. *Getty Images*

Below: Peter Schmeichel decides he knows where Mario Basler's free-kick is going, so moves in that direction. Mario Basler's free-kick goes in the opposite direction, and Bayern Munich lead United 1-0. *Getty Images*

Above: Ryan Giggs, moving off the right wing and onto his left foot, is tackled by Steffan Effenberg, as Michael Tarnat watches. *Getty Images*

Below: "Sheringhaaaaaaam!" Teddy Sheringham wheels away after equalising in the Champions League final, as Oliver Kahn appeals for offside. *Getty Images*

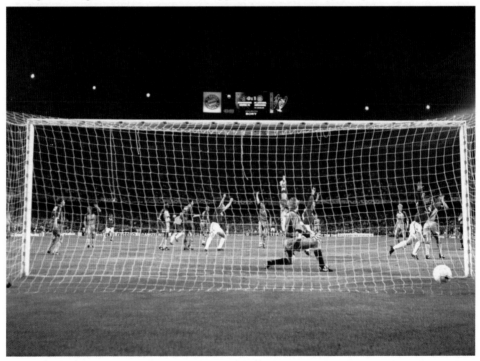

Above: "And Solskjær has won it!" *Getty Images*

Below: United's players set off after Solskjær as Bayern's begin their slumping. *Getty Images*

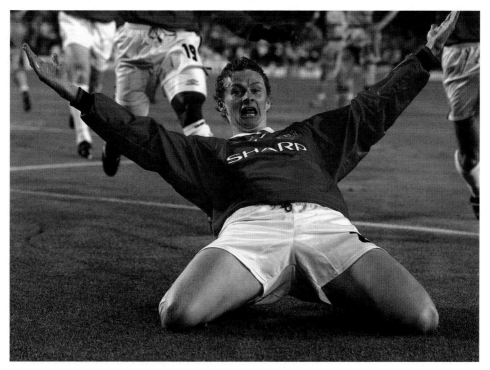

Above: Ole Gunnar Solskjær overdoes Mario Basler. *Mirrorpix*

Below "And the Munich players are on their knees, they don't know what's hit them! Manchester's hit them!" *Getty Images*

Above: Joy. *Getty Images*

Below: The Promised Land. *Mirrorpix*

Above: "Manchester United have won the European Cup! I don't believe it, but it's happened!" *Getty Images*

Below: Paul Scholes and Roy Keane have a go. *Getty Images*

Above: "The celebrations begun by that goal will never stop. Just thinking about it can put me in party mood." *Mirrorpix*

Below: Manchester celebrates. *Mirrorpix*

"Is 1999 to be the year of these young United princes?" wondered Clive Tyldesley before kick-off, and they began the game as if they felt so, the teacher's cardigan of a pitch blamed for various incompetences through the 1990s suddenly making no difference to anything. Calm and determined when behind, they were frenzied and feral when not ahead, tearing into Inter after the proper fashion, the Red Arrows on warp.

With only six minutes gone, one of Keane's hard, low passes was deflected upwards by a defender, and Yorke leapt to nod the loose ball out to Beckham on the right. Allowing it to bounce twice, as it took its third, he somehow flipped over a perfect cross like it was nothing, Yorke's diving header spinning into the far corner. Fergie would later explain that United rarely scored early in Europe because he considered it more important to "establish the pattern than go gung-ho", but they simply couldn't help it, intent on doing Inter a mischief. And, after establishing a pattern of conceding early goals, instead, they now had one for themselves. The difference was palpable.

A couple of minutes later Simeone crunched one wide, but then more ferocious football saw Beckham given time and space to prepare another cross, headed just past the post by Yorke. Jangling around midfield, Keane was giving Cauet, Baggio and Simeone no time to settle, wire bowl of hair even more unnerving than early-season skin-head; assassin versus serial killer, psycho versus psychotic.

But next, Inter enjoyed a brief period in the ascendancy, before United came again. Giggs, drifting right, pulled away and let the ball run across him to Cole, who shot against Bergomi. Scholes and Colonnese then indulged in a small bit of argio-bargio after a stern exchange of high feet, Zamorano and Keane booked as a consequence of the ensuing conversations.

Immediately afterwards, Zamorano tried getting crazy with Stam, apparently ignorant of his unimpeachable locosity. Wearing 1+8 on his back, after Baggio nabbed 10 from Ronaldo who took his 9, he used that very symbol of weakness and vanity to barge the chest of an actual hard bastard, the definitive macho man remaining still and composed.

Yet it hadn't always been that way. "It wasn't until I was about 16 that I began to grow and develop as a player," recalled Stam, known until then as Little Jaapie. "I always watched professional football and my father played at an amateur level, but I didn't think I wanted to become a pro. It was only later when I went to Zwolle that I began to think about it. For me, a late start was a good thing. A lot of kids who start too early get bored. I'd done all the things I wanted to do, I'd enjoyed myself, having fun and playing as an amateur and that was important."

But he was always a serious, focused sort. "You just have the urge to do things well," he explained to *Observer Sport Monthly*. "'Look, when I was working on a project at school, I had the urge to do that well. And if I'm fixing something up at home or whatever, making something, I want to do that well too. If I'm hanging a lamp and it doesn't work, nobody can talk to me for an hour, almost. And with football I have that urge and that will to win. With all sports."

Perhaps because he was so small for so long, he needed to be cajoled into using his physical gifts. Theo De Jong, who persuaded Stam to sign for Zwolle when he was still a right-back, would make a point of goading him, giving him the same instruction repeatedly until he snapped. "He would just shout, 'Get out of my head' and his next tackle would hurt. But he's not an angry, shouting sort of guy. Laziness, fooling around, that will make him angry, but on the pitch he will do his job and expect everyone else to do theirs."

The next passage of play was more even, until, just after the half-hour, United almost doubled the advantage, Cole's leg-extension appearing on the end of another bespoke Beckham cross. But Pagliuca – dropped by Arrigo Sacchi from Italy's World Cup squad after telling a magazine that he'd enjoyed "bountiful" sexual partners – saved with his foot.

The evening now nurtured a pleasing tetch, and on 38 minutes, Irwin imparted a tickle Djorkaeff. Pursued by Inter players seeking justice, the referee booked him, then Cole and Cauet exchanged shoves before football broke out once more; Schmeichel saved a Zanetti shot and Keane thudded straight at Pagliuca following Scholes' miscue. Then, in injury time, Beckham broke free again to describe another perfect cross that the relevant defender ignored, Pagliuca came and went, and Yorke's prodigious forehead did the rest.

"No one matched him, and there were some terrific players on the pitch," Fergie said of Beckham after the game, and he was right

– this was yet another decisive display. His eventual expropriation and fetishisation would gall the vanguard, pathetic fawning not the way in which United relates to its heroes, as such, it can be easy to forget quite what a United player he was, a man with everything who played like he had nothing and in the context of the squad, the midway point between Keane and Yorke. Consistent, elegant and decisive, aggressive, inventive and fearless, the off-pitch accoutrements could not obscure the rage and disrespect that underpinned his on-pitch persona. Gary Neville once commented that conversation with a teenage Beckham taught him that people not from Manchester could love United as much as he did, and even if the intensity waned for a time, the bond is indisputable.

He doesn't need to be compared to be enjoyed, but given our neurotic predisposition with the same, it's worth noting that in most select sides of the Fergie era, the wide roles are awarded to Giggs and Ronaldo without too much debate. But though Giggs was more devastating at his best, he never produced a season remotely the equal of Beckham's 1998–99: an assist away to Munich, assisting three and scoring one of the six goals managed against Barcelona, assisting one and playing a crucial role in a second out of the four scored against Juventus, scoring in the Cup semi-final replay, scoring the crucial equaliser in the final league game, easily United's best player in the European Cup final, provider of the crosses that led to both goals – along with general excellence. Not everyone appreciated everything about him, but, like almost every other British footballer of significance beyond simply being good at football, he simply could not have played for anyone else; only United could create him and only United could wear him.

Straight after the restart the lead ought to have increased, Yorke tricking away from two men on the right and crossing for Giggs, whose header past the post was so deliberate as to appear deliberate. Scholes was then booked for a scythe on Cauet and a few more half-chances were organised and spurned, the midfield just too much for Inter. It's hard to argue that Busquets–Xavi–Iniesta wasn't the best of all time, but equally so that Beckham–Keane–Scholes–Giggs wasn't the most complete.

But its flow was interrupted by Galante's cross from the left, finding Zamorano, who alone just past the penalty spot, he launched into a flying headbutt that appeared destined for the net, until Schmeichel's improbable, probable, and quite brilliant star jump flapped the ball clear, to evident disquiet.

United then concocted a further succession of near-things, Giggs weaving inside and slicing wide, Bergomi blocking a left-footer from Neville and Stam heading Beckham's cross by the post. Then Yorke, suddenly on the left, fooled yet another defender with his outside-dragging cross for Cole, and Winter was fortunate to block when the shot happened to coincide with his unwitting presence in its path.

Baggio had done almost nothing until this point, and attempting, a stroll through midfield, was hunted down and deposited onto his back by Keane in a vignette that summarised the story so far. But then Berg intercepted a Djorkaeff cross from the right, and from the resultant corner, Simeone thrust a diving header into the net, and suddenly Inter were in the tie.

Except that they weren't, because the referee disallowed the goal. Television commentary concluded that it was on account of Galante coughing aggressively in the direction of Berg, television pictures suggested it was on account of Bergomi blatantly glancing at Beckham – or in other words, United got away with one.

They responded by replacing Scholes with Butt and a minute later Lucescu brought on Ventola for Zamorano. Then, with 15 minutes remaining, Beckham encouraged the referee to book Simeone, Yorke narrowly avoided finishing a Neville cross, again halishing for a hat-trick, and Pagliuca pushed away a whack from Giggs. Careless in possession, Inter were clearly nowhere near as fit as United, Cole and Yorke in particular chasing all over the pitch with startling enthusiasm.

Inter's second change was the introduction of "teenage winger Andrea Pirlo", replacing the almost anonymous Divine Ponytail. "Every time we had the ball and went forward, I moved into midfield to pick up Baggio, rather than stay back as a natural right-back," explained Gary Neville. "It would detract from my attacking play. There would be very few overlaps from me past Becks. But Baggio didn't get a kick in the game, and Irwin did the same to Youri Djorkaeff on the other side."

Yet Inter could still not be counted out. No sooner had Galante cleared after Cole's shot slipped from Pagliuca's grasp – one of the bountiful errors that pockmarked his career – than Ventola scooted away from Berg and forced Schmeichel to save with his studs. Absolutely, he was back.

Then, with only injury time remaining, Cauet slid a pass down the outside of Stam, for Ventola at inside-right. Again Schmeichel saved his effort, but this time could only parry the ball back into play. It broke to Colonnese, striding into the box, and Schmeichel hurled himself right, in the way of the impending shot, except that it never came; Colonnese cunningly jinked outside and around his other side, to slide an easy, deliberate finish into the net. Except that Henning Berg was on the line, in precisely the right position to clear an easy deliberate finish. United had escaped again, and yet another great game was over.

But no one was getting carried away. "I think that's my job, just to put them on Coley's head or Yorkey's head," said Beckham after playing the game of his life. "Yeah, just happened to be in the right place at the right time," said Yorke after scoring the goals of his life.

The presence of Simeone had, though, prompted Beckham to engage with matters metaphysical – on the way off the pitch, the two had swapped shirts. "We didn't say anything to each other but I had decided before the game," he explained. "When the final whistle went we were standing next to each other. It must have been a sign."

*

The day before the Cup quarter-final with Chelsea, Dennis Viollet died, aged 65. He scored 179 goals in 293 games for United, including 20 in the Babes' first championship season – four of which came against Anderlecht in the club's record win. The following year, he managed 26 as United won the league again, and his tally of 32 league goals in 1959-60 remains a United record.

Like many of his team-mates, Viollet's experience of United post-Munich was not uniquely positive, an unexpected phone call from Tony Waddington of Stoke informing him that he had been sold. But though he retained his love for the club, the family he knew were already gone – and he adapted, claiming a Second Division winners' medal before moving to America where he excelled as a coach.

Prior to the Munich reunion at the 1997 European Cup final, he had suffered dizzy spells, before disappearing at the airport. When he got home, a brain tumour was diagnosed.

*

Though United might have beaten Chelsea twice in the league, they could equally have lost twice, and accordingly, the next meeting involved not only the oddity of tactics, but those deployed solely to disrupt the opposition. Joining Keane and Scholes in midfield was Phil Neville, detailed to man-mark Gianfranco Zola, the reasoning presumably that if he were eliminated from the game, United's remaining nine players were better than Chelsea's.

Following their exertions against Inter and with those still to come in mind, Cole, Yorke and Giggs took a rest, with Solskjær alone up front – a role for which he was not quite ready. Chelsea were also not at full strength, without Babayaro, Leboeuf, Wise and Vialli, and the result was a drab game.

United made the majority of the running, De Goey denying Keane and then putting off Scholes as he collected Beckham's lofted pass over the top. Beckham then launched a Scholes cut-back over the bar, before, with half-time imminent, Gary Neville hurled himself at a Beckham cross, glancing a header off the far post.

Not long into the second half, Roberto Di Matteo was sent off for two borderline bookable challenges, with Scholes, recipient of the second, acutely unimpressed with the decision. Four minutes before the end, the same fate would befall him, the referee Paul Durkin again alerted as to the depth of his disappointment.

"It's a shame two players were sent off in a game which was never dirty," said Gary Neville. "There was no malice at all. If you are asking players not to make tackles when it's Manchester United versus Chelsea in an FA Cup quarter-final, it's just not going to happen. It's not as if the referee had to get a grip of the game because it was never out of control. Basically, you want the referee to keep as low a profile as possible."

Durkin, though, was having none of it, actually prepared and allowed to say so. "I have looked at television re-runs of all the bookings and they were consistent and accurate," he said. "I really don't want to get into a slanging match… but players already on yellow cards should know they are treading on thin ice."

It was not a good afternoon for Scholes. He would attract specific managerial criticism for his carelessness in front of goal, missing three good chances in the second half as Fergie sent on reinforcements – including Sheringham, making his first appearance since the start of January – to the avail of bugger all.

Even so, the pretence after the game, in which Vialli participated, that the need for a replay somehow made Arsenal title favourites, was peculiar. However, in the dressing room, things were couched differently. United were due to play Liverpool in midweek, who, out of the Cup, had been two weeks without a game. "I said to our players and staff that a replay was the best possible result for us. The last thing I wanted was to go to Anfield with them waiting for us all fresh and fired up. As far as I am concerned, Liverpool can wait until later in the season!" By which time, presumably, the title would be secure.

But even before the second game, Arsenal set about proving the dissembled message. Away to Sheffield Wednesday, the score was locked at 0–0 after 83 minutes, before three goals in the next five, including Kanu's first for the club – a typical duping of defender and keeper – gave them a crucial win.

The cup replay may have been positively spun by Fergie, but entailed significant grief for United's support – there has probably been no domestic away end as empty since. But as ever, it was worth the hassle and not just to avoid the embarrassing guilt at missing it.

After messing with the line-up at the weekend, Fergie reverted to his strongest available, which meant only one real selection dilemma, Scholes preferred to Butt. For Chelsea, Poyet was still unavailable, but everyone else was there.

United started well, and with three minutes gone, Lambourde pulled Cole down 30 yards from goal, left of centre. Beckham curled the free-kick hard into the middle of the box towards Leboeuf, who, uncomfortable under the high ball, knocked it up but not away. First to respond was Cole, also knocking up, but timing his jump to do so softly and forwards, to Yorke – now unmarked. Watching the ball over his shoulder and all the way onto his metatarsus before anyone even knew what one was, he carefully guided a volley across the Dutch Ogrizovic, and into the corner.

It was a while before the game got going again, the highlight of the opening period a disputation between Schmeichel and Keane after the former piled through the latter, in the process of heading clear. The consequence was shots from Zola and then Morris.

Next, Di Matteo took possession from Flo, 30 yards from goal and in plenty of space. Spotting Zola, unmarked and on the move across the line, he slid a pass into the box, right of centre, that gave him only the keeper to beat. Yet somehow, that became impossible, Schmeichel springing out so quickly that Zola's only available option was to drive the ball into his sole.

Chelsea were dominating worthwhile possession, forcing a number of corners and sending over a similar number of other crosses, their narrower formation with the deep-lying Zola facilitating control of a midfield battle largely passing Scholes by. But they could not create any clear chances, Di Matteo's shot on half-time about the best of them – and that was easily saved.

Myers replaced the injured Leboeuf for the second half which made little difference, Chelsea retaining control of the game. And on 49 minutes, Lambourde came close to equalising, beating Berg to Wise's left-wing corner and heading wide when he might not have done.

Then, on 56 minutes, the crucial moment. An excellent Morris pass, swept first time from centre-field to the left wing, fed Babayaro, who controlled and prepared to cross, Neville not doing enough to block. And it arrived perfectly, Flo rising on the run to head home the equaliser – except that he missed the ball, which continued to the back post, arriving perfectly for Wise to slide home the equaliser – except his finish hit the feet of the prone Flo. Had he only waited until the net was asleep in a drunken stupor, he might have found it easier to hit.

Fortified by fortune, United came forward, Keane thudding into Wise and finding Irwin, taking possession back to pick a pass inside for Giggs, left side of the box and on the run. Crossing first time, low and hard, the ball stuck in the feet of Cole, but allowed him to lay back for Scholes, his sliced drive en route to another dimension but blocked before it could get there, allowing Chelsea to break. Charging forward with United commited to attack, Di Matteo fed Zola, whose pass to Flo was instant, but forced him wide. Squaring up Neville, he could only lay back for Morris, and his cross, aimed towards Babayaro at the far post, was easily collected by Schmeichel.

Then, on 59 minutes, Berg lifted a searching ball towards Yorke, on the right touchline. Lambourde was there first but diverted it behind him to where Desailly dallied and Cole lanced in to relieve him of possession before sending the ball on to Yorke, suddenly through on goal and at the corner of the box. With stupefying confidence, he took the chance at its most difficult point, as early as possible and from under his feet, torqueing his entire body into a first-time power-flick with the outside of his right boot that soared and arced over De Goey and into the next round, Fergie all shaking arms and half-jumps.

Shortly afterwards United almost scored again, a great ball down the line from Irwin to Giggs inviting a first-time cross that a sliding Cole almost reached. But Chelsea had yet to give up, Flo knocking down a Le Saux cross for Morris to control – by which time Schmeichel was in his grille, saving via bottom-bounce.

With 67 minutes on the clock, Chelsea had managed 12 attempts at goal, seven of those on target, compared to three and two for United, demonstrating a hitherto unseen ability to get the job done when deserving to solely on account of the essential statistic. Then, two minutes later, Chelsea wasted another opportunity, Lambourde slicing wide from close range after another beautifully curled Zola free-kick, before Di Matteo shot past the post following an interchange involving Zola, Morris, Babayaro and Flo.

And that was it: Chelsea had been beaten at Stamford Bridge for the first time since the previous April. The grief was handled badly outside the ground, bricks flying and coach windows shattering, but the sense of United's invincibility was growing.

*

The night before the weekend game at Newcastle, the Monopolies and Mergers Commission delivered its verdict to ministers as to whether Sky's bid for the club ought to be accepted. It was thought that Stephen Byers, the Secretary of State for Trade and Industry, would accept whatever the recommendation turned out to be, given government policy of allowing business to do whatever it wanted, and that directors of United would simply be asked to leave the room when officials of other clubs were discussing telly-related business. "We demonstrated there are no competition or public interest grounds to block the transaction," wheedled David Gill.

Newcastle had spent the entire season messing around in mid-table, and though they'd won their last game at Nottingham Forest, Ruud Gullit still made four changes, bringing in Dabizas, Georgiadis, Solano and Kershaia. Despite flying to Milan the following day, United were at full strength, and for now that meant Berg, not Johnsen

After just three minutes, they almost took the lead, Giggs' cross from the left arriving into the space between keeper and defence, but Yorke, for whom it was intended, was caught on his heels. Then, on the quarter-hour, Stam crushed Hamann 25 yards out, giving Newcastle a free-kick, right of centre. Behind it were Shearer and Solano, before Shearer moved off and Solano curled a shot over the wall and in off the near post.

After Schmeichel was summoned from his goal to kick clear when Ketsbaia nudged away from Stam, United improved, and on 24 minutes, won a corner that was cleared into touch on the right. Neville threw it high and straight to Berg, still inside the box and unmarked. He craned his neck underneath it and flicked on, Yorke bungled a scissors kick, the ball bumped off Hamann, and Cole forced home from a couple of yards.

Schmeichel did not reappear after the break, suffering from a bad back – though Fergie, not wanting to give Inter any encouragement, told the press that it was flu. The remainder of the game was even quieter than that which had preceded it, the second half almost entirely devoid of action. Then, on 59 minutes, Berg skipped a straight pass into Cole, only just inside the Newcastle half and with his back to goal. He knocked it off to Beckham, who came inside and flighted a flat, crossfield ball to Giggs. Extending his left foot as it dropped, caressing it to the ground, he shifted the angle to curl a cross around Barton, at first glance, too close to the keeper, who dived to catch – only for Cole to nip in front of him and intercept, poking into the empty net.

Though there were 39 minutes still to play, there may as well not have been. United, conscious of conserving energy, played out time, and Newcastle were incapable of stopping them.

Fergie was not altogether surprised by how lacklustre they were, having heard that Gullit was unpopular, with Shearer in particular. "Certainly Shearer was a shadow of his normal self," he wrote, "and I was disappointed with his performance. I know he is capable of producing a lot more than he did. When you see that kind of thing, you have to worry for the manager's future."

At Goodison Park, goals from Parlour and Bergkamp gave Arsenal victory over Everton, Uriah Rennie attracting controversy after the soft sendings-off of Don Hutchison and Emmanuel Petit, Petit claiming to be finished with English football on his way off. And at Stamford Bridge, Chelsea were beaten by West Ham, a result widely expected to end their hopes of the title.

Elsewhere, the Milan derby finished in a 2–2 draw, Ronaldo making his first start in two months, and managing 45 minutes. "I'm hoping to play for the whole match," he said of Wednesday's second leg. "It will be difficult to do so, but I'm not ruling it out. And whatever happens, I'm certain I can go out there and do my job well. I'm convinced that the rest of the team are going to do the same. They are very, very motivated."

*

Luck and ill luck are regularly cited as instrumental in sporting success or failure, usually without good reason; where margins are small, the decisive factor is almost always competence under pressure. So United weren't lucky to move past Inter, in the same way they weren't lucky to knock Chelsea out of the FA Cup; rather, both opponents faltered at crucial moments.

"When an Italian tells me it's pasta on the plate, I check under the sauce to make sure," said Fergie before the game. "There will be a lot of scheming and diving and referee-baiting; they'll go through the whole Italian repertoire."

"Maybe Ferguson has done it because he is afraid," retorted Inter coach Mircea Lucescu. "That is what you have to ask yourself. Surely there can be no other explanation." It's unlikely he was still as convinced, when, at full-time, Ferguson came onto the pitch to join in the celebrations and Gilles Veissière was one of the first men he congratulated, the fine he would later receive for "unnecessary provocation" well worth the £2,155.

If United came into the game on a roll, Inter had hit the rocks; "their form has been so bad recently it is hard to guess how they intend to play", surmised Fergie. There was also plenty of speculation regarding the health of Ronaldo, who, though passed fit, "looked vacant, utterly uninterested in the happenings around him, as if he didn't want to be in that place at that time." Butt, on the other hand, was absolutely desperate, initiating a tunnel row after learning of his omission not just from the starting 11 but the matchday squad.

And from there, the pitch only increased, Fergie describing "a clamorous tension" as the players waited to come out, with Simeone, "the aggressive Argentine", "screaming exhortations at his team-mates". And United had good reason to be nervous. Italian teams were the acme of world club football, and they'd never before eliminated one, let alone this one, on this ground.

Behind closed doors, the players had been warned about the intimidation they'd feel from the crowd, and the various projectiles they'd need to dodge – "welcome to bedlam" were the words used by Clive Tyldesley to open his commentary. Even before the game, United's directors were pelted with projectiles, from a home end flying banners reading "Fourth Reich" and "Yorke is my dog" – both made to look very silly by one in Curva Sud that said "MUFC we're too sexy for Milan".

Though Jaap Stam, at least, of course, was sanguinello. "People need to try a lot harder than lobbing coins, oranges, even plastic bottles of piss in my direction if they want to provoke me. I tend to block it all out and just concentrate on the game."

And United planned to play as normal. "I expect them to express themselves, I expect them to enjoy themselves," Fergie told ITV, and he was also insistent that his full-backs be brave enough to demand the ball, reassuring them of their ability to perform regardless of the atmosphere. But as against Porto and Juventus in 1997, he took the precaution of starting Johnsen in midfield, concerned about Ronaldo dropping deep and claiming his man to be the world's best at eliminating that kind of menace. It was only the fifth time that Inter had been able to field Ronaldo, Zamorano and Baggio together; they had scored eight goals between them during the previous four. Also playing was a young wing-back called Silvestre; had what is known now been known then, much tension could have been avoided, simply by shouting "Oi, Mikael! Look over there!" at the appropriate moment.

Perhaps his condition was contagious, because within minutes, the usually reliable Johnsen sent a dozy back-pass towards Schmeichel, out just in time to thrash away. But now United were in the game, Keane soon carrying the ball forward and sending it left to Giggs, Yorke almost reaching the ensuing cross with his forehead.

Next, the first burst of Ronaldo, Berg folding his legs into a tackle, after which United, knocking the ball around to jeers and a constant pitch of wild noise, almost took the lead. Cole slid in to win the ball on the left, Giggs veered away from Colonnese and slung to the back post, but Yorke couldn't quite dislocate his ankle around it, prodding wide instead.

On 15 minutes, Baggio found Cauet who discovered Zamorano, in behind Berg. Taking a soft touch inside in preparation for a shot, he was moving across the area left-to-right when Schmeichel t-boned across his path, between him and the ball and nowhere near the ball. Lots of shouting, screaming, gesturing and cajoling, but no penalty given. Yep, Fergie must have been afraid; there could be no other explanation.

Minutes later, Baggio released Zanetti, sliding by Giggs with Irwin nowhere to be found and measuring a cross that was perfect for Zamorano, diving to head home. But at the last millisecond, Berg inserted a leg in front of him, diverting the ball to safety and now fully atoned for his comment the previous spring that he wasn't "that bothered about not playing too much" as it meant he'd be fit for the World Cup. And whether Berg across this tie, Phil Neville's cross at home to Arsenal, Cruyff's equaliser at Derby or Brown's alleviation of the autumn defensive crisis, every member of the squad contributed qualitatively to the cause, reflecting the origin and principles on which United was built. From each according to his ability, to each according to his needs – and beyond.

But the danger was not yet clear, Johnsen forced to head away and Giggs ineptly dangling a leg in the direction of the loose ball, allowing the waiting Zanetti to eptly collect and turn inside. Letting it drop and bounce, he then swerved a flowing right-footer with no apparent force – how fighters describe the delivery of a knockout punch – which smacked the middle of the middle of the post.

United, though, remained a threat, Yorke holding possession and releasing Johnsen galloping outside him along the left. His cross, clipped low and hard, was close to perfect, Cole leaping into a slide, but he could only push the ball wide.

At half-time and channelling Jack Worthing, Fergie lamented "30 seconds when we were torn apart a bit", but you could see his point; the game was footballing DMT, general calm interspersed with short episodes of high mentalness. The second half began in similar vein.

First, a Beckham cross was narrowly missed by Cole, then a Silvestre free-kick barely reached the wall, then Baggio slipped Ronaldo in. He ran away from Neville, as he would repeatedly in the Bernabéu a few seasons later, and shot at the near post, but Schmeichel thrust up a giant forearm to prang the ball to safety.

Finally, on 59 minutes and following a strong tackle from Neville, Ronaldo was mercy-subbed. "On his day he can beat anyone," Fergie had said before the game. "So, first thing, you hope it's not his day. But you also organise to ensure you minimalise the damage."

Replacing him was Ventola, who many in Milan wanted to start, in preference to Zamorano. "What they would call in Italy *un uomo serio*, a dedicated young man," cooed Brian Glanville, "who has been studying jurisprudence at Bari University."

And within seconds, he'd scored. Cauet scooped a ball over the top of the United defence which gripped and pitched and leapt out of some day-five rough, Keane's jack-knife getting nowhere near. This allowed Ventola – staying admirably calm amidst the shock of such an error from such a man at such a moment – to steer a finish across Schmeichel and into the far corner.

"I thought 'oh my god'," Gary Neville later confessed, noise in the ground growing and Moriero replacing Bergomi, who stomped off with intimidating intent. But this was original Fergie and, accordingly, he was having none of it, defusing the situation with an attacking change of his own, taking Johnsen off for Scholes' "fresh legs and good imagination with his adventurous passing".

Almost immediately, Cole broke clear but dragged his shot wide with Yorke waiting at the near post, then Zanetti weaved into a shooting position and whipped his right foot across the ball, but couldn't find quite enough draw, drifting it just wide.

And then came the chance. Ze Elias sought Ventola on the edge of the box, almost dead centre, but Berg beat him to it, Baggio first to the loose ball. Smuggling it away sideways from Scholes and Berg, it went directly into the path of Ze Elias, to his left, who knocked it past Neville, strode, looked up, selected his spot, and carefully tucked his finish across goal and wide. Pressure, not luck.

Minutes later, Cole and Yorke found themselves space in the Inter box, wasting the opportunity by intricately trying to conceive the perfect goal, but minutes later still, a goal that was perfect arrived.

United won a throw deep inside the Inter half, Colonnese ramming the ball into Beckham's face as he came to retrieve it. Leaving it for Neville, it went along the touchline to Yorke, who held up and returned.

"Neville with the cross, Andy Cole waiting underneath it… *it's Paul Scholes!*"

The world paused. He was unmarked. He was in front of goal. He couldn't miss.

"The ball seemed to take an age to come down," he later wrote. "Scoring should have been straightforward but somehow it wasn't. I don't know what I was trying to do. I just wanted it on target but I scuffed my shot badly, maybe even catching it with my heel. As the ball rolled towards the goal I realised that I had unwittingly wrong-footed their keeper."

"He's done it! Matchpoint Manchester United!"

The United end erupted, the ground emptied in seconds, and the players, first informed that they would win the competition by Fergie in the immediate aftermath of Monaco, knew for sure that it was on. "I think everyone will be scared of us," said Cole afterwards, Bobby Charlton adding, "if it's not this year, it'll be soon".

Obviously, Roy Keane was convinced. "Having the ball shoved in your face like that is hard to take," he said. "But fair play to Becks. He walked away and that's what it's all about. We knew their players would be hostile and would try to intimidate us, but how Becks reacted shows that we have come through the learning process to succeed in Europe. Of course, you need skill and ability. But in European football, especially in the atmosphere that confronted us in the San Siro, you need more than that. Now we can handle anything."

And Clive Tyldesley felt it, too.

"It all adds up to a growing belief that *this* could be *their* year. Each season, each adventure, each match, they seem to learn a little more, seem to find their way around Europe a little better. The joy of the success will intoxicate them and their legions of supporters tonight, but it won't satisfy them… they believe they're ready to win the giant trophy again. The semi-finals are three weeks away, but can't come quickly enough. Manchester United are *through*."

As the players left the pitch, the few Inter fans that remained showered them with fruit and bottles, only for Schmeichel to realise that he had left his lucky towel in the goalmouth. But in general, he was a happy man, the decision to defend higher up the pitch limiting his workload. "That has made it far easier for me, so a large percentage of what I am called upon to do is to act like a sweeper. Now it is rare that the opposition get clear-cut chances," he explained. And this also allowed Roy Keane to get on the ball closer to the opposition goal, rapping out the passes that underpinned so many of United's post-Boro goals.

Celebrations in the dressing room got underway and continued all the way home, the players arriving back in Manchester in the early hours of the morning. But for Yorke and Cole, the night before was only just beginning, Yorke black booking a girl to join them at home, who would later reveal her shame exclusively to the *News of the World*.

After a time, the "very religious" Cole toddled off to meet his girl-friend and son, on a later flight back from Italy. Then, the following week, Yorke attempted to arrange a second viewing – complicated, given his punishing work schedule.

"But we've got so many games coming up," he told her. "We're playing Saturday at Wimbledon away. We come back. Then I play Juventus on Wednesday in the semi-final and we've got Arsenal in the semi-final of the FA Cup on the Sunday."

Clearly, the girl in question was the girlfriend of a City fan, and clearly, he was desperate to display his desolation: "It was bad enough her sleeping with someone else, but going off with two men, and United players at that, is the lowest of the low. I'm a devout City supporter and I can't believe she has done this to me," he told the *Sun*. "She has completely humiliated me." Still, at least all those years of early FA Cup exits had stood him in good stead: "I'll just concentrate on City now and hope they get promoted to Division One," he resolved.

And then there was Paul Scholes. It had been clear for a while that his talent for the sumptuous and instinct for the scruffy was matched by few, but not until this game did he out himself as a scorer of the genuinely crucial goal. And perhaps no United player since can match his subsequent philanthropic record: Spurs in 2003, Arsenal in 2004, Barcelona in 2008 and Manchester City in 2010 are amongst the top goons of the last 15 years, the first three amongst the most important goals.

No less a natural than Ryan Giggs considered him as "the most talented player I've played with", and perhaps no one has provoked as many outrageous and articulate homilies from as eminent a group of peers. Described by Lionel Messi as "one of our teachers", he was revered at Barcelona for the cerebral simplicity of his play and natural ease of his technique. "It is about the game, a way of playing," he explained. "The pleasure of striking a ball or finding the right pass," what he termed "effective football". And this phrase, more than any other, summed him up; clever or straightforward, difficult or easy, spectacular or understated, he just did whatever was necessary, at the precise time that it became so.

Kicking folk, on the other hand, was different, the head-patting chuckles that would emanate from commentary boxes insulting to his boyish pleasure in inflicting pain, his inability to refuse such opportunities verging on the pathological. "He will do something if he gets the chance – even in training," chuckled Fergie.

And he'd been at it a long time. Growing up, he was generally the smallest kid on whichever pitch he found himself, compensating via pre-emptive strike – the Nevilles recall playing for Bury Juniors against Boundary Park Juniors, and specifically, their violent ambush by a pair of ginger rascals.

By the end of his career, Scholes' personality was as much a cliché as the tackles it helped him get away with, and equally underestimated: not just unassuming, but witty and bluff. "I suppose as footballers you just get on with it, don't you… We're quite cold people, aren't we?" he said, explaining the players' placid reaction to hearing of Fergie's retirement. "Or is that just me?"

*

The next day came the draw for the semi-finals – also in the pot were Juventus, Dynamo Kiev and Bayern Munich. "I don't care who we get now. I am just so happy to be in the semi-finals," said Ferguson beforehand. "We could get Melchester Rovers and I wouldn't mind."

In the event, it was Juve, and it was clear that things had changed. "We have the experience of playing against them four times in the last two seasons," said Ferguson. "The players know all about them, and to be honest, we have also improved. It will be a hard game for us but I hope we can make it hard for Juventus." And Juventus knew that they would, Filipo Inzaghi commenting that he'd have "preferred not to play Manchester United at all" and Angelo Di Livio finding solace in the happiness of his daughter, "a Spice Girls fan".

Things were getting very warm.

*

United's game at home to Everton was on the Sunday. On the Saturday, early and late goals took Arsenal past Coventry, and the following lunchtime, the players watched Chelsea whack Villa 3–0. A win, though not *imperative*, was certainly imperative.

Luckily, Everton were pathetic, limping through a run of ten defeats in 15 games as Walter Smith established his mark. By its end, they were in the relegation zone, before four wins in six games helped them to finish 14th.

That being the case, United's team was an unintelligible Fergie special, the season's only real such type and not his fault. Giggs and Blomqvist were injured and Keane and Scholes suspended, so Johnsen continued in central midfield, with Beckham and Butt alongside. Up front, Yorke started behind Solskjær and Cole in what the *Guardian* called "the Cantona hole", but his team-mates – Gary Neville excepted – wallowed in one more akin to the K variety.

So the first half was a drab affair, with very little created. Everton, who lost Bakayoko after five minutes, defended deep and in numbers, United doing very little to tax them – "pedestrian", was Fergie's summation. Myrhe had just one shot to save, from Solskjær at his near post – and that was headed wide. Schmeichel was also tasked with just one serious intervention, from Materazzi's free-kick, Berg getting rid of the loose ball before Unsworth could reach it.

At half-time, United made a tactical change, Solskjær moving to the left wing; typically, he understood. "I don't think we play at our best when there are three of us up front because we run into the same spaces and it gets a bit crowded," he said. "When we play with three strikers who all play quite a similar game it is bound to happen."

And they improved immediately, Gary Neville seizing on Unsworth's lax clearance to force Myrhe into a save, and then, in the 54th minute, arrived a goal. Cole, wide on the left, dipped inside Short and flipped in to Yorke, in the middle of the box and with his back to goal. Leaping to control on his chest, as the ball ran away, he spread for

Beckham, who crossed directly into the forehead of Ball, stood only a couple of yards away. But Gary Neville assumed possession and picked a low, hard pass into Solskjær, on the edge of the box, right of centre, and in sufficient space to turn. Playing a one-two with Yorke, he strutted onto the return, decided what was happening, and punished a finish across Myrhe and into the corner.

This caused Myrhe to become angry with his defenders, and he promptly evened the score with his second-goal conduct. Phil Neville, in for Irwin, hit a crossfield pass to Beckham, headed down for Gary Neville to slide a pass down the side of Yorke. He then raced away from Dacourt and inclined inside, before hearing the screams on his outside and slipping a return through Short's legs. With Myrhe far enough away from his near post not to be guarding it and far enough away from the ball to have no chance of snatching it, it was run past him and into the side netting for Neville's first strike in nearly two years. It was no more than he deserved for an excellent afternoon's play.

"As an individual, I was feeling right at the top of my game," he wrote in his autobiography. "That match at Inter was a night when I felt total confidence in my ability. It was a like a utopia moment when you can do nothing wrong. You feel completely in control. Your dummies come off and every pass seems to fly to feet. I felt great, and why not? We were top of the league and through to the semi-finals of both the FA Cup and the Champions League."

Next, Short fouled Johnsen 25 yards from goal and just right of centre. Up stepped Beckham, to curl over the wall and inside the near post, Myrhe getting a hand to it but without sufficient strength or angle to keep it out. This was his first goal since Brondby at the start of November and only his fifth of the season, four of them free-kicks and all from outside the area. For the first time in ten games, United had scored more than twice.

Soon afterwards, Beckham was replaced by Greening with Cole departing for Sheringham, returning after more than three months out. Within two minutes, Greening had hit the post, but it was Everton who scored next, Hutchison drilling a free-kick right-to-left and high into the net while Schmeichel arranged his wall.

After the game, the majority of the squad departed to join up with their countries – but even that could not detract from Fergie's good mood. "They will come back two weeks from now ready for the challenge," he demanded. "We're looking very powerful."

*

In February 1998, England played Cameroon at Wembley, a dull game on a cold night, and therefore, the home crowd had no choice but to stand up if they hated Man U. Meanwhile, on the pitch, Paul Scholes was busy scoring, and was at it again when England played Poland. His hat-trick took them a step closer to the embarrassment of Euro 2000.

*

On the 30th of the month, Fergie was given the freedom of the city of Aberdeen – known as Furryboots City, after the local greeting "Furryboots, ye fae, like?" An estimated crowd of 20,000 gathered to thank him for his efforts, the extent of the achievements required to prove him worthy of the United job, particularly resonant at the start of the Moyes era.

"Look at big Fergie, he looks a right tosser," said a man within earshot of the *Guardian*'s reporter, his official outfit attracting a fair amount of attention. Would his players rib him about it when he got back to Manchester? "Let them try, if they're brave enough," he semi-joked.

Also that day, United announced that the cost of a season ticket would increase by £2 a game, Martin Edwards gracefully blaming the rise on players' wages and justifying it on the basis that it was cheaper than watching football in London, where wages were higher and none of the grounds remotely the size of Old Trafford. During the calendar year, the club had spent £1.3m on buying houses for players and £1.75m on professional advice with regard to the takeover.

"It's a disgrace," said IMUSA's Lee Hodgkiss. "We will be getting in touch with the club as we do every single year to discuss ticketing issues. We would like them to look at reinvesting some of the profits in the business and not just ask the fans to fund everything through higher ticket prices." The club asked the fans to fund everything through higher ticket prices.

APRIL

In 1894, the Australian state of Victoria instituted a minimum wage, but not until 1 April 1999, did the British government acknowledge a moral obligation to treat the poor and powerless justly and with sensitivity. United, though, were going to have to earn their maximum remuneration, with games against Juventus and Arsenal on the agenda.

But first came Wimbledon. Though Beckham had played half an hour for England with an injured buttock, he was fit for the game – and the victim of more shrillness after appearing on the front of *Time Out* magazine in crucifixes and rosary beads, underneath the headline "The Resurrection of David Beckham". So close to Easter, this was apparently offensive to some, the restraint of free expression apparently less so.

Jaap Stam was unavailable, sent home prior to Holland's friendly with Argentina after being caught on the ankle in training by Johan Neeskens, so Berg and Johnsen played at the back. In midfield, Scholes joined Keane, with Blomqvist returning to the left and Giggs to the bench.

Wimbledon were in a bad way. A month earlier, manager Joe Kinnear had suffered a heart attack prior to a game with Sheffield Wednesday – one they won to go sixth in the table. But their form had been in decline since before then and three straight losses followed, then another six in the eight games remaining after United, causing them to finish 16th. Kinnear, at home and losing weight on a diet of fish, salad and crackers, would be forced into retirement and replaced by Egil Olsen, who led the club to relegation at the first time of asking. Then, in May 2002, its shell was usurped by the appalling MK Dons, everything that really mattered moving to AFC Wimbledon. Kinnear's appointment as Newcastle's director of football, some 11 years later, would have been surprising, were George Osborne not Chancellor of the Exchequer.

"It has been a torrid time," first-team coaches Mick Harford and David Kemp wrote in the matchday programme, "but with an improved performance, your support and United's coach breaking down on the way to the ground we could be in for a good afternoon after all." Meanwhile, owner Sam Hammam agreed a deal with the players, whereby they would eat sheep's brains, intestines and testicles should they lose by five clear goals.

But United, and Schmeichel in particular, proved to be accommodating opposition. "Going to England would be good for my development and I am delighted to be connected with Manchester United," Ajax's Edwin van der Sar had entreated in the week. "They are a very big club and if I were to leave Ajax and go to England they are the club I would want to join. If I were to get the opportunity to move there I would be open to it. Of course when Peter Schmeichel leaves there will be a big hole there and it would be a massive job to take over from him. For a while you would be fighting the name."

But, in the meantime, his defenders were fighting the reality; from the first seconds of the game, he looked nervous, kicking directly to John Hartson – luckily it was only John Hartson – and they responded in kind. After just five minutes, Blomqvist chipped an aimless cross for Sullivan to collect, and his long kick bounced between Neville and Euell. Rather than get rid of it immediately, he allowed it to bounce again, forcing him to nod back to the advancing Schmeichel – but fearful that too solid a connection would result in an own goal, did so too softly. This allowed Euell to catch up, knocking the ball one side of Schmeichel and racing around the other to slide in, Neville's head and hands already getting acquainted before Irwin could intervene.

And it almost got worse for United, Schmeichel saving superbly from Euell after Hartson had shrugged off Johnsen. Then, blithely seeking Berg and perhaps seeking to avoid asking Schmeichel to kick, Irwin passed across the back four directly to Gayle, who ought not to have have shot wide.

After which, United started to play. Berg might have done better with a header from Beckham's corner, then Sullivan saved from Neville, threw himself in front of Keane as he rushed into the box, and leapt to push away Scholes' 25-yard drive. But, moments before half-time, United equalised. Yorke laid off to Beckham, right of centre and 40 yards from goal. Taking a touch to control, he curled over a cross for

Cole, which both he and Perry missed, but collected by Irwin close to the byline. Slipping the ball between Michael Hughes' legs as he stormed over, his whacked cross hit Blackwell's thigh, Beckham racing to crane-kick into the net as it dropped and before he could recover.

United emerged after the break with similar intent – "the siege of the Wimbledon goal was almost comical", wrote Oliver Holt in *The Times*. "A pinball game of madly rebounding shots and blocks and a sprinkling of wonderful saves from Neil Sullivan."

Blomqvist worked himself a shooting position with a deft sidestep just outside the box, drilling a drive that sent him the wrong way – but a trailing leg diverted the ball wide. Then Cole hit the side netting, after which it was time for Solskjær, United rattling out three goal attempts in quick succession.

First, Yorke headed only just wide, then Sullivan touched a Scholes effort around the post. And even when he was beaten, his defenders were on hand to help; a cross was palmed away, but only as far as Beckham, the outcome almost assumed. But, from nowhere, Blackwell insinuated body between ball and goal, sending the shot looping well over the bar.

Though the players left the pitch with a frustrated trudge, they were still well-placed, and in the performance of Keane had real reason to be confident; the law of averages insisted that he could not be denied too many more times. "He is the best midfield player in the country without any doubt," said Robbie Earle after the game. "He has got the edge on Patrick Vieira because you can't rattle him; you can't wind him up like you can with Vieira. Maybe a couple of years ago, but not anymore. The responsibility of being captain has helped him mature as a person and a player. He doesn't question himself like I think he used to when Paul Ince was at Old Trafford. Ince used to call himself 'The Guv'nor' and I don't think Keane liked that because that is how he saw himself. Now he is, without any question. Since the bad knee injury he got last season, he has reassessed himself, like you have to. He sits and holds in front of the defence, dictating the play. He is without question their most influential player. At one point, he even apologised to me after coming in a bit late. That took me by surprise. Two years ago, I would have reacted to him and then he would have been in my face and he would have got into trouble."

Keane in Robbie Earle's face sounded more like trouble for the latter than the former, but otherwise his judgement was sound. And Vieira's had not been a good afternoon – away to an improving Southampton, Arsenal could manage only a draw. Kanu was culpable in missing their best chance, opting for precision rather than power and elevation when in front of goal, allowing Benali to clear when he ought to have been running for cover. Central to Southampton's point had been Mark Hughes, who, reported *The Times*' Matt Dickinson, "had disturbed Tony Adams' serenity, dumped Patrick Vieira on the floor and gone 12 rounds with Martin Keown".

In general, Arsène Wenger was an unhappy man, having refused to allow Kanu to play for Nigeria the previous week and threatening to ban his England players from travelling to England's imminent friendly in Hungary. And his mood was unlikely to have improved by Chelsea's win at Charlton – they were now only a point behind Arsenal, and five shy of United, but with a game in hand on both.

Meanwhile, in Tuscany, a weakened Juventus side lost 1–0 at bottom club Empoli, the winning goal scored by defender Stefano Bianconi – but with Juve focused solely on Europe, no one was too fussed about their losing. "It's an easy alibi to seek, but it's perhaps also a fair one," excused their new manager Carlo Ancelotti.

Fergie, though, was ready for the pressure, in typical style making his boldest proclamation following a setback. "I have always expressed caution in the past about the strength of the squad to make a realistic challenge for all the trophies," he declared. "But now I believe we have a great chance of landing the Treble."

*

While United prepared for Europe, Arsenal closed the gap in the title race, edging past Blackburn – with ten men, following the dismissal of Keown. This gave rise to behaviour exceptionally exceptional, even for the FA: ordinarily, the ban for his offence would have been one game, but because he'd been dismissed earlier in the season, it was automatically extended to two, though his first red card had been rescinded. Somehow the disciplinary committee ruled that for these purposes, it still counted, on account of its presence in the record books.

*

That first time you beat your dad at something – chess, tennis, a fight, whatever – it means something and there's no going back. Just ask Freud. So, when United beat Juventus in October 1997 after losing to them twice the previous season, then easily won the group that they shared, they felt ready to usurp. But Juventus somehow skulked into the quarter-finals following a late Inzaghi goal in the return fixture, the second of two best-placed runners-up and ahead of Paris Saint-Germain only on goal difference. United then went out in the first knockout round, while Juventus reached their third consecutive European Cup final.

Typically, it was similar this time around. Going into the last round of group games, Rosenborg and Galatasaray had eight points and Juve had five, from five draws. To progress, they needed to beat Rosenborg at home – fair enough, they did – but also needed Athletic Bilbao, owners of a measly three points, to win against Galatasaray, who had eight – and they did. "Juventus have qualified?!" incredulised Gary Neville after United's game with Bayern, his face falling so far as to require a team of geologists to extract it from the earth's core. They stab it with their steely knives, but they just can't kill the beast.

"Just standing next to them in the tunnel was intimidating," said Gary Neville, describing the September 1996 game as "the biggest battering I've ever had on a football field". But good though Juve were, the pandering was still peculiar, not at all in keeping with the general approach. "The first time I played with them," recalled Bryan Robson of the local boys, "you're thinking 'right, I'm gonna have to look after a couple of them.' Well, I think it was the first five minutes, Scholesy smashes one of their centre-halves, then you've got Gary Neville belting their winger all over the place, we get a free-kick from about 20 yards out and Becks goes 'Er Robbo, I take these.'"

Perhaps the respect – or "awe", as Neville called it – emanated from Fergie, who compromised his team for that first meeting and was never anything but respectful; "Class oozes out of them," he would observe. And even when goaded by an Italian journalist to repeat his pre-Milan allegations, he was having none of it. "You get so serious about these things," he said. "It was just a bit of fun, but it obviously upset someone. You want to know what I think, but do you want to pay my next fine?"

It hadn't been a great season for Juve, their worst domestically since 1990–91. Alessandro Del Piero didn't play after October, and by February, Marcello Lippi was out of a job, replaced by the cuddly but dubious Carlo Ancelotti. But still, they were quite a team, particularly when compared with Inter's collection of individuals; "a rather different cup of cappuccino", wrote David Lacey.

With Fergie's attention for the previous couple of weeks dictated, if not consumed by the game, preparation was different. On the day itself, the players were summoned far earlier than usual, nominally for a massage, but principally because he didn't want them "lying in bed and feeling lacklustre". Not an accusation that could be levelled at chunks of United's support, also gathering earlier, for a pre-match chinwag with the travelling Italians.

Back at Old Trafford, Fergie was announcing the starting line-up. Berg was chosen ahead of Johnsen, and as a mark of his confidence, Scholes preferred to Butt. "If we have a good start to the game, if we settle into it well, I think we have a fabulous chance," he said. "The priority is to score goals and we won't change our style that way." And the crowd were similarly chipper, "We shall not be moved" in evidence even before kick-off; there was a growing sense that after everything that had already happened, momentum was elemental and unstoppable.

And although it amounted to nothing tangible, the dynamic between the sides had been altered by the previous season's encounter. "A hugely significant milestone," said Gary Pallister, while Gary Neville noticed that standing in the tunnel this time, he felt ready to knock them out.

The feeling was fleeting. Though United did actually start well, with some playstation passing, Juve soon took over, as though their entire season until this point was just an elaborate hustle. Zidane, who hadn't played for three weeks – "not exactly a smooth mover at the best of times", said Clive Astaire in commentary – stroked a chip from distance narrowly over Schmeichel and the bar, the introduction to a performance of gliding menace and invention. Alongside him, Conte was everywhere and Deschamps carried more water than the entire nation of Gibeon, but the real star was Edgar Davids, the pit bull en pointe, whose mix of gentle and mental was more than United's outnumbered midfield could handle. "It is an honour to play with Zidane," he had recently self-effaced. "But then he feels the same about me."

After 15 minutes, Inzaghi spun away from Berg, forcing Schmeichel to tip behind at his near post, and shortly afterwards, Zidane, bald patch projecting above his head like a halo, flattened Keane who, appeared to enjoy it. United responded in kind, Scholes getting stuck into Davids and Beckham diving in on Pessotto, before Deschamps was unluckily penalised for a foul on Cole, Beckham's free-kick clipping the outside of the post.

But minutes later, Juve took the lead. Wide on their left, Di Livio sent a back-heel through Gary Neville's legs, collected by Zidane, who, attracted Berg towards him and out of the danger area, then quickly moved the ball on to Davids. Quickly looking up, he toe-curling a poke through Scholes' legs into precisely the area vacated by Berg and to where Conte was now waiting, away from Keane, to drag across Schmeichel into the far corner.

Not content with a single-goal lead, Juve pressed for more, Inzaghi forcing another save from Schmeichel at his near post to earn himself a mapoleh from the jilted Zidane, in perfect position for a pass. He retorted by convulsing on the floor following an unfortunate encounter with the torso of Stam.

However United neither panicked nor crumbled, Giggs and Yorke taking advantage of an Iuliano error to knit together a one-two followed by a cross, Cole heading just wide as Peruzzi plopped out. But in the main, their straight lines couldn't handle Juve's curves, and in the stands, a new record was set for how early hearts were sung out for their benefit.

Next, on 37 minutes, Pessotto leapt to intercept a Keane pass just outside his own area, Zidane taking the loose ball forward and right, then squaring to Deschamps. Spotting Davids ahead of him, he threaded a pass between Keane, Scholes and Berg, swept forwards and left with an immediate turn, to where Pessotto now reappeared. On the far left of the box, he moved towards goal, of curling hard and only just wide. Though not quite defenestrated, United were hanging onto the sill, their fingernails set about by a steel stiletto.

And just before half-time Juve almost scored again, Inzaghi arriving at Zidane's low cross ahead of Neville to slide it just past the post; the whistle was a relief. For the only time since the side settled in September, United had been thoroughly outclassed – "a real tousing", Fergie called it later – and the same could be said of what went on in the dressing room.

"A few words were spoken," Roy Keane said afterwards, with pained expression. "Basically for everyone to pull their finger out, you know, and start to work that bit harder. Doesn't matter if you got skill, you've got to work as hard as them."

Fergie's plan had been to play with three in midfield "at all times" and with a wide player pushing up, to make three up front. But, "intoxicated by the atmosphere", Beckham and Giggs did so at the same time, rather than according to whose side the play was on. And with Keane on Zidane detail, Scholes was left alone against Davids and Deschamps, also aided by two narrow wide players. So, in the second half, Beckham joined Scholes and Keane inside, Giggs understandably tasked with penetration, Johnsen also came on, for the injured Berg; he would not play again until the following season.

Yet, despite it all, Fergie was still confident. "All I think we should try and do is get one back," he told ITV. "If we can draw the game, then we can always score."

And gradually, United clambered into the contest, Juve unable to resume the flow. On 54 minutes, Johnsen headed Beckham's cross over the angle, then Scholes jagged a clever pass at Cole, who transferred into his stride and shot wide.

Next, Peruzzi turned away a Giggs header from a Beckham corner, before Scholes, very much involved now, sent Cole slithering free in the inside-left position, fading an effort just wide after racing outside Iuliano. Easily the better of United's strikers, he then teased Ferrara, again down the left, reached the byline and cut back a cross, Iuliano smothering Giggs' effort with his hand. While innocence and guilt were vehemently protested, the ball broke to Scholes to sneak in a shot, pushed past various grounded bodies but also the post.

United's improvement was such that there were no further changes until the 79th minute, Sheringham replacing Yorke immediately following a Zidane shot, clouted across Schmeichel and wide. And after five more minutes, Juve almost happened upon another opportunity, Neville ceding possession to Inzaghi, Stam coasting across to remedy the situation.

Then, with only four minutes left, United equalised, Keane scudding a shot from the edge of the box at which Sheringham flung himself, as he'd done on the opening day, and again rerouting the ball into the net at speed. By the time he discovered his offsideness he was posed on one knee in front of the Stretford End, counting on his fingers the seconds taken by the referee to decide as though the delay made the confiscation of his happiness unreasonable.

But he had made a difference. Both passer and target man, the uniqueness of his style was hard to defend against, the calm calculation a handy option in a team that played at such frantic pace. "Yes, he did well," Ancelotti said later. "But that was largely because we were beginning to tire when he came on." He did not explain why his side were so poorly conditioned, nor why he didn't consider proper conditioning to be important – and given what we now know, that it was even the case seems entirely inconceivable.

When Giggs zoomed down the left and a combination of Sheringham and Cole nodded back for Scholes to head straight at Peruzzi from six yards, it looked as though United's chance of an equaliser was gone. But then they fashioned another shooting chance, again for Scholes, Iuliano violently throwing himself into its path like a soldier absorbing a grenade to save his mates, Ferrara blocking Sheringham's follow-up.

But of course, just when it looked like it wasn't coming, it came. Inside the second of three added minutes, Amoruso frantically scythed an attempted clearance behind him and Johnsen shoved Esnáider into a tame back-header, Beckham hooking over his shoulder and to the near post, from on the right byline and just outside the box. Though Peruzzi came, Sheringham had flicked on by the time he arrived, a Cole–Scholes double-team ensuring that the men under the bar couldn't head clear, and the ball dropped onto the left lace of Giggs, who dematerialised a deceptively difficult finish into the roof of the net, prompting a primal Old Trafford roar.

Just reward for United's endurance, perseverance and competitive courage, there was additional satisfaction in nicking a late semi-final goal against Juventus. Paolo Rossi doing the same in 1984 stood out as a major disappointment in a decade of major disappointment, but the hope now was that revenge would be concluded in Turin two weeks later. Sheringham wasn't sure – "the pressure will be on them in front of their own fans, they'll have to turn it on against us, and you never know," he hedged – but Fergie was emphatic. "It does give us a great chance," he said, while pretending to seriously consider the options – but was also just buzzing with what he'd seen, "a fantastic game of football, top-level stuff with no nastiness, no cheating".

And Ancelotti was pleased too, just not as pleased as he might have been: "We could have killed them off in the first half, so that is my biggest regret," he said. "I would have accepted a 1–1 draw until I saw the way the first half went… I don't think United are as good away as they are at home." Let's just leave that one to marinate.

After the game, the players stayed the night at Mottram Hall – an unusual measure, but an unusual debrief was required. "Detail. Always thinking. Typical," wrote Roy Keane. During the discussion, Beckham and Giggs were chastised for not working hard enough when not in possession, and Keane asked to apologise for haranguing Irwin, whom he'd identified as partially responsible for Juve's goal. Obviously, he refused – "If this was an analysis of the game, let's analyse it" – and though there followed a brief atmosphere, the two of them laughed about it after returning to the room that they shared. "Are footballers sometimes childish?" Keane wondered. "Of course, they have to be, otherwise they'd just start believing that they were only playing a game! And who knows where that might lead us! (Almost certainly not to trophies.)"

*

Two days later, almighty relief: Murdoch's bid to buy United was blocked by the government. Rumours had been circulating for a week that the decision would be in favour of Sky, that even Blair's corporation-cosying, Murdoch-fellating Cabinet couldn't allow it indicating just how wrong it all was. Those who'd fought so hard on behalf of everyone were now available to enjoy the season's dénouement, and everyone was free to engross themselves in any glory that turned up, without the nagging feeling of nausea.

*

The morning of the Arsenal Cup semi-final, another Yorke shagging story. He had convinced the girl in question that he was a) a local postman, and b) called Brian. "People were coming past and saying 'hello' to him and he said it was because he delivered their letters. I believed him. He seemed a lovely bloke".

"Next day he rang and said he was a footballer. I said 'so what?' Then he said, 'For Manchester United. I'm really called Dwight Yorke.' He said he'd lied because he didn't like people just being with him because he was a star. Brian was the first name that came to him as he has a cricket friend called Brian Lara."

Vaguely weird, but not *that* weird – until paired with this, from the Cole combination: "He told me he only had two friends in Manchester – Andy Cole and his toy monkey. He called it Brian and was always cuddling it. Once he put the monkey on his knee while I was stripping off."

*

It's rare in football for two great teams to reach a concurrent peak; more common is an interregnum as one gradually declines while another matures. Of the cross-border rivalries, Benfica took over from Real Madrid at the start of the sixties, and the best sides of the seventies – Ajax, Bayern Munich and Liverpool – succeeded one another. Domestically, this happens even less frequently – had the Munich air crash not happened, then United and Wolves might have been the first, but otherwise, the only other genuine candidates are Liverpool and Nottingham Forest 1977–80 and United and Chelsea 2006–08. Accordingly, the FA Cup semi-final with Arsenal was one of the most anticipated of all time, like interrupting an epic novel to quickly dash off an epic vignette that distilled it, yet possessed a character all of its own.

In the event, the game was boring, miserable and tight, like the worst kind of teenage girlfriend. Its start was marked by the fearsome sight of yellow balloons waved by balloons in yellow, after which went on not a lot – though even Martin Tyler was forced to acknowledge United's "long periods of superiority".

But there was still some good controversy. Beckham, on the left touchline after taking a corner that was headed clear, picked up possession before moving away from goal as Parlour harried him, releasing Giggs, just to his right. In the middle, Yorke was in an offside position, but no flag was raised until Giggs, seeing Dixon come across to cover, turned the ball outside him and eased by on the inside. The linesman then unflagged, Giggs' cross was headed on by Yorke, ahead of Adams, and rammed into the roof of the net by Keane at the back post. The linesman then reflagged.

Gallantly, David Elleray blamed the confusion on his assistant: "He thought the ball was going to run out of play for a goalkick, so he dropped his flag. But Ryan Giggs was so fast that he caught up with the ball, crossed it, and, in the ensuing play, a goal was scored. But the assistant, having dropped the flag, put it back up again to indicate it was offside. I went over and consulted with him and he said it was offside in the build-up. I am happy to accept this view."

"A piece of retrospective legislation which stretched the game's statutes of limitation," wrote David Lacey, a generous interpretation of a generous interpretation; even Tony Adams conceded that the goal ought to have stood. The officials considered Yorke onside when Giggs received the ball, and given his retention of possession, he can only have remained so as play continued, the speed that enabled him to reach his knock-on – not especially extreme, especially for him – irrelevant. The suspicion was that the officials simply hadn't bothered to observe that his first pass was not, in fact, a pass at all, but part of a dribble. The absence of any United players anywhere near him might have suggested as much, though in their defence, this was mid-20s Giggs. Ah well, *gam zu letovah*.

But Fergie was aggravated, his ire not assuaged even once the season was over. "A lot of things disturb me about Mr Elleray," he wrote, "but chiefly his influence over referees. I don't think we are seeing the best referees in the Premiership. What we are getting is a lot of David Elleray's friends." And Martin Edwards was vexed too, "making really out-of-character comments about the referee". Truly, the mind boggles.

Otherwise, Schmeichel made an excellent save from Ljungberg, through one-on-one just before the end of normal time, and soon after the start of extra time, Nelson Vivas – only playing because Petit was suspended – was himself sent off. And that was about it, the replay that United's players had been ordered to avoid scheduled for the following Wednesday.

But now it was happening, Fergie was ready for it. "By the time we go to Turin, we'll be champing at the bit – we'll be eating people!" he declared. "Never underestimate the British endurance. Juve will have to run a million miles to beat us!" No doubt there were men in white coats doing all they could to guarantee precisely that.

In the meantime, Chelsea won at Wimbledon the clinching goal scored by Poyet, making his first start since Boxing Day. They closed to within a point of Arsenal and two of United, Arsenal having played a game more.

And so to the replay, the open net of a final against Newcastle awaiting the winner. "Don't watch it alone," warned Ferg, in the days when he cared what we did. "The more difficult it is, the more resilient they become," boasted Wenger, in the days when he said things because they were true, not because he was desperate to make them so.

There's an argument to be made that the United–Arsenal replay represents the zenith of football in England: two of its best ever teams conjuring a spiralling, thumping, coruscating, defibrillating orgasm of a game, gushing and thrashing with everything that could possibly happen when 22 men convene to boot a pig's bladder around a field.

Incredibly, neither club sold all their tickets and there was chuntering in the United end when the team news arrived. Irwin hadn't recovered from a knock inflicted by Parlour in the first game, Scholes was again on the bench, and so too were Giggs and Yorke, with Cole left out altogether, Sheringham and Solskjær starting up front. It could never work.

Except, of course, that it could – and Tony Adams knew it. "I was concerned," he wrote afterwards in the *Observer*. "I had got used to Andy Cole and Dwight Yorke after two hours of football and felt that I could handle them for another two. Now United had a new dimension with two fresh pairs of legs, two players fired up, and they relished it. I knew Ted would feel he had something to prove after not playing for much of the season."

Meanwhile, Roy Keane stomped and pistoned around the pitch like Roy Keane in his pomp, like Roy Keane in his pomp against "Airsenal", arms pumping, head in sideways motion, and United deservedly went in front on 17 minutes. A long Schmeichel clearance was killed on the move by Beckham, first on the bounce and then his thigh, and with a pass slipped under Winterburn, he found Sheringham, somehow always close to his team-mates. He cleverly worked the outside of his foot around the ball to keep it protected by his body, earning space free of Adams and the woolly-gloved Petit, then simply stepped well away. But no one had even conceived the possibility of what came next, Beckham running onto it and unfurling an out-swinging full-toss that moved early and kept going, shrieking the wrong way past Seaman, done with the eyes from 25 yards. "What a goal!" burbled Tyler, but only after pausing to contemplate the implausibility of what he'd just seen.

Before the game, Beckham was one of two players selected by Fergie for a special word, the gist of which he explained to Hugh McIlvanney in *The Sunday Times* the following weekend: "David, in his eagerness to have a crucial impact on a game, can occasionally over-elaborate. He has abilities that set him apart from every other player in Britain. Nobody else strikes the ball as well. The range and accuracy of his delivery, whether he is shooting, passing or putting over crosses, provide us with a weapon that is liable to win any match. In essence, my message to him was that he is at his deadliest when concentrating on the simple application of these tremendous skills."

Arsenal had not been behind since the first week in January – in 17 games, they'd conceded only five goals, their fabled five producing the most miserly season of its long career. And like United, they were unbeaten in all competitions through the period, the beauty of the rivalry at this stage was how certain each side was of its superiority, both fully committed to attack.

But on this occasion United were dominant, Adams later criticising his team for "not squeezing the lines, that is each unit – defence, midfield, attack – pressing their opposite numbers enough." Luckily for them, United were wasting chances with gay abandon, Solskjær uncharacteristically rushing one shot, then *missing the target* when fed by Keane just after half-time. Shortly afterwards, Blomqvist's effort was saved, following yet another Pythagorean pass from Sheringham, before Solskjær showed his strength in holding off Keown, hammering a trademark low shot close to the keeper's legs that looked an easy save but wasn't. Seaman hung on, but only just.

In between times, Anelka snatched at a cross to lash high and wide, but when the equaliser appeared, it was out of nowhere, Bergkamp's shot from distance deflecting off Stam and scuttling past Schmeichel. Though United almost replied immediately, Sheringham just failing to connect with Beckham's low cross, for the first time Arsenal were in the game. And within a minute, they thought they'd taken the lead, Bergkamp's shot spilled by Schmeichel into the path of Anelka, who shuffled around him to tap in. Though the flag had gone up immediately, he was well into the crowd parading his magnificence with his friends before the terrible truth came to light, the United sections already swaying with laughter and thumbless hitchhikers. Given his first-game antics Elleray had no choice but to accede, but the delay made a mockery of Sheringham's Juve whinge; at 72.02 the ball crossed the line, celebrations continued until 72.33, and only at 72.48 was the verdict official.

Immediately afterwards, United were reduced to ten men, already-booked Keane sliding in on Overmars. Determined to deny the referee the pleasure of flourishing a second yellow card and then a red, he turned on his heel. Determined to enjoy the pleasure of flourishing a second yellow card and then a red, Elleray set off in pursuit, but Keane was already halfway towards the tunnel, Arsenal fans climbing over each other to flob at him.

Martin Keown claimed that as soon as Keane was dismissed he felt that Arsenal wouldn't win, expecting United to be fired by injustice, but there wasn't one. It was hard to argue against either booking, and in any event, they were already fairly keen to win.

For the remaining 17 minutes, United were penned inside their own half as Arsenal went in search of a winner, but they created little of note until, with seconds remaining, Parlour dragged himself outside Phil Neville who couldn't help but crumple into a foul, conceding a penalty. "We've got Dennis Bergkamp, we've got Dennis Bergkamp," twanged the Arsenal end.

"I couldn't believe how fortunate we were to be going to the final when we didn't really deserve to be in this game," wrote Adams. "'It's our year again,' I thought. Guilt doesn't really enter it when you're a professional – I'd have taken 2–1, thank you very much – but I think I would later have felt a bit sorry for United."

For all Schmeichel's greatness his record at saving penalties was dismal – for United the Uefa Cup shootout against Torpedo Moscow in 91–92, Everton away in the 93–94 League Cup, and from Sheringham at Spurs in 94–95 its full extent. But iceman Bergkamp had scored only two of his last five penalties, so took no risks with this one, limiting power and friction by side-footing at comfort-able saving height, Schmeichel reading his intention and trepidation to push it away. Allowing himself a moment's elation, Giggs and Beckham bouncing up and down too, all were shooed away with great vengeance and furious anger – another innovation, setting the template for the reaction that has since become cliché. "You've got Dennis Bergkamp, you've got Dennis Bergkamp, ha ha ha," hooted the United end, Fergie on the pitch before extra time telling the players that losing to Wenger was absolutely forbidden.

If describing this game is trite, to bother to address what happened next is tritest, but here we are so here we are. Arsenal pushed forward seeking a winner, United attempted to hang on for penalties, Yorke loitering around upfield and everyone else massed around their box.

The cause was not helped by the efforts of one RJ Giggs, Esq, who, on as a second half substitute for Blomqvist, had contrived a performance careless even by his exulted standards. He was the second player identified as requiring a pre-match prod:

"With Ryan, in contrast, my advice was that he should always be trying to do the difficult things," Fergie explained. "If he does not make frequent attempts to do something apparently undoable, he is not being true to himself. There will be plenty of times when the effort fails but when it succeeds the best opposition the game can offer will be helpless. He took the breath away from Bobby Charlton and me when we first saw him a dozen years ago and he is capable of doing it every time he is at full surge. Of course, I am glad he has worked on acquiring a more rounded game but he must never forget how exceptional he is. Talking to him on Monday, I told him he was the forward that defenders in the Premiership least wanted to face because of what happened when he ran at them. I urged him to do that whenever he had a glimpse of an opportunity. How could anybody foresee what he did in the second half of extra time? When he set off on that gallop, we were hanging on for dear life and hoping it would come down to penalties. It would be madness to say I even dreamt he could give us that ecstatic climax. All I did before the match was try to plant in Ryan's head the belief that he is entitled to be far more ambitious than 999 footballers out of a thousand. With his talent, he has an absolute right to attempt feats of extravagant brilliance on the field."

So it was that intercepting a rather weary one from Vieira, on the burst and to the left of the centre-circle, he ran with it instead, into the Arsenal half and keeping far enough away from Dixon so that he wasn't drawn across, before swaying off towards him in the process of stepping by Vieira's extended leg. Swaying and stepping back and forth, ball cantering along in front, Dixon guessed wrong and went right, then Keown picked outside when it was inside, twisting himself to the ground as Giggs pulled himself between them, like a man sneaking onto a departing train. But even a one-on-one meant little, Giggs the world expert in ruining brilliant goals via the careless application of easy finishes, until suddenly a deceptively difficult one spat, roasted, hissed and burned into the roof of the net as Adams plunged in, realising the danger only once it was too late. Chest hair, swinging shirts and pitch invasions.

"He just bobbed and weaved and kept going, and when he needed a finish, *my god* did he give us one," growled Andy Gray. "The ultimate expression of the incredible natural gifts he has always had since he came to us as a 13-year-old," kvelled Ferg, his allocation of inspiration again uncannily precise.

The man himself found it impossible to explain. "There was no technique or anything, I didn't think about it – it was just, purely, players were coming towards me, I was just beating them and just when I came to the area I just smashed the ball – it was... instinct, really." An experience you could match to works of genius in numerous fields, sporting and not; somehow, things happened.

He's a funny one, Giggs. In some ways the personification of youthfulness, in others a venerable presence, it's hard to square the dressing room joker with the serious-faced man out of whom the piss was and is never taken.

But that toughness is something he's always had, fortified by a week-long exposé of his family life in the *Today* newspaper, one of two his career outlasted. Even in 1994 – a year in which he received 6,000 Valentine's Day cards – Barry Davies described "the smile diffident, the eyes determined", and he was right.

And, despite it all, he has remained relatively grounded through the success, his best memory still the moment when Fergie first came to watch him playing for Salford boys, as a 13-year-old. There are very few men able to prompt Scholes into effusion, but Giggs is one. "When Gary, Nicky, me and David came into the set-up, we idolised him," he recalls. "In some ways, I still do."

Partly because he was so good to begin with, partly because of injury and partly just because, his career never exactly peaked, more plateau than parabola. If a player stays at any club for long enough, there'll inevitably be moments that are absolutely his, but suddenly Giggs had produced two within a week, serious brilliance at times of significant clutch from a man considered something of a flake by plenty. In a way, it misses the point to assess Giggs according to quantitative and even qualitative standards, the elation of witnessing objective beauty a more nebulous but no less meaningful experience. But its combination with the most intense purpose awarded it an entirely different quality, eternal moments as well as eternal feelings.

For all their possession in extra time, Arsenal couldn't cobble together much in the way of chances; Bergkamp forced Schmeichel into a flying save in the first period, and after the goal, Adams, all bohemian lyre-playing hair, headed wide from a corner, when, had it been in the corner, Schmeichel could not have saved. Then Lee Dixon's matter-of-principle foul on Giggs put him out of the Juventus game, and then it was all over, precipitating another pitch invasion.

"Sometimes," wrote Keane in his autobiography, "you invest so much of yourself in a game that it acquires a significance way beyond the prize at stake. This contest was a good example of that. OK, it was the FA Cup semi-final, but that trophy meant nothing like as much to us as the Championship or the Champions League. But it was Arsenal, the reigning League champions, who'd trounced us 3–0 at Highbury, and held us to a 1–1 draw at Old Trafford. Theirs was an important scalp. Beating them on this occasion became an end in itself. How fucking good are we?"

As the United players returned to the changing room, Adams and Dixon waited by the door, shaking hands with each of them. "Looking back, Ryan's goal was meant to be," reckoned the former. "I did my best, played my part, but in the end I felt strangely powerless over the outcome. A higher power was at work." A novel way of shifting blame, but his poise reflected the beauty of a grown-up rivalry, the teams far more similar than different. "I always felt the game was destined to go to penalties," he wrote. "Looking back, I'm glad it didn't because a tie like that, with two heavyweights slugging it out, deserves to be settled in proper play."

Next come the spraying of champagne, the brothers Neville now sufficiently experienced to put their clothes away before joining in the spontaneous merry-making. "The time to give up is when you're dead," Fergie told them.

Meanwhile, the managers got on with their interviews. "The two teams are very close to each other and in the end the luckiest won," said Wenger. But he didn't specify as to which particular aspects of United's outrageous fortune – the excellent disallowed goal in the first game, the general superiority in the first game, the brilliant and original goal in the replay, the total domination for the best part of an hour in the replay, the deflected goal conceded, the penalty bottle and save, their stubborn defending or the all-time great goal – he was referring.

Typically, Ferg rose to the occasion too; naturally bullish, this particular interview was positively bodacious (look it up, it's worth it).

"This isn't what you need, really… you needed a result, but you didn't need extra time, ten men, a real battle like this," Gary Newbon informed him.

"Look, who's to know what's gonnae happen in football, Gary?" he replied. "It could all blow up in our face at the end of the day, but can you forget moments like this?"

A sheepish "no" is faintly audible.

"Oor supporters will be talking about that for years, the players will be talking about that for years, that's what football's about, trying to reach peaks and climaxes to a season, which we are doing at the moment. We're in a final, we got something in the bank for ourselves, now we go and try and win this league now."

It was the last FA Cup semi-final replay. Well done, football.

*

That same night, Chelsea drew at Boro, Zola missing a one-on-one that left him punching the ground in frustration. They were now a point behind United, having played a game more.

*

Sheffield Wednesday: the perfect next opponents. After winning four from five in January and early February, taking them to tenth in the table and safe from the threat of relegation, they responded with five successive defeats and one goal scored, before beating even worse Everton. Accordingly, United rested Schmeichel and Johnsen, van der Gouw and Brown coming in, and left out Beckham, Yorke and Cole too, while Giggs and Irwin were injured.

Wednesday were at full strength, such that it was, Dejan Stefanovic, whose friends and family lived in and around Belgrade, returning after time off in the light of the Kosovo crisis – but he was selected for the bench only. Up front were Booth and Carbone, Cresswell held in reserve.

Before kick-off Fergie appeared on the pitch to thank supporters for their efforts against Arsenal, after which the game purported to begin. Neither side played especially well, the rain not helping, but both keepers were forced into early action, Srnicek denying Keane from 30 yards and van der Gouw flying across his goal to tip Carbone's effort behind. Almost immediately afterwards, Carbone threatened again, a dipping shot dropping narrowly over the bar.

For United, and along with Keane, obviously, Sheringham stood out, taking advantage of Beckham's absence to shoot from a free-kick, drawing a save from Srnicek. Immediately afterwards, he headed over, and then, on 34 minutes, was instrumental in United's first goal.

In space, almost precisely on halfway and dead centre, Scholes flighted a pass towards Blomqvist on the left. Controlling on his chest and moving inside Atherton, he allowed the ball to bounce twice before lifting an up-and-under in to Keane at the back post. Though his cutback was mishit into the ground, Sheringham reached it prior to the pair of defenders behind him as it reared up, diverting backwards for Solskjær to drill hard into the net, following through into Jonk's studs.

Then, a minute before half-time, Phil Neville slid square to Keane, who found Solskjær on the right, almost level with the edge of the box. Pausing to investigate what was happening therein, then pausing again when the answer turned out to be nothing, he ignored Gary Neville's run inside him and bent a perfect cross to coincide with Sheringham's arrival, duly glanced into the far corner. Somehow, and though it failed to make Fergie's United top 10^{2*}, it would be placed 9th in Andy Gray's top 20 goals of the season. But indisputably, it was in Sheringham's top 1.

2 1. Giggs v Arsenal, Villa Park; 2. Cole v Barcelona, Nou Camp; 3. Yorke v Chelsea, Stamford Bridge; 4. Yorke v Liverpool, Anfield; 5. Beckham v Aston Villa, Old Trafford; 6. Keane v Brondby, Parken Stadium; 7. Cole v Spurs, Old Trafford; 8. Giggs v Nottingham Forest, Old Trafford; 9. Scholes v Liverpool, Old Trafford; 10. Solskjær v Nottingham Forest, City Ground.

The second half featured little more than the elapsing of time. Scholes had a shot that Srnicek saved, then, just after the hour, one that he didn't. Keane, in possession in the Wednesday half, slightly left of centre, appeared to be moving towards his own goal, before wrapping hip and thigh around the ball to dart a pass at Scholes, facing him just in front of the D. Using a dodgy first touch to spin and escape his marker, he poked into Sheringham and set off behind him. Intuitively grasping his intention, Sheringham's control first turned, then opened his body, facilitating a gentle return with the outside of his foot, not dissimilar to his pass for Beckham at Villa Park. Again, Scholes' run had taken him around the outside of the defence, and one touch later, he flogged another low finish across the keeper, Walker contributing a slight defelection. 3–0 was the final score.

Also that day, Martin Edwards laid the groundwork for the summer's parsimony. Apparently, the unlawful nature of Sky's proposed takeover would mean that there was no money available for transfers, despite the regularly full crowds, potential maximum number of games played and likelihood of substantial prize money. Blame was attributed to the expansion of Old Trafford – ordered to make more money – and the new training facility at Carrington. Oddly, for someone who claimed to a) love United and b) have no care for the specifics of his own wealth beyond general satisfaction in its existence, he was not volunteering to supplement the shortfall with any of his own money or dividends.

"It will be difficult after this season for an English club to succeed in the European Cup," he whimpered. "We will have to replace Peter Schmeichel but that might be the end of our summer spending," the team thusly beginning its descent even before ascending to its peak. Elsewhere, Mohamed Al-Fayed had recently pledged £17m to help Fulham strengthen, apparently equivalent to the amount that Parma wanted for their promising young keeper, Gianluigi Buffon.

Edwards had tried to sell United at least twice, sold Mark Hughes, refused his managers money when the going was bad and was now refusing money when the going was unparalleled by any team in the history of English football, all the while disenfranchising loyal supporters. Could it possibly be that he was a thick, entitled nomark who understood nothing of business, yet had benefitted from astounding luck?

All this went down predictably well with Fergie. "He hasn't said anything to me about money, and I haven't said anything to him," he responded when asked for his throughts – "tartly", according to the *Observer's* Paul Wilson. But otherwise, he was in good spirits. "It's good for Teddy and Ole to get the goals, they will be confident of playing in any game now," he said.

Also that day, and without Zidane, Montero, Pessotto and Deschamps, Juventus eased to a 3–1 win over Lazio. "Manchester United have one chance to survive in Turin, and that is to play without making a single error," said their manager, some *Sven-Göran Eriksson – what The Times called "the football of their dreams".*

But Fergie was on it. "Juventus have just had a fantastic result against Lazio, so we know we're going to have to perform. They are a high-class team and I'm sure they will try and beat us. We need a momentous performance; we need to hit the heights – but we're doing that quite regularly at the moment."

Later in the weekend, Chelsea ceded a two-goal lead to Leicester, and really did now have no chance of the title, three points behind United still having played a game more. In midweek, they would lose at Mallorca, ending the defence of their Cup Winners' Cup, before another league draw, this time at Sheffield Wednesday, effectively ended their season. But Arsenal were still very much there, responding properly to their Cup disappointment and dissecting Wimbledon 5–1 with four goals in ten second half minutes. "Acceptance is the key for me these days," wrote Adams. "It hurt to lose and you acknowledge that it hurt. But the feeling doesn't last long and then you get on with the next one."

*

All the way through the tie with Juventus, even after the first-half kicking at Old Trafford, Fergie remained believably convinced that United would win. "Some people are achievers who want to progress all the time. They want to win all the time", he explained. "That is the kind of human being I have here. Others are quite happy to settle for what they have. Maybe they get to one Cup final and say: 'That's fine, we'll go home and get a rest now'. I can't understand that. At Manchester United, there is a tradition of having players with courage – fighters. That's why the club is so successful. It isn't just about ability. It can't be about that alone. We endorse that ability but we also recognise the effort that gets you the big trophies."

The players spent the build-up in the usual manner, competing at table-tennis and cards, then went for a stroll around Turin on the morning of the game, Keane walking alone and staring hard. But Fergie was still relaxed, or affecting relaxation, even in the tunnel: "I feel good about it," he told ITV. "They'll come at us a hundred mile an hour, they'll try to finish us off as they always do in the first 30 minutes… It's gonna be a great night, I hope."

Obviously, Juventus were confident too, *La Gazetta dello Sport* bragging in advance about a fourth consecutive final appearance. "False modesty is not a Juventus trait," wrote the *Guardian*'s Jim White on the morning of the game. "Indeed, after their magnificent performance at Old Trafford in the first leg, the air of certainty Juventus have already as good as qualified for their fourth Champions League final on the bounce is such that their coach, Carlo Ancelotti, has been trying to caution against complacency, telling them that 'they are not invincible'."

But Edgar Davids was having none of it. "Manchester United are supposed to have the best midfield in Europe," he scoffed, "but we had the better of them at Old Trafford. We were like a steam train running over them. I have no fears of them anymore. I want to get at them again. The higher the stakes, the tougher the fight, the better overall feeling I get. I can produce. I am a winner."

And Didier Deschamps felt similarly. "If we made a mistake in not killing Manchester United off when we had the chance, then it is one I expect to correct tomorrow," he said.

In Turin, excitement had been mounting, the match a sell-out despite a ground whose capacity was 20,000 more than its average attendance that season. But the club claimed that they could have sold 200,000, a local ticket seller forced to call police after trouble broke out at his store, while 2,000 were "destroyed in order to keep the two sets of fans apart". And by the time of the game, things were seriously cooking, flares, synchronised sprinklers and much noise.

Juve made two changes from the first leg, Brindelli in for the suspended Mirkovic and Ferrara replacing Montero, fit enough only for the bench. But most of the pre-match fuss surrounded Zidane, whose Spanish wife wanted to go home, which incited Gianni Agnelli to speak to the press that "Zidane is suffering because he's under the thumb. I took him aside and asked: 'Who is the boss in your house – you or your wife?' He said since he'd had his two sons, his wife is. I'd love to have him at Juventus next season. The problem is the wife; I have no authority over her."

United lined up as expected. Giggs was close but unfit, so Blomqvist played wide on the left, while Cole's ankle was sufficiently recovered for him to return, and Yorke did too, though Fergie conceded that they were suffering "a flattening-out period". Accordingly, Sheringham was taken to one side as the players gathered in the team room and told that he'd not be starting, while in midfield, Butt was compensated for his Milan omission, preferred to Scholes.

"I don't think players ever see things from the manager's point of view, they look after themselves," he said. "I know I do. I am selfish about wanting to play every game. It's never nice to be told you are not in the team, but you've got to find a way of keeping your spirits up and staying fresh for the next one."

Though he never quite sustained the improvement it looked like he'd made in the autumn and winter, it's arguable that he and not Scholes was the first-choice partner for Keane – he was certainly preferred in many of the most important games, including all four against Arsenal, playing every minute of the Cup tie.

The evening began relatively slowly, United looking comfortable, until on four minutes, Zidane sent a diagonal ball right-to-left, where Inzaghi had pilfered a half-yard from Stam. In the time it took him to control the pass, Stam reclaimed it, and averted the jeopardy, but not for long. After Davids found Pessotto, Beckham conceded a corner, taken short by Zidane to Di Livio. While United's men on the posts vacated their positions – after all, who could have expected a corner-type cross, of all things, from a man in possession near the corner flag – everyone else did nothing, allowing Zidane to measure a ball to the back post, where, as Gary Neville recalls, "Inzaghi nipped ahead and scored as I tried to rugby tackle him." "Gol de Filippo..." began the stadium announcer, and the crowd belted out the rest.

United came straight back, Keane, Yorke and Beckham exchanging passes, before Keane found Neville. He lifted a cross in to Cole, who made good contact with an overhead kick, but could only direct it at Peruzzi's pie holder, and absorbed like so much before it. But United continued to push the pace, the pattern of the game already set – all the more so when Pessotto fed Inzaghi on the left corner of the box, his back to both goal and Stam. Feinting to turn inside, he then went outside, and with the split-second acquired by the artifice, hit an early shot that turned what would have been a block into a deflection, the ball looping in for 2–0.

"Manchester United need a minor miracle now," lamented the commentary, but that wasn't so; they'd played well enough in the opening 11 minutes to suggest that two unanswered goals were not beyond them. "We felt unbeatable," said Schmeichel, and why wouldn't they? They were. No flapping, shaking or sulking, just hard, fast, skilful football taught by Matt Busby.

So a swift move between Beckham, Keane and Yorke ended with Cole given wrongly offside, then Blomqvist chested down facing his own goal and swivelled into a reverse pass for the overlapping Irwin. His ball into Yorke was stepped over, lifted over the top by Cole and collected by Yorke with leaping chest control, setting up a volley lashed just wide – a contribution good enough for Ron Atkinson to restore him to nickname terms following a brief demotion provoked by a poor piece of control.

You could feel it now, United were coming in the air tonight. Butt, joining things, bringing one sentence to an end and starting another, flicked on a Schmeichel punt and suddenly Yorke was in on goal. Ferrara, though, was not an Italian defender for no reason, taking a millisecond to pull on his shoulder, just enough to disturb his balance, before joining him on the grass. No foul said the referee.

Permitted hardly a kick since scoring their second goal, internal Juventus voices must've been looping John Williams with Jules Winfield, and on 24 minutes, Keane and Blomqvist exchanged passes to win a corner on the left, which Beckham curled into the near post. Rising early and rising alone, clearest eyes fixed clearly on the ball, Keane will-powered in a glancing header, symbolically placing Zidane on his anus at the same time before running back to get going again without so much as a double-footed hop and arm flap, pausing only to pass Beckham a nod of acknowledgement.

The archetypal captain's goal was the defining moment of what would become his signature performance, "an amazing insight into the strength of his character", said Stam. Keane later said that the fuss over it was "quite embarrassing actually", typically contrarian but typically accurate. Newcastle in December 1995, Liverpool in the 1996 Cup final and at Anfield in 1997, Arsenal twice in 1999–00 and Madrid away in 2000 immediately come to mind as superior efforts, along with several for Ireland in qualifying for the 2002 World Cup, against Portugal, Holland and Cyprus. Coming off at half-time in the last of those games and giving out about someone's misplaced pass, Gary Breen attempted placation. "We're two-up, Roy," he ventured. "That's not the point," came barking back.

But to identify specific games is almost to miss the point; it was the reliability of the brilliance that was so alarming, far more than its particular iterations. And it was this that made him such an inspirational captain. Giggs once appeared to joke that "fear was Keaney's greatest strength," before making it clear that he was being serious. "A lot of it was," he said. "He would tell you whoever you were."

But the "Alan Hansen generation" had good reason to tolerate this rounded mouth, jerking arm aspect, because without him there would likely be no such moniker. Won with kids in the team, delivered by grown-arsed men: Schmeichel, Keane and Cantona. And this was recognised within the team if not without, Gary Neville later admitting that "we were nothing without them".

Yet, any moron can shout and bully, this only a small part of Keane's leadership style. He was a popular figure in the dressing room, proficient in laughing at himself and others, but like Robson and Cantona, his influence was underpinned by the confidence others took in his presence. Ole Gunnar Solskjær rated Keane as the best player he ever played with and who he'd pick if given only one choice, while Giggs acknowledged his principal contribution to be "his example on the pitch... just his performances." But still there was more to it: "If Keaney wasn't playing well, he would still contribute to the team, drive the team forward and get performances out of players who maybe weren't playing to their potential. I think that was Keaney's greatest strength" – and the mark of the true leader.

Keane's leadership was founded in an obsessive attention to significant detail learnt from Brian Clough, a man who once made him cry after a careless back-pass cost a late goal. "I only ever hit Roy the once," he said. "He got up so I couldn't have hit him very hard."

"If you weren't doing your stuff, Clough would spot it," Keane wrote in his autobiography. "A seemingly innocuous mistake that resulted in a goal conceded three or four minutes later, a tackle missed, or a failure to make the right run, or pass, would be correctly identified as the cause of the goal. It was no use pointing the finger at someone else – which is second nature to most players. He knew; you knew he knew. Every football match consists of a thousand little things which, added together, amount to the final score. The game is full of bluffers, banging on about 'rolling your sleeves up', 'having the right attitude' and 'taking some pride in the shirt'. Brian Clough dealt in facts, specific incidents, and invariably he got it right."

"Bluffer" is the ultimate insult in Keane's world, acting truthfully and according to principle the only standards that require satisfaction. But this refusal to compromise is psychologically demanding. He recalls being unable to concentrate in his first FA Cup final, unsure whether his brothers had got in after spending the time prior to it sorting out his friends from Cork first, desperate not to be thought a big-shot – part of the reason he so often found himself back home for nights out. Similarly, living in digs in Nottingham, he asked his landlady whether he might decorate his room, and when she agreed, painted the walls and ceiling black, claiming it to be the only way that he could relax. It was no great shock to learn that he is a compulsive leg-shaker.

Or in other words, his public persona belies an insecurity, the kind of insecurity that meant his first words on entering the United dressing room took the form of a pre-emptive strike: "I don't like you, you don't like me, let's just get on with it."

And now, lean, pinched and demonic, burning calories with the pure intensity of his being, he was the very personification of the red devil, scared of nothing, and a worthy addition to a lengthy line of hard bastards including Frank Barson, Maurice Setters, Nobby Stiles, Jim Holton, Joe Jordan, Bryan Robson, Remi Moses, Norman Whiteside and Mark Hughes. And this had always been his manner. Before his debut for Nottingham Forest, made at Anfield, no one in the team had heard of him – "he was this young kid pushing the skips and helping with the kit", recalled Brian Laws. Then, Clough told him to try on the number seven shirt "to see what he looked like", concluding that "You look a million dollars. In fact, you look that good, you're playing." Stationed on the right wing and opposing

John Barnes, then the best attacker in the country, some might have been cowed. Keane was not cowed. Within five minutes, Barnes had not only been banjoed but "told what he was going to do to him", just the start of an "incredible debut".

Also paying attention were United – "We tried to buy him right away," Fergie told *FourFourTwo* in November 1999. "He played against us three weeks after that – that's why we watched him at Liverpool, because we were due to play them at Old Trafford. They beat us 1–0, and at the kick-off the ball went back to Robbo and he cemented Robbo right away. Now that's not a reason for signing a player, but it told you something about his attitude. Playing in the big arena didn't phase him one bit and Robson didn't intimidate him in any way – which you would find quite surprising 'cos in Robbo's halcyon days he tended to do that to everyone – including his own players – the kind of personality he had. From that moment on we targeted him."

Growing up in a tough city like Cork, smaller than other kids and rarely hugged by his father, Keane quickly learned to protect himself. "Aggression is what I do," Keane once said. "I go to war. You don't contest football matches in a reasonable state of mind." And opponents knew it, team-mates knew it, and the crowd knew it; it's unlikely any player has ever imposed his personality to such an overwhelming degree. In any place you called home, it'd be his word that found you.

The trope is not uncommon in elite sport. Writing for ESPN about Michael Jordan, Wright Thompson observed "the way Jordan has always collected slights, inventing them -- nurturing them. He can be a breathtaking asshole: self-centered, bullying and cruel. That's the ugly side of greatness. He's a killer, in the Darwinian sense of the word, immediately sensing and attacking someone's weakest spot. His whole life has been about proving things, to the people around him, to strangers, to himself."

And the same was so of Keane, his edge inspirational to his team-mates not as elementally possessed but able to push themselves as remorselessly, given suitable stimulus. "Anybody looking to throw in the towel had the perfect opportunity," he later wrote of going 2–0 down. "Anybody seeking to prove that they were worthy of playing for Manchester United also had the chance to fucking prove it."

So it was that Beckham told Neville "we can do this" – suffixed, of course, by the obligatory "you know" – as Stam recalled, "there was no sense of panic". recalled Stam. "Our mental strength had an effect on the Italians, I'm sure of it," he wrote. "They were used to teams rolling over after going 2–0 down. Not us. Everyone in a red shirt still wanted the ball, we all wanted to get forward and no one was hiding."

After 28 minutes, possession percentages appeared on the screen: Juve 38, United 62. Then Cole held the ball up, preparing Yorke for a shot which he dragged wide, and it was all very weird: away to Juventus in a European Cup semi-final, and it's one-sided. Every now and again, a person at the scene of a road accident finds someone trapped under a car, and, instinctively focusing every reserve of strength and adrenalin into the maelstrom of the moment, discovers the ability to lift it. That's what United were doing.

But a minute later, Juve almost scored again. Di Livio crossed from the left, Schmeichel attempted some sort of volleyball set, missed, and the ball hit Conte on the head. But as it looped goalwards, Stam raced after it in pursuit, slotted in behind, and headed off the line.

Soon after, Blomqvist played an ill-advised square ball towards Butt, who let it go, Zidane nipping in to steal possession before it could reach Keane who brought him down with a lunge that was probably unnecessary. Booked and accordingly out of any potential final, he responded in typical fashion, briefly distributing viscous chunks of his mind before proceeding as before, the game another where the compulsion to win obscured the bigger picture. That, and his desire to justify the debt he owed his manager, while restoring his club to where he felt it belonged.

Gary Neville was a man after his own black heart. "The way it was reported," he wrote, "Roy had been even more heroic following his booking – in contrast to Gazza crying at the 1990 World Cup in the same stadium – but I didn't see it that way. He'd done his job, outstandingly. Emotion hadn't come into it."

There followed a brief quiet period, before Neville – who had another exceptional evening – clipped one of his aimless passes around the corner. Only this time, Beckham leapt to nod it down, to Cole, whose first touch happened to prod it into an ideal crossing position. And his cross was ideal, a pass almost, cutting out Ferrara – whose face flashed horror then resignation – to where the Jumpman was waiting to do the rest. "They have seen Juventus' away goal, and they have raised it!" shrieked Tyldesley.

People are odd things, and sporting form is one odd aspect of that oddity; it comes and goes for different people at different times, often with neither warning nor explanation. After United beat Wimbledon in the 1994 FA Cup fifth round, Fergie commented afterwards on the rarity of almost every player performing at close to his best, and in his time at United, there mightn't be even ten occasions when that's been the case. The 6–2 win at Arsenal in November 1990, perhaps two wins in 1993 against Spurs and Norwich, 1–0 over Everton in 1994, 3–2 against Juve in 1997, Fiorentina at home in 2000, 6–2 at Newcastle in April 2003, Roma at home in April 2007, Aston Villa at home the following season.

"In your very best performances," wrote Keane, "you often find that extra bit of inspiration when you forget the tactics, the game plan, even forget what you're playing for and just play. The way you did when you were a kid on the streets when there was nothing at stake except, in some vague way personal vindication. When you reach that level of deep, deep concentration it's amazingly liberating. You summon up all you've ever learned about the game from somewhere deep inside and just play." Unequivocally, this was that.

And the tempo of Keane's passing permitted neither side a moment's respite, ordering Irwin forward and finding him down the left. His pass into Cole created the chance for a snap-shot which, though hit well, Peruzzi saved down to his right.

Then, Neville and Beckham combined, Beckham sliding quickly down the line for Cole. The ball then travelled through Butt, Neville again and Keane, before Neville hit a long pass towards Blomqvist. Ferrara headed clear, but Birindelli's error allowed Yorke to pick up possession 25 yards from goal. He floated clear of Iuliano, advanced, and spanked a low shot off the inside base of the far post. Blomqvist then combined with Cole to initiate another stepover routine involving Yorke, but Iuliano intervened, and perhaps the finest half of football United have ever played, perhaps the finest half of football United will ever play, was over.

At full-time, Fergie would fully agree – "All my life I have based my football creed on passing the ball, possession with rhythm and tempo. For 30 minutes of the first half, my ideals were almost totally realised" – but at half-time, he only half-agreed. "We're playing great football," he said in the dressing room, before turning to the defence.

"But you lot had better sort yourselves out... keep going at them, they're not used to it and they don't like it."

And they didn't, Keane later recalling that Juve's midfielders all vanished; "I went for a fifty-fifty ball with Davids. It was a no contest." Nor did Zidane enjoy playing against Stam – "what a beast!" he would later exclaim.

Yet the first chance of the second period was created by Juve, Inzaghi taking a pass from Di Livio and shooting against Schmeichel, beginning a brief period of home supremacy. It ended with Yorke flicking on a Beckham cross and Cole attempting to control, when a shot would've served him better.

Then, on 62 minutes, Stam headed a Di Livio cross clear and the dithering Blomqvist was robbed, Conte pulling his shot for Inzaghi to tap in at the far post – but he was offside. That would be Blomqvist's final involvement, withdrawn for the calm authority of Scholes' passing, quickly inspiring a move involving Neville, Beckham and Yorke that spanned the width of the pitch and ended with Irwin clicking right-footed against the inside of the post and left-footed into the side netting.

Though trailing, Juve were unable to build momentum, United always quick to move the ball forward. On 76 minutes, a frustrated Ferrara stuck his hand into Cole's face, Cole pursuing him to return a shove, after which Scholes caught Deschamps and received a yellow card. He too would miss the final – but ah, *gam zu letovah*.

"I didn't really make a bad tackle," he recalled, "but when I challenged him, he gave a bit of a scream, which some foreign players are liable to do, and I firmly believe that's what got me booked. I have to admit it came as a crushing blow, but there was never going to be any Gazza-type tears from me. You can get upset and disappointed, but it's only football and you have to keep perspective." Seconds later, he won the ball, stepped away from his man, and prompted an attack with an astute pass.

With 11 minutes remaining, United almost scored a third. Fonseca, brought on as Juve prepared to defend a corner, sliced off the line when Yorke arrived first to Beckham's cross. He then almost contributed at the other end, first crossing for Amoruso, but Johnsen was alert and headed clear, before collecting a reverse ball from Zidane on the left byline, and his low cross was missed by Inzaghi, Stam allowing it through his legs, and away from goal.

And that was as nervous as it got. United knitted together passes one after another, but passes with purpose, one move ending with a Cole shot. Then Juve tried another attack, and when the ball went behind, Schmeichel punted a clearance downfield. Met with a weak header, the ball dropped to Yorke, who inhaled deeply to slink through the tiny gap between Montero and Iuliano. Through on goal Peruzzi pulled him down as he went by, but before the referee could award a penalty, Cole dashed into view, caught up with the loose ball, and slipped it into the net.

"Full speed ahead Barcelona!... Manchester United are in sight of the European Cup final again!"

And that was pretty much it. Juve resorted to off-the-ball kicks, shirt-pulling and pinching, their fans a hail of lighters and suchlike. Meanwhile, Beckham volleyed wide then called Davids a fucking wanker, which resulted in minor tunnel shenaniga, Davids doing some face-shouting and some of his team-mates refusing to shake hands. Accordingly, unruly celebrations in the United dressing room paid no heed to nicety when considering the proximity of their opponents. Butt, Beckham, Sheringham and May posed for a photo, Butt imploring them to flex, before Yorke arrived to make a noisy circuit, shaking every hand and finishing with Bobby Charlton.

Juventus became the first Italian team in 20 years to lose a home knockout tie in the European Cup and, for the first time in eight years, the final would not involve an Italian team.

While the players frolicked, in the United end there was a brief silence, punctuated by a lone voice. "Forty-one years ago, a team lay in the snow, battered and bloodied and some of them died, some of them survived. Charlton and Matt Busby, they went to Wembley, we beat Benfica and won the Cup, all those years ago."

And it was impossible not to think of Munich, even in the moment and even for those remembering something that they couldn't actually remember. For those who experienced it, the trauma remains beyond comprehension, but the feeling is acute even for those who didn't, envious and empty, and often, a first encounter with death; the realisation that it meant never coming back, happened to United, people you knew, and you.

But the richer history is, the more it means and the more deeply it is experienced, the paradox of tragedy its role in inspiring stories, songs and love, elements of life that resonate deeply with the human condition, sharpening identity and purpose. And unlike most mythological characters, the Babes actually existed, their legends not legend but fact. They were not a device to teach things, though they do, nor a construct to encourage belief in things, though they do, nor a yarn to inspire unity, though they do; they are, because they were, and that is something special and rare.

"Where others would have sagged and died," wrote Geoffrey Green of the Babes' final league game against Arsenal, "United, as so often over the years, refused to wilt at the crisis. They trimmed their sails, steadied the boat with a firm hand on the tiller and rode out the storm. Step by step over the last 20 minutes they took charge again like champions. By sheer force of character and will-power they superimposed their skill to dominate events once more."

Lines that could equally have been written about this United side. To watch a football team over a period of time is to watch men grow and develop, to observe them at their best and worst, and though they were not integral to the community in the way of the Babes, they nonetheless represented something of the people who watched them.

In 1997, those survivors who could returned to Munich for the European Cup final. "Everyone needs to know one thing about three of the men sitting here with me," said Kenny Morgans. "Bill Foulkes, Harry Gregg and Bobby Charlton were out of the plane to safety when they realised that many of us were still trapped inside. They went back into that inferno to pull us out. That's what we mean by team spirit." And, quite literally, what it means to be United.

*

United were in the European Cup final!

"We always make it hard for ourselves," parroted Keane. "But we kept battling on and we always felt we'd get goals, and even at 2–0 down, I'll be honest, I still felt we'd get there." And elation had yet to be usurped by devastation, testament to the spirit within the team. "It doesn't really matter because the club has got there," he caid of his suspension. "It was a bit of a late challenge, but United have got there."

Keane's contribution was not lost on the Italian press, singing "Keano! Keano!" when Fergie arrived at the press conference afterwards, followed by "Oh Andy Cole!", also praised in *Tuttosport* for "a truly wonderful display of football".

As you'd expect, Fergie was almost drowning in pleasure. "It is a very proud moment for me," he gurgled. "This is the level we want to play at. My players were absolutely fantastic, absolutely magnificent. I thought the first 45 minutes was the best in my career as a manager. It was absolutely terrific. We gave them a start. But I am proud of the way they recovered and kept their composure, and I think they deserve to be there."

Carlo Ancelotti did his best to be gracious, clearly having failed to heed his own pre-match advice. "We met a team that was tactically superior to us. We were not able to impose ourselves on them as we had done in the first leg, and perhaps we made a mistake in supposing we could do so again. I was surprised that Manchester United could play like that, especially after going two goals down."

Meanwhile at Anfield, Liverpool lost to a last-minute Leicester goal, in front of a crowd of 36,019 – roughly 9,000 below capacity – though, in their defence, there was some pretty decent entertainment on the telly.

United were in the European Cup final!

*

Two days later, controversy, disgrace and disgust abounded in the football world after Cyril the Swan, the Swansea mascot, appeared before a disciplinary hearing at the Football Association of Wales, ordered to come in full 9ft tall outfit. Already accused of shoulder-charging Norwich City's Bryan Hamilton earlier in the season, this time he was charged with celebrating a goal against Millwall by dancing on the pitch; it required four hours to find him guilty and fine him £1,000. Swansea were fined an additional £1,000 after fans threw missiles onto the pitch during the same game.

*

A day before United visited Leeds, Arsenal faced a thorny fixture away to Middlesbrough, who were seventh in the table and unbeaten at home in 35 games. But, despite the absence of Bergkamp, Arsenal won 6–1, Kanu's size 15 boots somehow scoring a flicked, back-heeled volley. This took them top for the first time all season, by two points, and they had also reduced United's goal difference advantage by nine-tenths in just a week. They had, though, played two games more – of United's last 12 games, only four had been in the league – and given the respective fixtures remaining, it was generally felt that should they win at Elland Road, the title would be very close to done.

But that was far from a given. Though Leeds had drawn their previous two games, at home to Liverpool and away to Charlton, before that had come seven straight wins, equalling the club record in the top division which had stood since the Revie days. The run had taken them to fourth place, only five points behind Chelsea and in with a chance of nabbing the final Champions League place.

Though the kick-off was extra-early, and it was a nice day too, the hostility did its best – though Stam remained unfazed. "I always have a laugh when I see 40-year-old supporters foaming at the mouth, giving me a 'wanker' sign as I look out the coach window," he wrote. "It's comical to think that a grown man still believes it's going to make any difference to me."

"I used to think the Arsenal–Tottenham derbies were something but this game makes that look like altar-boy stuff," said David O'Leary, who announced in the morning that he had signed a new five-year contract. It was timed, apparently, to invigorate his players – as one might expect of a man nicknamed Jack, on account of a preoccupation with his personal alrightness. Later that day, he would refer to his period in charge as a "reign".

In the Sky studio, George Best reflected on the Juve game, which he'd watched in his local pub "for a change". Calling it "the performance of the decade, maybe of all time", he drew the obvious comparison with the 1968 comeback in Madrid. "The boss said to us 'you're still in with a chance', and we came out the second half and slaughtered them."

Despite sustaining an Achilles injury Jaap Stam was selected to play, only to drop out following the warm-up, to be replaced by David May, starting his first league game of the season.

Also injured was Scholes, whose knee problem meant that he was fit enough only for the bench and unavailable for England's midweek friendly in Hungary, a game from which Beckham and Gary Neville had already been excused. Consequently, Wes Brown would make his debut, and he replaced Johnsen for United, who, along with Solskjær, was already away with Norway in advance of their meeting with Georgia.

For Leeds, Jimmy Floyd Hasselbaink passed a late fitness test – he had missed only two games all season, and Leeds had scored in neither. But Hopkin and Ribeiro were injured and Haaland also off with Norway, so McPhail came into midfield, while the defence was as expected – and one that had conceded just eight goals at home all season.

Though this was the first point of the season at which it was impossible to deny precisely how good United were, Leeds were not remotely bothered and turned it up from the start, the crowd cheering every tackle and error. With three minutes gone, Kewell roved away from Keane, who either slipped or fell into him, but he simply absorbed the momentum, rolled over and back to his feet, dinking a cross for Bowyer at the back post. Finding himself underneath it, he headed just over.

United really couldn't get going, only now realising the extent of the physical and emotional puff expended in Turin and relieved to see the flag go up when Hasselbaink was probably onside and definitely through. Then, on nine minutes, Smith lifted him a pass over the top and he easily evaded May, forced to pull him down and accept a yellow card. Gary Neville once identified him as the only member of the squad comfortable telling a joke in front of everyone – hardly surprising given the numbers in front of whom he didn't mind defending.

It took 13 minutes for United to rustle up an attack, Irwin combining with Blomqvist to get past Jones, his cross blocked behind. Beckham's low corner was missed by Keane at the near post, his hop and skip distracting the defenders so that Brown could miss it in the middle. Sliding in at the back post was May, but he managed to avoid making the proper contact, allowing Martyn, already on the ground, to poke away, with Cole then unable to get his foot around Jones with enough power to force the ball over the line.

Next, after lesser beef between Beckham, Harte and Bowyer, Hasselbaink lumped Neville in the body as punishment for its use to shield the ball on the floor, for which he was booked. Then Beckham wandered inside and played Cole in, Radebe doing well to hook clear, before Kewell found space behind Neville, and with everyone expecting a cross towards the middle, instead picked out Bowyer on the edge of the box, only for him to slice a shot well over the bar.

And again Leeds came, Hasselbaink pulling left, easily away from May chugging along behind, and Butt doing well to win a tackle with McPhail after the ball was pulled back. "Fuck all, you're gonna win fuck all," chorused the ground.

Then, on 32 minutes, Leeds took the lead. Butt, on the left, attempted a square ball to Keane that was well behind him, and Kewell took possession. Moving through the centre-circle towards goal, Hasselbaink made him an angle by running across May, who declined to pursue in favour of trying to block a pass already past him. Delivered into the space at inside-right, Brown stumbled as it came into his range, and when Schmeichel chose to come out, Hasselbaink flicked a foot to intimate a shot, turned it into an additional step, taken quickly, and scored off the base of the near post before he could adjust. If only he'd seen him do similar when the teams met at Old Trafford, it might just have been preventable.

Thereafter, United played with greater aggression. First, Yorke escaped Radebe down the right, gained the byline and stepped inside Harte as Cole stepped outside, ready for a pass. But an extra touch meant that it was no longer on and instead the ball went towards the back post, where Jones headed behind before either Butt or Blomqvist could act.

Then, with two minutes until half-time, Leeds almost scored again, McPhail given time and space to measure a left-wing cross that Kewell headed only just wide as Irwin looked on, before Blomqvist – who'd given Jones a hard time – pulled off him, onto Beckham's raking pass. Woodgate managed to nod his centre behind, and Yorke met the ensuing corner running from far to near post, but couldn't quite twist his brow into a glance, thudding wide instead. That was the last action of a first half that Dermot Gallagher said was the fastest he'd ever refereed.

"I didn't miss the point of asking them if they were the team we had talked about after Wednesday night," recalled Fergie of his dressing-room monologue. "I asked them to consider whether this was the spirit everyone had been remarking on after the great recovery against Juventus."

Immediately after the restart, Kewell lost Butt and whacked a shot from distance not that far over the top, but United maintained general control. On 48 minutes, Blomqvist won possession from Bowyer and found Keane, who sent a pass out to Yorke that he set back for Beckham. His smoothly bent cross was cleared, but eventually returned to Blomqvist, whose better cross forced Radebe to head behind under pressure from Yorke, clattering the post as he did so.

But Leeds couldn't get hold of the ball, Keane fed by Butt and orchestrating another attack, spreading play right, to Yorke. Receiving the return outside the box, still right of centre, he arced an unforeseeable pass over the top, Butt now at the far post where it pitched perfectly into his path, and though Martyn pushed out his header, Cole was on hand to poke home from close range as against Newcastle, also injuring Woodgate, who was subbed shortly afterwards.

United kept at it, Blomqvist running onto Cole's lovely stabbed return pass before a heavy touch ruined the opportunity. Then, Leeds created their first promising situation in a while, Bowyer almost sneaking a ball through to Smith that Brown was in quickly to block.

Just past the hour, Hasselbaink drifted in behind Neville but could only smash high, and then Smith knocked Schmeichel over on the touchline as he tried to see a ball into touch. With United losing the impetus, Phil Neville replaced Irwin, and before Keane was booked, pursuing Bowyer and pulling out, only for him to fall anyway.

On 82 minutes, as Scholes stood on the touchline toking on his inhaler, Brown tarried in possession and was caught by Smith. Breaking two-on-one with Hasselbaink, who again created the angle for a pass with a diagonal run, when a feint sent May scurrying in that direction too the space opened up for a shot, which he hit straight at Schmeichel's sprawl.

In the final seconds of regulation time, Wijnhard took a pass from McPhail, burst away from May, and hit a shot as he fell that whumped straight into Schmeichel's arms. Then, in the third additional minute Butt collected Wetherall's headed clearance and found Yorke, wide to his left. Seemingly playing out time, from a standing start, he set off inside away from Jones to find Sheringham, who stretched into a return that put him through on goal. Allowing the ball across his body to finish tidily with his left foot, it looked inconceivable that he might miss, and then he missed, and then he grinned.

"Good chance from Dwight," laughed Fergie afterwards, "but I think we can forgive him." Yorke was one of five players – Beckham, Keane, Petit and Ginola the others – who were up for the PFA Player of the Year award, the dinner for which was to be held that night. Did Fergie think he might win, wondered Geoff Shreeves. "The *PFA* Player of the Year? I don't think so." He didn't, and Keane was astoundingly denied entry to the team of the year, people still labouring under the misapprehension forged in his absence that Petit and Vieira were superior.

David O'Leary, meanwhile, was looking to the future. "I hope," he said, "with the backing of the club, that they will allow me in the summer or back me over the next five years to be able to bring quality players into this club to add to the quality I've already got because that's our yardstick today. You see their squad, you see who's sitting up in the stand and we've gotta bring quality people in if we're gonna chase them."

"I think he might talk the chairman out of a few quid," prophesied George Best in the studio.

MAY

There were seven games to go and 26 days in which to play them, after which life might never be the same again. "This is a special season," wrote the manager in his first programme notes of the month. "No matter what happens on the last lap, you should enjoy it because you might never see the like again." He was right, of course, though the ability to take pleasure in the football part of football is governed more by temperament than choice.

With a full week off prior to playing Aston Villa, the players had a rare opportunity to rest and recover. "Training is minimal now because it's simply not an issue," explained Fergie. "Mental fitness and freshness are the key. If the players feel strong in their minds, they will be strong on the pitch."

With Stam and Berg injured, May accompanied Johnsen in defence, while Keane's suspension meant that Butt and Scholes were in midfield, though the former had played for England in Bucharest in midweek. Solskjær, hurt in Tbilisi, was not risked – "It's not very popular to come back with an injury," he observed – and with Cole still not fully fit, Sheringham started alongside Yorke.

Villa were still without Ugo Ehiogu, not quite ready three months after fracturing his eye socket in a collision with Alan Shearer, as you did, and Lee Hendrie was also out. In net, Michael Oakes replaced the dropped Mark Bosnich, still linked with a move to United on account of out-of-contract cheapness – though, earlier in the week, Edwin van der Sar had again claimed that United had contacted him. The difficulty, of course, was that he would cost money, when, of course, United had absolutely none – if you asked Martin Edwards, but not if you asked IMUSA's Andy Walsh.

"Martin Edwards' temper tantrum in the last few weeks over the failure of the Sky deal is contemptuous of Ferguson's achievements over the last ten years," he said. "Edwards should sit down with the manager and discuss these matters before he goes and shoots his mouth off in the press… The club is not Martin Edwards' club. It is loved and its soul is owned by thousands of people around the world… and such an announcement, when we are on the verge of such major games, does nothing for the stability of the club."

Though United played well enough, missing was the cohesion provided by a settled line-up – or, put another way, Roy Keane wasn't there. But after their mid-season mincing, in a run that saw them scramble one draw from eight games, Villa had also found some form and were audacious enough to actually try, Old Trafford's first league visitors so to do since Newcastle.

For all United's initial pressure, they created just one chance in the first quarter of an hour, Sheringham nodding back Blomqvist's cross only for Scholes to shoot straight at Oakes. Then, on 19 minutes, and from just outside the box, just left of centre, Beckham whipped a free-kick over the wall and towards his usual near-post netting, but Southgate, hanging around on the line for precisely such eventuality, headed away. But Villa were unable to clear the resultant corner, headed clear at the near post but only as far as Blomqvist, outside the box and just left of centre. Fooling Joachim as he rushed back to tackle by pausing, studs on the ball, he then angled over the top for Scholes at the far post, who'd sneaked in front of the defenders. Knocking back across, he sought Yorke but found the path of Watson, unable to avoid running the ball into his own net, red face and orange hair clashing in an embarrassing fashion faux pas.

But over the next period, Villa realised that a kicking was most likely not in the offing so augmented effort with quality, and just after the half-hour, they drew level. Watson pushed forward down the right and found Draper, the ball moving into Dublin and back to Watson, who fed Stone outside him. Suddenly in space as United appealed for offside, his cross was volleyed against Scholes by Joachim, sending the rebound in at the near post from closish range with Schmeichel headed towards the far.

Then, a minute after half-time, a moment. Wright fouled Yorke 30-odd yards from goal and wide on the right, this time determining Oakes that he was fine not only without goal-line help, but a wall too. And given the angle, compounded by the distance, it was almost fair enough, were anyone but Beckham behind the ball. Beckham was behind the ball. And, with the keeper roughly in the middle of the goal, he raced up and placed a rasp into the far top corner for another brilliant, original finish. "Our goalkeeper felt he could deal with it on his own," said John Gregory. "The problem was, he didn't."

"David Beckham is Britain's finest striker of a football," explained Fergie afterwards, "not because of God-given talent but because he practises with a relentless application that the vast majority of less gifted players wouldn't contemplate." But the *Guardian*'s Ian Ross knew better, describing "a young man whose vanity away from the pitch is to be deplored."

When, after a further 17 minutes, United couldn't extend their advantage, they elected to preserve it, Phil Neville replacing Blomqvist, and within two minutes he had won a penalty, subsiding after a nudge by Stone. Up stepped Irwin to hit a not appalling effort to Oakes' right, who, guessing correctly, clawed it out from above his head. This was the first time Irwin had failed to score from the spot, and he would miss only one other, against West Ham at home the following season, on that occasion scoring from the rebound.

But the loss of Blomqvist hindered United, who struggled without the width he provided – "we did well to survive that managerial mistake", said the manager afterwards. Fortunately for him, Villa were unable to take advantage, though he was forced to spend much of the last five minutes on the touchline blaring at his players to behave themselves.

"We're asking them to win the last four games," said Fergie in the press room. "Their energy levels, their attitude and their will are good. So let's do it."

Also that afternoon, Ian Wright was sent off for two bookable offences in West Ham's 5–1 loss to Leeds. After being restrained by Trevor Sinclair, he repaired directly to the referee's room in order that it might become trashed – a consequence, no doubt, of the magnanimity heist he'd suffered earlier in the season. "I was disappointed at being dismissed, at letting down my manager Harry Redknapp, my team-mates and the West Ham fans by not being on the pitch to help win the game and get us into Europe," he explained. "I hope and pray to God that I can be forgiven for this stupid and reckless act." Whether he afforded the referee the same toadying courtesy was never revealed, but Rob Harris' car was attacked as he left the ground and Wright was later banned for three games.

Then, the following day, Arsenal scraped by Derby, the game enlivened by footage of Wenger telling his players precisely what he thought of them. Suddenly, he wasn't quite so urbane.

*

United's game at Anfield was to be Fergie's 500th in the league, though it's questionable whether he was quite as chuffed now at having deferred it, given how seriously the points were required. But he was certainly chuffed the day before the game, the club announcing that he had signed a new three-year deal.

"I am delighted that the matter has been settled and that I have a contract that will take me to 60 years of age," he said. "My hunger for success remains undiminished and I will be striving to ensure that the next three years are as successful as the last 13 have been."

But Schmeichel wasn't buying it. "It wouldn't surprise me at all if he is still there at 65," he wrote in his autobiography. "Yeah, it's nice for him to go for two or three weeks to the races or the South of France, but, after that, the feeling is going to come back to him. He can't sit back and relax."

It had not been a good season for Liverpool, eighth in the table and beaten at home ten times in the league. Before losing in the Cup at Old Trafford – "a turning point", said Houllier, the first in a journey comprising more corners than Hampton Court – they had been minding their own business in sixth place, falling after a run of four defeats in six games, then had played only once in March before more misery in April. Aside from the Leicester defeat, they also managed to avoid beating Nottingham Forest, conceding another late goal, and lost at home to Villa, prompting Houllier to tell the *Liverpool Echo* that the contest with United was "David against Goliath", causing predictable consternation.

They had, however, won their previous two games, turning one in nine into three in 11 – the first at Blackburn and the second at Anfield at home to Spurs, coming back from 0–2 down, though against ten men. The winner in that game came via Paul Ince's clever header – he was pushed forward in the absence of Michael Owen and Robbie Fowler, both out for the rest of the season. Owen had pulled up after injuring a hamstring against Leeds, while Fowler was serving a double suspension, the first for the Le Saux homophobia, and the second for the admittedly excellent goal-line sniffing celebration. Or pretending to eat the grass in imitation of Rigobert Song, if you believed Houllier.

Liverpool also had problems in goal, Houllier seeing no problem in making his search for a new keeper public knowledge, despite the two already on his books. He would end up with Sander Westerveld – a "safe option", he reckoned – and perhaps the first man in history not to be converted into gibbering jelly by the legendary Scouse wit, admitting a lack of mirth when publicly nauseated by folk he didn't know.

"Some people think it's funny to make jokes about goalkeepers when they come up to me, but I've just about had enough," he complained. "If someone two metres away from me drops their glass of beer on the floor, as was the case on Saturday night, you can bet that a wise guy has asked if it was me. Even my postman gets in on the act when he gives me my letters. 'Watch you don't drop them,' he says. I don't like these comments and they don't exactly help your confidence either."

For this game, Houllier preferred Friedel to James for the second time in a row, after several months out in punishment for his September Old Trafford panic. In front of him was a back three of Babb, Staunton and "young Carragher", Song at right wing-back and Matteo on the left. In midfield, and in the absence of the injured Gerrard, were Ince, Redknapp and Leonhardsen while McManaman, still in the doghouse, roamed behind Riedle.

For United, Stam and Cole returned, along with Keane, on whom Kenny Dalglish was amusingly solicited for praise in the studio, pre-match. He played alongside Scholes, with Butt, May and Sheringham missing out. Only Giggs and Berg were unavailable, along with original referee Paul Durkin. In his stead, David Elleray was appointed – he'd awarded Liverpool a shifty penalty during the previous season's Anfield meeting.

As the players gathered in the tunnel, a topless Ince prepared to lead out the home side, bravely confronting the superstition that insisted he be last in line, while Fergie stood at the door of United's dressing room, distributing back-pats to each player. The ground then made a suitable din, telly cameras locating a man on the Kop holding a sign that read "18 times" – perhaps he's still there now.

Within two minutes Scholes had greeted McManaman, disturbing the isosceles triangle sitting atop his head, and then Blomqvist was incorrectly adjudged offside after chesting down Neville's long pass and cutting in. But otherwise, Liverpool started the faster, denying United space and time.

Their pressure on the ball even prompted the rare transgression of a stray Keane pass, but it was United who had the game's first shot after 14 minutes, Neville volleying wide from a clearing header after Cole and Yorke combined to set up a break. Next, Scholes rapped Ince on the Achilles – "he's anything but a dirty player, but he doesn't half mistime some tackles", patronised Martin Tyler.

Gradually, United assumed control of the game, Scholes moving away from Redknapp and spreading the ball wide before consecutive flicks from Neville and Keane gave Beckham space, but Babb getting back to cover. But, before long, they were ahead. Matteo nudged Beckham over just by halfway on the right touchline as he chased a return pass from Cole. Instead he tipped the free-kick short and inside to Keane, accepting the return, to relocate him, now in goodly space, by passing forwards and hard to the exclusion of Redknapp and Leonhardsen. Waiting for Beckham to make up the ground and pass him as McManaman pretended to pursue, Keane then rolled a ball of ideal weight into his path that Beckham appeared simply to allow to hit his foot, cross fondled without backlift or follow-through and arriving at the far post precisely as Yorke did and Carragher didn't. Yorke took a token skip into the air, headed home easily, and pranced. Martin Tyler's excitement was less.

Not long after play restarted, Beckham almost crafted a second, again from the touchline but this time in his own half, unleashing a long pass while back-pedalling into the space between Friedel and Cole. But Babb was alert to the danger, dashing between the two to nod behind.

Then, on the half-hour, Redknapp arrowed a crossfield ball to Song, who was diligently tracked and foiled by Blomqvist, replicating the work-rate of the missing Giggs. But the other flank brought Liverpool's principal threat, McManaman and Matteo combining to good effect and forcing Schmeichel to move sharply for a cross that Riedle only just missed at the near post.

With only a few minutes until the break, United almost managed a second. Scholes read a square ball from McManaman aiming to set Redknapp for a shot just outside the box, sending a simple side-foot out to the right and into space. Cole chased it down and turned inside Staunton, stabbing back outside for Beckham, as Ince slid in. Taking a touch, he slung over another perfect cross, to the near post this time, Yorke again running away from Carragher and jumping, hanging and heading down, Friedel doing well to shovel behind.

United began the second half with controlled possession, but an aimless pass from Gary Neville allowed Liverpool to create the first scoring opportunity. Cut out by Babb, Matteo then fooled Beckham down the line and found McManaman inside him, who moved the ball on to Ince. With Matteo now in an advanced position, Ince delivered him the ball and continued moving, ready for the pull-back. But on its way, it kicked up off the turf then slowed, and now, forced to drag it from behind him, shot over the top.

United were still a threat, though, and won a free-kick when Leonhardsen twisted Irwin to the ground, retaining an arm around his neck for a fair while afterwards. Tapping short to Keane, the ball went back to Stam who returned it, space now open in front of the Liverpool area. Spotting Beckham moving inside, he fired into him, prompting a fairly aimless pass, stabbed high around the corner to the opposite corner of the box. Leaving the ball to each other, Song and Carragher both then let it bounce, letting Blomqvist head away from them and move towards goal. This left Carragher with no choice but to slam a shin into his liver. "It's got to be a penalty," lamented Martin Tyler. "It must have been an obvious penalty to have been given at Anfield by David Elleray!" wrote Fergie.

As the players gathered before the kick, Keane said something to Carragher who pushed him as he passed. Ince then arrived to initiate a short donnybrook that ended with Keane's shirt getting ripped and Ince forced to endure a talking-to from Staunton, wearing his best indignant face.

Meanwhile, a nervous-looking Irwin composed himself, chest hair spilling over the V of his jersey, and began his usual run and immediate turn. Except Elleray hadn't indicated readiness, moving to defuse a row and forcing a semi-pause. Friedel then swayed to his right and committed left, but Irwin's kick was too precise and billowed the side netting a foot or two off the ground. Again, the commentary was in the style of a state funeral.

Not in the game since United's second goal, Tyler implored Liverpool to go forward, suggesting they throw "a bit of caution to the wind", the rest presumably saved for a rainy day. And they did make an effort to attack, Carragher striding down the right, but Blomqvist, running his little gnome feet off, caught up and slid around his legs, winning the ball cleanly and incurring no sanction.

As against Spurs, Ince was moved closer to Riedle, after which Berger created and almost took Liverpool's first opportunity in some time, running right to left across the face of the box and swinging into a shot that flew only just wide of the near upright. Next minute, Berger, McManaman and Matteo built down the wing, Matteo's clever pass finding Berger on the left of the area close to the byline. With Riedle and Ince racing towards him, three men were drawn out of the middle, such that when Berger tapped into space towards the back post, Blomqvist and Leonhardsen were effectively duelling for goal. Again, Blomqvist slid and curled around legs to poke the ball away as Leonhardsen jumped to finish, and amidst no appeals whatsoever, Elleray whistled for a penalty kick – the first against United in the league all season. Andy Gray was outraged, Martin Tyler was not, and Jamie Redknapp smashed it home for Keysie.

Suddenly a game which had appeared over was not remotely so, Liverpool again loading up on their left, this time with Leonhardsen sweeping across from the other side and Matteo and Berger combining to give Ince a chance to cross. Picking out McManaman at the back post, straining, leaning and clambering over Blomqvist to reach it, Blomqvist did just enough, holding his nerve, standing his ground, seeing it away, and other clichés.

Talking of which, Martin Tyler had by now segued into soliloquy about penalties against United. Did you know that none had been awarded to an opposing Premier League side at Old Trafford in five seasons? Well, Tyler did, and he was determined it be thought relevant to an obviously dodgy one just conceded away from home.

With 15 minutes remaining, Matteo set off down the wing again, crossing towards Riedle at the near post, where it was as well Stam cleared, because Schmeichel had wandered off. From the corner, Riedle headed wide, but Carragher would not allow Irwin to let it run out for a throw, so he beat him to it and knocked the ball along the line, playing a pass a sixth of a second after a whistle he claimed not to have heard, and finding himself sent off for a second bookable offence. Elleray never did say how he could be so sure to the contrary, and even Phil Thompson sat shaking his head. Irwin would miss the Cup final.

Immediately afterwards, Liverpool made an opportunity for Ince, his shot scooped away by Schmeichel and the loose ball somehow evading McManaman, before Cole hooked clear. Then, United made a double change, Phil Neville and Butt replacing Blomqvist and Cole as they endeavoured to secure the points, and two minutes later, Liverpool removed Staunton for Thompson. "David Thompson, David Thompson" chorused the crowd, to the tune of "Steven Gerrard, Steven Gerrard".

Despite the hairy circumstances, United were not really hanging on, passing well, and with the exception of Schmeichel, looking calm. But then, with a minute left to play, Matteo spread the play wide to McManaman, who skipped a pass into Berger on the left edge of the box that he and Johnsen missed. Suddenly, United were under pressure, Riedle reaching it ahead of Stam and ducking inside him. With Schmeichel opting to come out, once the ball had been nudged square, away from him and Butt, there existed a split second to realise the horrible reality before Ince slid in the equaliser, beside himself with righteous lunacy.

"The second before I scored I knew I was going to get the equaliser because it was an open goal and I just got this rush of adrenalin because I knew I couldn't miss," Ince told the *Liverpool Echo*. "I've had a lot of stick over the last two years, been called a 'Big-Time Charlie' and all that. I knew someday I'd have my day and today was that day and I am just ecstatic."

Some felt the way that he celebrated was out of line, but it's hard to condemn him for wanting revenge over beef started – or at the very least, made public – by Fergie, and milked by supporters who'd taken plenty of pleasure in his performances.

Then, in the third minute of injury time, things almost got very much worse. Thompson crossed from the right and Carragher, advancing into an astonishing quantity of space as Johnsen and hearts stood still, headed wide. He would compensate for this profligacy in the next fixture between the sides, notching a brace of own goals, half the number he managed for his own team in an entire career, and setting him en route to the proud record of scoring more goals against Liverpool than any other player.

"I think it's fair to say that we'd have won the game but for the referee," Fergie commented afterwards, establishing causation of the tort, "and we're just not gonna let him deny us our opportunity to win this league. We'll recover from it."

Nor was Martin Edwards best pleased, poking his head above the door to complain: "If Arsenal or Chelsea win the Premiership this season by either one or two points, I trust they will strike a special commemorative medal for Mr Elleray because he will have done it for them."

Anyway, the draw, followed by a defeat to Sheffield Wednesday in their next game, meant that Liverpool failed to qualify for Europe, while general excitement reached even higher pitch. *Gam zu letovah.*

But at the time, not so much. Arsenal had won 3–1 at Spurs, Kanu had scored a brilliant goal, and they were now three points clear – having played a game more, but with a better goal difference, in control for the first time. They had also won five on the trot, United just two in the same period.

Elsewhere, Chelsea sneaked past Leeds, Gus Poyet's winner highlighting the significance of his earlier absence. This secured them third position and a spot in an expanding Champions League, to feature two group stages and much tedium, but wasn't what they were after. They lost only three games all season, a feat bettered by only three champions in the last century.

The following night, David Ginola was named Footballer of the Year – "that's quite amazing", said Fergie when claiming apparently genuine ignorance of its award a day or two later. "The Football Writers' Association proved today that its members know just as much about the game as the folk who actually play it," said the *Guardian's* Fiver. "The Frenchman, who caught the eye with magnificent displays of mesmeric trickery down the left flank all season (apart from in the Worthington Cup final and an FA Cup semi-final) beat noted chokers Dwight Yorke and David Beckham into second and third place respectively."

United's next game was away to Middlebrough, and with Arsenal not playing at Leeds until the Monday, needed a result – if possible, scoring a few in the process, though given an extra game and inferior opposition, it was reasonable to expect them to win the league on goal difference, if it came to it.

On the other hand, Boro were the last team to beat United and were strong at the Riverside. Dumped in a particularly miserable piece of cold wasteland, its name fooled no one; Moley, Ratty and the boys were not tempted to relocate.

"It's getting really tense now," intoned Richard Keys over a montage to prove it, set to Massive Attack's 'Angel' to prove it. Fergie, though, was typically relaxed and at the top of his game, telling Sky that he "had a feeling it was going to go to the last day anyway", as though it was all part of a prophetic plan. But were the players looking tired? "No, no' a bit, I must say that, they're looking very well."

And as for Arsenal, well – he knew, for sure, that Leeds would give them a game. Either that or he was debuting a manoeuvre later to become known as the reverse Keegan. "They've a lot of young players who're making careers for themselves, and great reputations. I think that they're a genuine team," he told them.

With Cole unable to train at his normal level, his place in the starting 11 was taken by Sheringham, and Giggs and Solskjær were also unavailable. At the back, May partnered Stam, Johnsen's groin injury keeping him out, and Scholes was picked ahead of Butt in midfield.

For Boro, Pallister was fit but Festa and Cooper were not, so the youngster Gavin retained his place as one of three centre-backs. Paul Gascoigne was also deemed unfit, Mark Summerbell, another youth team graduate, retaining his place, and up front were Ricard and Deane, the latter with an excellent scoring record against United.

Pre-match cheerleading to 'Rule Britannia' and 'Land of Hope and Glory' ensured a febrile atmosphere, but the game started fairly slowly. Then, after five minutes, Keane allowed Sheringham's pass to escape underneath his studs, and pursuing the loose ball was fouled by Summerbell, his right ankle wrapping around a pair of sliding legs and causing him to limp away. Beckham floated over the free-kick, which was cleared despite being dropped by Schwarzer, and Ricard then tried a shot from well inside his own half. Seconds later, karmically he was retributed, levelled for his effrontery by Scholes, who was booked.

United then worked the ball from left to right and back again, before Keane – who had hurt his ankle in a tackle with Stockdale and would soon depart – had a shot pushed away by Schwarzer. Sheringham tucked away the rebound, only to be wrongly given offside.

But United carried on about their business, Pallister forced to head Blomqvist's cross away from the prowling Yorke, and then, a minute later, Beckham picked up a loose ball on the right of the box. Nodding it outside Gordon, he somehow managed to hook a controlled, flat cross for Yorke at the near post, only for him to miss his header and shoulder wide instead.

With 27 minutes gone, Boro won a free-kick just to the left of the centre-circle, which Townsend hit long towards Deane. With Stam barely jumping, he achieved the desired touch, and Summerbell, with a run on Scholes, took it down on his chest, shooting through May's legs and across Schmeichel, the ball clipping the outside of the post. "United have *dominated* this first half," growled Andy Gray, "should be up, but *could* be down."

Then, in injury time, Blomqvist was fortunate to win a free-kick after wasting a chance to cross. Schwarzer was first to Beckham's ball in, choosing to punch when he might have caught, and it dropped to Butt, outside the box and near its right corner. Jumping to ride the bounce and bring it under control, he directed a garryowen towards the back post, where Sheringham, unmarked, might have gone for goal. But instead, he nodded across for Yorke, unmarked, who headed down and in, the move more common to volleyball than football. Replays subsequently showed Yorke to have been in an offside position at the moment Butt played his pass, prompting various discussions of phases and interference, confusion and tedium that has been duly compounded in subsequent years.

On 56 minutes, Neville almost dropped United in it, a short back-pass forcing Schmeichel to hurry into a clearance, his dander not dampened when caught on the ankle by the chasing Ricard. Shortly afterwards, Blomqvist lost Townsend following a throw, allowing him to cross towards Gordon, who, refusing to condone a right-footed effort, arranged his body into one with his left that went nowhere near goal, ruining what turned out to be Boro's last real chance.

Neville and Yorke – now on the left after Cole replaced Blomquist – both trundling efforts at Schwarzer. In the absence of Keane, United's dominance of possession was orchestrated by Scholes; to paraphrase Rio Ferdinand's lovely aphorism of a decade later, his passes were telling people where to go. And drawing a man in on halfway before nudging clear of him, he slipped a short reverse ball to Sheringham and moved the poked return onto Beckham, who caught it as he spun and off the ground, volleying a flick over the top for Cole. Letting it drop on the left edge of the box and opting not to shoot, he then brought it down with his chest before lobbing the keeper after the next bounce; but, too close to goal after the ball had run away slightly, he could only clip the back of the bar, before booting the hoardings in vex.

And that was pretty much it, Boro – "working harder than they have worked in any game", according to Schmeichel – had only a couple of sniffs of sniffs, otherwise entirely neutralised. At full time United were top on goals scored, they and Arsenal entering the final week of the season with records that were almost identical.

Two days later, Arsenal went to Elland Road, the chatter all about whether Leeds would lie down to help deny United the title. But O'Leary had promised that he would "try to kick their butt" – yes, he really said that – and David Batty chided that "We're proud at Leeds".

And they played like it too, the teams producing a thoroughly brilliant game. Though Harte slammed a penalty against the bar after Keown lummoxed into Smith, Arsenal couldn't capitalise. The substitute Kaba Diawara missed three great chances – one of them forcing an improbable headed goal-line block from Woodgate – before, with four minutes to go, Hasselbaink headed in Kewell's cross at the far post. Suddenly, United were a maximum of four points away from the title, and even a draw at Blackburn would eradicate the possibility of a final-day goal-race.

*

A penultimate league fixture at Ewood Park was far from ideal, with anything but a win for the home team relegating them and Brian Kidd. At the weekend his team, at home to long-gone Forest, had lost after which he finally lost it.

"As a player I never suffered the words I had to dish out in the dressing room after the game," he said. "I have played rubbish, missed sitters, missed a million chances, but I have always tried to have a go. That didn't happen against Forest or, last week, at Charlton. I thought they were a frightened team. I have got people too ready to make excuses instead of fighting for the cause. A good dressing-room spirit can cover a multitude of sins; you will get results by sheer fight and hard work. But you cannot manufacture hearts and I didn't see enough of that out there. The inmates have been running this place for far too long."

And if that sounded like a paean pining for United, well, it probably was. Watching Steve McClaren poised to assume your credit cannot be a good look, and perhaps his inability to dominate his new men reflected qualities more suited to an assistant's role. But his contribution to his old club's position was unarguable, whatever the mean-spirited revisionism at the top.

United made five changes from the Riverside. Johnsen replaced May in defence, Giggs returned – he'd started only half of the season's league games – Cole came in for Sheringham, and the middle of midfield comprised Butt and Phil Neville. All 11 selected were eligible to play in Barcelona and though Keane was injured, the line-up was perhaps a trial for that game. Before this one, Fergie told Martin Tyler that there was "a lot of thinking to be done" ahead of the Bayern game, contradicting his usual policy of quick calls, and this performance would prove it.

Incredibly, for a side requiring goals and a win, Blackburn left the prolific Kevin Davies on the bench, and also Kevin Gallagher, who had missed a penalty against Forest to put his side two goals up. Starting up front was Matt Jansen, who had chosen Ewood in preference to Old Trafford, though Jason McAteer, sold by Liverpool against his will, was absent, injured in training. They lined up in a defensive 4–3–3 formation, Fergie taking the opportunity to undermine Kidd further.

"What struck me more than anything," he recounted, "was the way they decided to play... I got the feeling that their priority was to make sure that we didn't win the championship on their ground. I wondered if anyone else had been influencing Brian."

In the tunnel, Lee Carsley indulged in light shouting before the teams emerged to 'The Final Countdown', all very dramatic and the gravity of the situation now definitive. But the game started slowly, and it wasn't until the fifth minute that anything happened, Beckham pulling outside and shaping to play in Gary Neville on the overlap, instead twisting to whip a surprise shot just wide of the far post, via a deflection.

In the tenth minute, United won a throw deep in the Blackburn half which Gary Neville shaped to take long, before finding Beckham close by. Knocking it away from goal, feinting to cross, then taking it away from goal some more, he coiled his foot and body around the ball to dispatch a scarcely believable centre directly onto the furrows of the advancing Giggs, just beyond the far post. Easily outjumping Croft, he headed firmly but against the post, Cole prodding a foot at the rebound but sending the ball over the bar.

It took until the 39th minute for United to happen upon their best chance. Schmeichel rolled the ball out to Gary Neville, who launched long towards Cole, and incredibly, he was through, the brilliance of his jumping instep control taking him into the box on its right side and clear of a defence not paying the remotest attention. A little wider than was ideal, it was still a shooting opportunity only a few yards from goal, but he didn't quite middle his effort, easily collected by Filan.

The second half began without Stam, his Achilles injury requiring his replacement with May. The first action of note featured Phil Neville catching Dunn with an elbow, then caught by the zoom of the camera spitting in the manner soon to be made famous by Bodie Broadus, and no doubt admired by his assistant manager Brian McClair, master of a related genre.

United's lack of creativity in midfield was beginning to show, Blackburn doing a better job of stifling the wide players, and on 56 minutes, Dunn ran onto a flick from Ward and shot hard, Schmeichel tipping over. Johnsen then headed a Beckham corner goalwards, kicked away by Carsley before Cole could divert it the other way – his last contribution before being replaced by Sheringham. The two exchanged a no-look handshake.

Jansen then escaped Beckham and Butt on the left, his driven cross too good for everyone, and next minute, Blackburn created their best chance of the game. A heavy touch from Yorke allowed Henchoz to assume possession, finding Ward, and he immediately set Johnson away down the right. After sprinting back like a meshuggener, Johnsen felt unable not to contribute when the cross came his way, so although

Schmeichel was in position to collect, he back-heeled a clearance straight to Ward on the edge of the box. Immediately, Schmeichel dived in front of him, and though Jansen was well-placed close by, he opted to shoot, chipping over his legs – and past the post now defended by Johnsen.

But the game was not yet over, United enduring a final fright when Johnsen headed Johnson's cross away, but only as far as Wilcox. Controlling on his chest and steering away from May with his second touch, the wait for it to come down allowed Gary Neville to intercede with a back-pass that forced Schmeichel to improvise a long barrier. Otherwise, there was time only for Beckham to be booked for kicking Davidson; Blackburn were down with Forest, to be joined either by Charlton or Southampton, and United needed one more win for the title.

Heading down the tunnel, Fergie handed out a no-look handshake of his own, Kidd now an enemy, and with Jack Walker crying in the stands, probably considered it a decent night's work, despite his annoyance at United's inability to convert possession into goals. Kidd was left to console himself with the gift of Schmeichel's gloves, while Fergie feigned ignorance of Blackburn's relegation, responding with a dismissive "oh well", when the terrible news was "revealed" to him.

So it was that he was in a good mood when he visited Kidd's office, surprised to find him in one too, and not minded to preserve his privacy. "Maybe he has been able to distance himself from the responsibility of the relegation that is Blackburn's fate, or perhaps he feels he has to put on a front following his momentous decision to walk away from the success he enjoyed with us," he delighted in wondering.

But that wasn't the worst of it – just a few months later, Kidd found himself sullied in Fergie's autobiography, a shock that he handled with dignity and class. "After working with a person for over ten years, you get to know a lot about them personally and privately," he said. "I've chosen to respect that relationship. Clearly he hasn't. I've more important and pressing things than that. I have work to do here. If you go down the road of 'he said that, and she said that', it's laughable. What do you tell your kids? I'm struggling for words, but I don't feel I have to justify myself. The way I was brought up by my parents from the streets of Collyhurst means that I don't start belly-aching. You take your knocks and you get up and get on with it. Don't explain and never complain. It doesn't hurt me what has been said. I know. I'm at ease with myself. You can kid everybody – but you can't kid yourself."

He was fired three months into the following season.

*

Beat Spurs to win the league – not words anyone could ever object to hearing. But they were the only Premier League side United hadn't beaten, and were actually in reasonable form, producing their best passing performance of the season in their previous game, a 2–2 home draw with Chelsea.

"I can still remember as clearly as if it was yesterday," wrote Gary Neville in his newspaper column, published the day before the game, "the feeling of utter despair that surrounded the Manchester United team after we drew with West Ham United on the last day of the season four years ago and so allowed Blackburn Rovers to win the title. I remember, too, how Alex Ferguson got on the team coach as it sat outside Upton Park and told us all not to forget how badly we were all hurting because that way we would never, ever want to let it happen again." He did not have to repeat himself for 18 years.

Before his final game at Old Trafford, Schmeichel was presented with a plate, but otherwise, things were fairly normal, Fergie beaming ostentatious relaxedness in a new navy suit and waving hither and thither as the players came out. Stam was not amongst them, told that he'd be resting his Achilles injury, possibly until the European Cup final. Again, he was replaced by May, and elsewhere, Scholes was preferred to Butt and Sheringham to Cole. This did not go down well.

The game did, though, start well for United, Ginola forced from the pitch shortly after kick-off, hurting his hamstring in a tackle with Neville. And things almost got very much better within minutes, Yorke firing Giggs' low cross towards the near post, Walker doing well to save. However, he then took a touch to control and Yorke jumped at him, blocking the clearance and sending the ball spinning onto the post. The angle at which it bounced off looked, for all the universe, like it would take the ball over the line, and yet, somehow, it broke the other way, directly into his path and he skidded to meet it while Yorke performed a grin.

Though the slickness of United's passing was too much for Spurs, it was not matched by their finishing. Giggs headed straight at Walker from a corner, and Yorke entirely forgot himself, thrashing wide when sent through one-on-one.

Then, on 24 minutes, Spurs – whom Keane later accused of not really competing in the tackle – took the lead. After Yorke was caught offside, Walker belted the free-kick downfield towards Iversen, left of centre. Beating May to the ball, he flicked into the box for Ferdinand, there ahead of Johnsen, and observing Schmeichel off his line, read the bounce perfectly, flexing his ankle to coax a chip in the opposite direction to which he was running and into the far corner, the crack of the net as ball and keeper hit it echoing around the ground with deep foreboding.

"They've been giving you stick all season, wait til after this game, it we win it 1–0, like they'll lynch yer," said Anderton to Ferdinand – this was only his fifth league goal, in his 24th league appearance, and his first of the calendar year. "I've scored here and I'm supposed to be happy," he replied. "They'll go potty if Arsenal win the championship on the back of me scoring this goal."

United gathered themselves. Scholes smashed a shot at goal that Walker pushed out, and then, attempting to glide Sheringham's cross into the far corner, cut the ball too thickly, sending it too straight, and again, Walker saved, Campbell completing the job by hoiking into touch.

Still only 35 yards from goal, Neville threw short to Keane, picking up the return and banging into Sheringham, a few yards outside the box and with his back to goal. Ball bouncing as he trapped it, he timed his pass to coincide precisely with the next one, gently lifting into Yorke who turned, juggling from chest to foot to chest to foot and finding Giggs out wide. Taking a touch and looking up, he saw Beckham arriving at the far post, curling a cross into his path only for him to hammer a header over the top with almost the entire goal at which to aim, causing visible shock and anguish.

Security in the knowledge that someone would deal with it because someone always did was beginning to weaken, and on the bench, even Fergie was struggling to hide it. But Keane continued to force the team forward, a surge setting up Scholes for another spurned chance.

Then, after Neville and Schmeichel had denied Iversen through block and save respectively, and with only three minutes until the break, Ferdinand sold Sherwood short, just to the left of the centre-circle. In a trice, Scholes was on to him, tangling the ball away and leaving him in a heap as Giggs assumed possession. Pointing to where he was going, Scholes moved inside as Freund and Edinburgh were attracted to the ball, so that when it was returned, he was unmarked and contemplating a shot, even though it was slightly behind him. Deciding instead on a delaying touch, he waited until Beckham was where he wanted him before zipping a pass to the right side of the box. He then controlled and set, before ripping a virtual free-kick over and past Walker, his celebration a combination of aggression, relief and pose.

By half-time Fergie had composed himself, determining to introduce Cole in place of an unhappy Sheringham. "His quickness gave me a feeling that he'd score," he explained after the game, and to Sheringham – "visibly hurt and displeased" – during the break.

His message to the rest was simple. "Let's just play like you do, we just need one more goal," he told them, "and if we haven't scored and it's ten minutes left, I'll just put Ole on."

"I just grew!" recalled Ole. "He just said that I'm gonna win the league for us! Probably made me the happiest of the lot!"

Above stairs, 'Sit Down' was again ringing out over the PA, followed by the squad's single, 'Lift It High (All About Belief)' – a sub-Britpop dirge to its last bracket, yet still better than Keith Fane exhorting the crowd to noise as the players returned. But Spurs attacked first, Ginola's replacement José Dominguez (who played on the winguez) taking on Neville, who easily shrugged him off to manufactured annoyance.

"No need for me to point out that it's five and a half years since Manchester United last had a penalty given against them at Old Trafford in a league game," said Martin Tyler, pointing out when there was no need.

In the meantime, United were on the attack, Giggs' cross missed by Scales and Edinburgh clearing for a throw-in, level with the edge of the centre-circle. Scholes came to meet Neville, tapping the ball back to him when it arrived and watching as he came inside to clip a searching ball over the top that found Cole in space, on the right of the box. Hopping and jabbing out a foot while shepherding it over his shoulder with his eyes, he brought it down delicately but slightly behind him, so riding the bounce, feathered another touch to transfer it into his path before measuring the perfect lob over Walker, high enough to get over him, low enough to get under the bar. Goal!

And *what* a goal, perfectly encapsulating Cole and his unity of opposites; unorthodox and textbook, jerky and smooth, measured and impulsive – and beyond the ambit of anyone else, all in three touches. "If I'd known he'd turn out like this, I would never have sold him," said George Graham after the game – but it must have been tricky given a squad containing Alan Smith *and* Kevin Campbell.

Cole, of course, had no real idea how he'd done it, unable to repeat the move when asked so to do by the BBC in the summer. "When I scored the actual goal," he wrote. "I also thought I had plenty of time, but that wasn't true. See the playback and I had a precious second, maybe even a split second. Subconsciously, I knew that, too. And that, in a strange way, made certain I was clinical with the finish. It was pure instinct. For instance, if I received the same kind of opportunity again, with the ball floating over in the same arc, next time I might well cushion it and belt it in one movement. You never know precisely what you are going to do as a striker, at any given moment."

His first goal at Old Trafford since Arsenal, he made the most of its celebration, heading for Stam, as arranged earlier, only to be intercepted by very excited team-mates.

The ground went for it too, but Spurs didn't fold because they had no need to. Almost immediately, they were down the other end, Iversen getting a toe to Campbell's flick following a Scales throw, Schmeichel there to collect as the crowd sung his name.

Though ahead, United continued attacking with purpose, Yorke advancing along the right touchline before laying back to Beckham. The inevitable cross was probably aimed at Cole, but Scholes thundered in ahead of him, surprising everyone – Campbell was already halfway through his attempted clearance – and Walker did well to save low to his right.

Next, a long punt from May found Cole with his back to goal, and touching off to Yorke, he spun to run onto the immediate return. Sliding in, Carr prevented the shot, but succeeded only in diverting the ball into what Scholes made his stride while Campbell contemplaed, and he struck an effort low and hard across Walker, whose save was excellent, given the proximity of the ball to his feet.

Then, just after the hour, the first scare. Sherwood found Anderton slightly right of centre, and he smacked a low ball for Iversen, who not only came from behind to reach it before Neville but also snapped a dextrous flick for Dominguez outside him. His cross was a good one, but Iversen managed only the merest flick, which rebounded to him off May's back and arguably hand, bouncing up obligingly, but he could only tickle a shot into Schmeichel's shins from close range.

Around the same time, Kanu put Arsenal 1–0 up against Villa, but at Old Trafford, only Martin Tyler was ruffled. United just kept attacking, winning another throw on the right which Beckham took to Neville. Playing it square to Scholes, he darted another quick ball into Cole, and with Yorke passing across him pursued by Campbell, spun the other way into the gap, jinked past Edinburgh and turned into a cross, caught by Yorke on his right instep to set up an overhead kick, which went only just over the bar.

Then, Neville chipped a pass for Cole down the right, just the right weight to tempt Scales into thinking he could nab it as it bounced, and unable to resist, he ploughed into thin air as Cole rolled him easily. Expertly smothering the bounce with his body, he reached the byline and moved across, taking another touch before inviting Scholes to larrup home. But Campbell flung his body in the way, forcing a shot wider than was optimal, dragged just wide.

That was Scholes' last contribution, replaced by Butt – partly as insurance, partly because he wouldn't be playing until Barcelona and needed to keep his eye in. Moments later, Spurs made a change, bringing on Young for Scales, and United an adjustment, moving Yorke towards the right and Beckham inside to match what was now a midfield three of Anderton, Freund and Sherwood.

"If Manchester United surrender an equaliser, Arsenal would win the championship," said Martin Tyler, apropos of nothing. Shortly afterwards, two good passes presented Carr with a crossing opportunity, May doing well to reach the ball ahead of Iversen as both slid in.

This was the cue for Fergie to get to the touchline and ban his men from sitting off, while Spurs' substitute Dominguez was himself substituted. United then forced a corner, Johnsen and his freshly-dyed tips heading over the bar, before Phil Neville came on for Giggs.

With only ten minutes to go and for no reason other than principle, United became nervous, like a batsman a few runs short of a century, dominance already proven beyond all reasonable doubt. So when Anderton hit a routine free-kick to the back post, there was genuine relief when Irwin kept it away from Iversen, and in the crowd too, singing now intermittent, shouting omnipresent.

Thing was, Spurs simply couldn't get hold of the ball, and with six minutes to go, Butt was in sharply as Sherwood waited in the centre-circle for Freund's pass to arrive. Playing the ball forward and left, Cole twitched inside Young and delivered a return, Butt now on the right of the box. But he shot as Campbell slid in, earning a telling from Beckham, there for a simple pass.

With Keane directing and the crowd beginning to calm down, Phil Neville took the ball to the corner with some stepovers, before almost sending Cole through – he was offside. Walker then booted the free-kick downfield, which skidded off Beckham's hair and allowed Iversen to head into the box. But with Anderton supervised from either side, five red shirts swarmed the loose ball, Keane obviously arriving first, before Phil Neville cleared weakly, straight to Sherwood. He found Carr, who crossed again, Butt heading away and Beckham heading aimlessly square, Keane again picking up the loose ball and thundering away as the final whistle blew at Highbury, confirming Arsenal's win over Villa.

Then, another kick from Walker was gathered by Beckham, who found Yorke, who took the ball for a walk before sending it back. There would be two added minutes, the first of which was wasted easily enough, Gary Neville spending a chunk shrieking "blow the fucking whistle" at Graham Poll.

But when Butt's hacked clearance went the wrong way and to Carr, Irwin was forced to bring him down, giving Spurs a free-kick wide on the right and 40 yards from goal. Forward came Campbell, ominously, but the delivery was too high – though he got a touch, as Gary Neville ducked in anticipation of him missing. Johnsen, though, was on hand to win the next header and United ended up with a throw, sent down the line to Cole. Campbell came across, tackled, and while Cole protested the award of a throw against him, the ball was back in play, lumped forward, and the game over.

Following a group hug on the bench, bounding onto the pitch was Fergie, making straight for Keane and wrapping an arm around his neck while pounding his back. Elsewhere, Yorke and Cole twisted each other to the ground in spinning embrace, Yorke later surmising with impeccable confidence that the moment was "something I'd looked forward to", Cole now the man who could, and they were the two who lingered longest. Poor Sheringham did his best to be similarly elated – usually first-time winners offer the most engaging joy, as per van Nistelrooy in 2003 and van Persie in 2013 – but, despite silencing the Spurs fans, pride was clearly fucking with him.

Of United's five titles in the Ferguson era, this was only the second to be won on the pitch and the first at Old Trafford, the delight was augmented by the misery of the previous season. The most enjoyable title wins tend to be those which follow disappointment – 1993, 2003 and 2007 the other particular standouts – and the dicier the better.

And then there's 2013. The distress of 2012 wasn't losing the league itself, relatively straightforward to regain, but the manner in which it occurred, via concession of an irretrievable eternal moment. *Gam zu letovah* simply could not work. But that was to reckon without Fergie, asserting it as "just another day in the fabric of this club" before arranging a month-long party by winning the next title early and chucking in a retirement too, transforming humdrum into special.

It's easy to view disappointment as the most obvious inspiration for achievement, but it can just as easily go the other way – Liverpool post-2009, for example, and Arsenal after losing at Old Trafford in 2004. So coming back from the previous season's collapse and the two 3–0s was no small achievement, nor besting the finest opponent of the generation, and even on the final day and facing a deficit, they'd persevered to find the two brilliant goals it took to beat an inspired goalkeeper, very different from the flapping of 1995. Well done, United.

"It was very tense. *Very* tense!" chuckled Ferg in the tunnel, going a goal down, of course, "in the nature of Manchester United" who "just make it hard for ourselves". Interviewed with Schmeichel, who would later make a speech promising the crowd "you will always be in my heart", his manager could not praise him highly enough: "the best goalkeeper I've ever seen in my life… an absolute gem".

But once the trophy had been presented, all was back to normal. "Winning the title does take pressure off us in a sense for the two games we have got left," he said. "We know we are going into next season's European Cup as champions. If the players think that the

FA Cup is the lesser of the two targets ahead of us, if a lot of them start thinking about Barcelona, they will soon wake up when I pick my team for Wembley next Friday. This club is not about egos. It is about maintaining success, about building on the bedrock that was laid down by Sir Matt. That is why I will make sure no one gets carried away."

How successful he was with that is moot at best. Stam, for example, claimed that he applauded through the lap of honour until his hands hurt – though it was when the players returned to the dressing room that the fun really began. "We threw off our jackets and shirts like schoolkids going for a dip in a pool on a sizzling hot day," recalled his ghostwriter, with such incredible evocation as to reduce corpses and statues to steaming, sulphurous tears.

"Where's all my team-mates? Where's all my team-mates?" demanded Yorke walking down the corridor, snatching a plastic cup of fizz from Fergie as he found them. Forced to share the focus of attention with Schmeichel, he posed next to him. "You can't wipe the smile off my face," he announced with a gurn, "two more games to go" the pair of them announcing in unison.

With the league in the bag, the dynamic of the season altered. "Winning all three wasn't really an issue for us," said Sheringham. "We was just talking about winning the next game, we had so many games coming up. It was just like, 'could we win the league', you know 'we've got to win the league this year'. It was just like, 'get this one out the way, get this one out the way', and they just kept on coming." Not anymore.

And Schmeichel was certainly into it. "This was my last game at the Theatre of Dreams, and we've won the league," he told Stam. "It's absolutely fantastic. I'm going to treasure this for the rest of my life. But let's make it just the start. We'll let our hair down tonight, and then we'll win the fucking Treble."

As ever, Fergie was more candid with the players than the press. "You've played with the quality we expect of Manchester United, but most of all you've played with the spirit of Manchester United," he informed them. "That's the important thing. Now when we go to Barcelona and Wembley, we'll enjoy ourselves."

Which they did, after first enjoying themselves in Manchester, embarking on a session featuring the inevitable karaoke and Elvis impersonations from Giggs and Butt. The night that United won the 2012–13 title, Gary Neville had a go at explaining how it felt: "You never want it to be your last. You go out there every season, and the feeling that they will have tonight, honestly, it's difficult to explain, it gives me goosebumps thinking about those moments, those eight nights when you're champions when you go out in Manchester... and tonight, every one of these players, believe me, they will have the night of *their lives*. They'll not sleep... they'll not sleep for 24 hours, they'll be absolutely having the party of their lives, and to be actually there is what you live for."

And they were still at it on Tuesday night, meeting up at Mulligan's in town to take on board more fluids. Last to arrive was Roy Keane, contemplating the ankle injury that might cause him to miss a Cup final, about which he was less than arsed, and brooding on the suspension that would definitely cause him to miss the Champions League final, about which he was distraught. A team-mate once commented that his mental state was gaugeable according to his level of kempt, in which there had been a noticeable recent reduction, and he was already fresh from a solid afternoon's stretching with Norman Whiteside.

A pub crawl began, finishing in Henry's. There, Schmeichel regaled Solskjær and Johnsen with tales of his dislike for Keane while Keane described the same scene as "Peter Schmeichel posing (what's new?) and boring the arse off people".

Keane's party was soon joined by some local ladies, one of them, with a male friend, insultingly demanding that he buy them a drink. "Meet aggression with aggression," he told himself, later conceding that this was not the common sense approach, but "with drink taken, common sense is not my strongest suit." Accordingly, words were exchanged and a glass was thrown, followed by a scuffle and the ejection of those responsible. After which the police arrived and arrested Keane – "I explained what happened. They listened. Unfortunately, after nine hours on the tear, I didn't make a very convincing witness."

Eventually, he was released in the morning without charge. "He is totally in control of himself and not distressed," said Chief Inspector John Davies. "Shall we say, in football parlance, he isn't over the moon, but certainly not distressed. Ask me about his innermost feelings and I have to say I don't know."

He was not alone.

*

The players spent the week before the FA Cup final messing around in Windsor with bits and pieces of light training. Less relaxed than the rest was Stam, desperate to be involved but concerned that his Achilles might not be ready. Luckily, Alan Shearer was on hand to clear up the confusion. "I think Jaap Stam will play," he deduced. "I think Alex Ferguson might be being a little bit clever," he psychoanalysed. He did not expand on what remote difference any deception could possibly make.

Having to do nothing to win the FA Cup but beat Newcastle was just reward for perhaps the hardest ever run to the final, certainly United's hardest since 1948. Then, Matt Busby's first great side went to Villa Park and sneaked an all-time classic, 6–4, before seeing off Liverpool, the holders Charlton, and a very able Preston team 4–1 – all three home ties, but played at Goodison Park, Leeds Road and Maine Road respectively – before beating Derby County, the 1946 winners, in the semi-final.

Newcastle, on the other hand, had enjoyed a slightly easier time of it, knocking off Palace and Bradford, then Blackburn in a replay, and Everton. Their semi was against Spurs at Old Trafford, where they profited from an error by referee Paul Durkin, who failed to award a penalty when Nikos Dabizas handled in the box. To his credit, Durkin was not above explaining himself and later apologised for his error, also taking the opportunity to point out the nonsense of George Graham blaming him for his team's elimination, before two Shearer goals in extra time – one a penalty, one a pearler, both at the Stretford End – tantalised him with what might have been.

Newcastle didn't win again all season, their last in the league coming against Forest in the second week of March, and also had injury worries before the final. In the event, Laurent Charvet was passed fit – anything to avoid fielding Warren Barton – but, ahead of a hernia operation scheduled for Monday of the following week, Duncan Ferguson was fit enough only for the bench, where could also be found Luis Saha, and Steve Harper was preferred to Shay Given in net.

As for United's team, Stam was doorstepped by Fergie after breakfast on the morning of the game before he could declare himself ready to play, told he'd get a run-out from the bench if things were going well. Again, his place went to May, while Phil Neville was in for the suspended Irwin. But Keane was fit, and started alongside Scholes, while poor Butt sat fuming in his suit, the only player who simply could not be risked before Barcelona. Similarly, Blomqvist was also left out, needed on the wing against Bayern because Giggs was to play in midfield. Up front, Cole was paired with Solskjær, with Yorke and Sheringham left in reserve.

Pre-match, the United dressing room was a relaxed place. "Basically it was the same routine we have heard time and time again," wrote Stam. "A simple, but effective message from Ferguson urging us to concentrate and enjoy the occasion."

As the players gathered in the tunnel, 'We Will Rock You' boomed over the PA, fireworks greeting them as they walked out – how else might the importance of the occasion possibly be gauged? Meanwhile, Fergie wore the air of a man who'd already won, Keane appearing slightly dishevelled and strongly disinterested.

Some bright spark had thought it a good idea to mow the middle of the hallowed turf into a peculiar rhombus shape, a diagonal mess abutting each end, and the jerseys had been attacked too. Newcastle's special embroidery was done in *Neighbours* font, the names and numbers on United's bloated with Botox.

Only Beckham bothered with the national anthem, Charles the designated freeloader, and Keane and Scholes giggled through his introduction, no doubt with meritocratic, republican sentiment.

From kick-off, Ketsbaia took the ball and set off on a glorious run intended to take him past the entire United team. He was stopped by Keane on the edge of the centre-circle, and roughly, that was that, Newcastle's only other apparent tactic lifted straight from Palace in the 1990 replay, that of facial entry.

In the first minute, Keane was tackled late by Speed, then Hamann bashed into Scholes before Speed crunched Keane once more – probably fairly, but scissoring and wrenching his left ankle. While he hobbled away, Shearer, now well into his one-dimensional dotage, won a header to knock the ball down for Solano, only just outside the box and left of centre, but the shot was not caught cleanly.

Keane then almost played Phil Neville and Schmeichel into trouble with a careless back-pass, Neville hustled by Hamann as he dealt with it, who booted him to get booked.

Shortly afterwards and with only nine minutes gone, Keane was forced to depart, the second United captain unable to complete the game in three Cup finals, after Steve Bruce in 1995. On in his place came Sheringham, with Beckham moving into the middle of midfield and Solskjær relocating to the right.

"Sir Alex turns round at me and says 'Teddy go and get warmed up'," he recalls, "and I'm like, 'who me, what, you sure?' So, before I knew it I was actually on the pitch."

And he'd been there less than two minutes when United won a free-kick to the right of the centre-circle, on halfway, which Beckham tapped infield to Scholes. He then sent it back for May to hit a hard, low, straight first-time pass at Cole, who moved off towards the left, away from Dabizas sliding into his heels and Hamann, chasing. Aiming a further hard pass towards Giggs, Sheringham intercepted, killing it deftly and coming back inside, before poking one side of a charging Lee and gliding the other. Seeing Scholes in support, he "played a lovely little one-two", Scholes shaping to shoot as the ball came across his body before leaning left and sliding a pass right, to the edge of the box. "Set me up nicely," Sheringham said. "I ran onto it and snuck it away nicely under the keeper" – who had no business chasing so far off his line, but did. "So from sitting there not enjoying meself, until two minutes later I'd scored the first goal in the Cup final, fantastic."

The previous season, Gary Neville sought his advice on finishing, after a succession of a bad misses. "You've just got to slow everything down in your mind," he advised. "You always have more time than you think." Now part of a functioning team that played according to an opposing philosophy, that approach was suddenly a whole lot more useful, the exception enhancing the rule.

Newcastle attempted to hit back, Lee crossing for Shearer, but Gary Neville stayed close and in front, forcing him to foul and became angry. Next, Griffin was late on Giggs, and with no free-kick given, Beckham made it his business to hunt down the ball and boot whoever had it – in the event, Ketsbaia. Despite the occasional balance issues, it's impossible to argue that he didn't play with the correct attitude, and was never reticent in backing up his mates.

The next foul came from Ole Gunnar Solskjær, on Speed and 35 yards from goal, left of centre. As he'd done in March, Solano took aim, but this time his kick was waved onto the roof of the net by Schmeichel, master of anticipation.

Harper then took the opportunity to race out of his goal and legitimately flatten Cole, to the pleasure of the Newcastle end, doubly gratuitous given that he was offside. Minutes later, Hamann played in Ketsbaia, who managed to avoid the ball as he stepped into the area, before Shearer backed into Johnsen and was lowered to the ground, then penalised. A further bout of radge followed.

Seeking another goal, United increased the pace, Beckham cutting across a shot set up by Sheringham's knockdown, which went wide. Then, Solskjær forced a throw deep in the Newcastle half, taken long by Gary Neville. Headed out by Dabizas towards Beckham, just by the right corner of the box, he spun into a first-time flick of the bouncing ball, over the head of the closing Solano and to Neville's feet. Taking a touch to control, he swept over a delectable cross for Solskjær at the near post, glanced so wide that it stayed in play.

Newcastle's next attack foundered at the feet of Shearer, May in sharply to dispossess him, and Phil Neville rolled the loose ball into Scholes a few yards ahead, who snapped the return at Sheringham. Cleverly adjusting his body position to check what was behind, he laid back for Scholes who sent a leisurely flick to Solskjær with the outside of his right foot. Fiddling the now airborne ball back to Beckham as Domi rushed in from behind, it went wide to Gary Neville, who, while in the process of controlling, looked over and ordered Sheringham to the near post, before finding him there with a perfect cross, swung over from very wide and a fair distance from the byline. But he couldn't quite get his head around it, guiding narrowly past the post.

Ruud Gullit was forced to make a change at the interval, injury robbing him of Hamann, one of his better players. Ketsbaia took his place in midfield, with Ferguson coming on, and after a messy start to the second half, he won a header in the United box, May stepping off to collect rather than challenging in the first instance.

Next, on 53 minutes, Gary Neville lobbed a ball forward to Giggs, roaming on the right, where Dabizas headed away from him, but towards the corner, to where he was hounded. As he went to clear, Giggs turned out of the way to avoid ceding possession via rebound, Solskjær collecting a tame effort by reacting faster than Lee. Advancing, he knocked a pass into Sheringham, his back to goal, and set off outside him hoping for a return, Sheringham very deliberately setting his foot to direct the ball the other way and into the path of Scholes, arriving on the edge of the box to thud across Harper with his left laces for 2–0.

The combination play between Scholes and Sheringham was no great surprise – they shared a mutual respect of footballing intellectuals. Both Shearer and *Jürgen* Klinsmann rated Sheringham the best of their respective striking partners, and he also features in Scholes' United Dream Team – no small accolade given the competition for places. "I've never seen anyone with the timing of Teddy," Solskjær once commented, but even so, he was having a particularly good day.

After that, it was pretty much one-way traffic, Gullit's resigned reaction one of a man who knew the jig was up. Nonetheless, Newcastle came close to pulling a goal back before United almost extended the lead, Schmeichel coming out to flap at Lee's cross. Continuing his charge to the edge of the box, he was easily sidestepped by Ketsbaia, whose low, hard shot struck the outside of the post – had it been on target, the sprawling May would not have reached it in time.

On the hour, Yorke replaced Cole, the two enjoying an embrace, before Fergie chipped up a ball sent out of play to milk the cheers of the crowd; this was not a man expecting a comeback. Then, Yorke harried the tiring Charvet into conceding a corner, headed clear to Scholes, who sent the ball left to Giggs. Breezing past Lee, he crossed for Yorke, who did well to crane backwards, allowing it to hit his forehead, but from inside the six-yard box couldn't get sufficient downward momentum, his effort passing over the bar.

Then, Beckham's out-swinging corner was headed out and dropped for Giggs, waiting in the D. Cocking his right foot, incredibly, he made a perfect connection, the ball scooting just wide of the right-hand post. And now, there was not the remotest chance that he might successfully execute the very same skill in the very next game – *gam zu letovah*.

Newcastle were finding it hard to track down a meaningful kick, and a mistake from Dabizas almost let Yorke in after Sheringham had attempted to lift him a through-pass. But the angle at which he was running forced him left, away from goal, Griffin catching up as he checked and buying the dummy, but obstructing its next instalment by virtue of being on the floor amongst his feet. So he played a simple ball back to Giggs, and with a cross or shot expected, he clipped cleverly to Solskjær on the other side of the box, who chested and hit, a deflection off Domi forcing a fumble from Harper, Lee on hand to clear off the line.

Gary Neville would later comment that it was a "strange game for a Cup final, just seemed like a practice match at times", Newcastle left with very little once the bustling had failed. In the week before the game, Alan Shearer had told the press that, "The mood is very good here. There's a belief in the camp that we can go to Wembley and win. There is an air about the place right now," but they were just as uncompetitive as a year earlier.

Stam then replaced Scholes, after which Giggs picked the ball up in the centre-circle and set off on a run, hoodwinking Charvet by making to shoot before ducking the other way. With Maric tugging his shirt, he somehow manoeuvred his body right with the outside of his left foot, like changing gear with the wrong hand, Sheringham then chipping over Harper and onto the top of the bar.

Next, Dabizas was forced to head Giggs' cross away from Yorke and Beckham curled just over from distance, before Newcastle, who'd been without a meaningful move in some time, sent Ferguson bundling through the middle. A bouncing ball made it hard for Stam to clear, managing only a nod to Maric, who deftly nicked the ball away from May, and suddenly he was through. Opening his body, he eased a deliberate left-footed shot past Schmeichel, but also past the post.

Little else of note happened in the remaining minutes, save a false final whistle alarm which had May and Schmeichel cavorting before time. When the moment did come, again, Fergie made straight for Keane, as did Schmeichel, replacing the armband taken on his substitution. It had taken United 106 years to win a double, a feat achieved only five times in history before their first. Now, they'd completed the feat three times in six seasons, winning their tenth FA Cup in the process.

Keane led United up to the royal box, to receive the sexy hourglass figure of the trophy – which he lifted at a curious angle, either away from the royals, Schmeichel or both. Then, as the camera panned to an applauding Shearer, it was passed decorously along the line to repeating cheers with none of the disorganisation of today.

As the players shuffled along the line of magnificent human beings, Sheringham and Giggs were allocated special words from Martin Edwards, though Solskjær appeared to receive no semblance of apology. Fergie, meanwhile, stopped for a word with Tony Blair, as nauseatingly happy as ever despite the defeat of his heroes, no doubt reminiscing about Hughie Gallagher, Jackie Milburn and old times.

Back in the changing room after the lap of honour, no one could pretend that the Treble wasn't on – "it could be historic and stuff like that", reckoned Cole. Yorke, meanwhile, had always known:

"I've maintained from the start of the season that we can win the Treble, nothing has altered those thoughts," he told the following day's *Sunday Mirror*. "I've dreamt about the Treble, I've woken up at night in a cold sweat and I know I am touching those winners' medals. If ever a club deserves to rewrite the history books this club does. Nobody, no one, no team will stop us, we don't know what it's like to lose, we won't lose. Winning is inbuilt in this side."

*

On the Monday, the day that Eric Cantona became 33 (and Bob Dylan 58), the United players flew to Spain. With Millwest fully booked, they ended up on Concorde at BA's pleasure, where Fergie was "given the run of the cockpit", to the sniggering satisfaction of playground veterans everywhere, waving out of the window in captain's hat like a child flying for the first time.

Staying in Sitges, the players spent the majority of their time relaxing with cards, pool and massages, mainly trying to forget why they were there. This was not so easy with so many supporters around, the unwanted attention – and, no doubt, nerves – causing Fergie to misplace his excrement, telling them that should the team lose, they'd be the first to complain. Feeling ashamed, he later apologised; *gam zu letovah*.

Otherwise, there were three sessions arranged by way of preparation at the first, they learned who would start, why, and how United could win; the second went through Bayern's tactics, looking in particular at how they'd beaten Kiev by scoring an early goal and shutting down the game; and finally, Steve McClaren explained how set pieces would work.

That night, the local lads and Beckham sat on the balcony of a hotel room, wondering if they'd ever find themselves in this position again, not just in the European Cup final, but playing for a Treble. "I had known the mood before big England matches to be horribly tense," wrote Gary Neville, "that feeling that the world will end if you lose. In Barcelona the stakes could not have been higher but the mood was focused. We didn't want to lose, we loathed the very idea, but we weren't afraid of the consequences."

For Fergie in particular, this was a defining time, the history enthusiast obsessed by his place in it. "No matter how much I tried to play down the Champions League final in Barcelona, as far as I was concerned Europe had become a personal crusade," he wrote. "I knew I would never be judged a great manager until I won the European Cup."

His obsession was such that after United's elimination in 1994–95, he told the cameras that he was "trying to make it the Everest", the architect of his own mental illness. Similarly, it was the first thing that he mentioned the first time that he met Stam: "Jaap, I want you to play for Manchester United," he told him. "I want you to command our backline and help us take that extra step and win the European Cup."

The day of the game, the entire city of Barcelona was draped in giddiest, grinniest red, the entire central area, statues, balconies and windows, sparkling in sun, beer and United – and occasional lederhosen. Though football matches are absorbed into folklore according to their own merits – what actually happens during them – where they happen also counts; the best World Cups of the modern era, for example, were both in Mexico, despite deeply non-conducive conditions. Likewise Barcelona, an evocative, romantic, vital, iconic city, captured even by the cadence and phonetics of the word, Bar-ce-lona, pleasure both oral and aural. Add to that a relatively easy and suitably inexpensive ticket, a first European Cup final in 31 years and an enormous group of people who've already been celebrating for ten days straight – the biggest airlift out of Britain since D-Day, off to sunny Spain to see Man United – and it's not hard to understand the atmosphere.

Back in Sitges, and after an early-morning cliff walk, the players were beginning to feel the occasion, returning to the hotel to discover the final verdict on who'd be playing. "We never reveal the team to the players until the day of the game," Fergie said. "For a three o'clock game, we tell them at one o'clock and before that I speak to the players I've left out. I do it privately. It's not easy, but I do them all myself. It is important. I have been dropped from a cup final in Scotland as a player at ten past two, so I know what it feels like. I'm not ever sure what they are thinking, but I tend to say 'Look, I might be making a mistake here' – I always say that – 'but I think this is the best team for today.' I try to give them a bit of confidence, telling them that it is only tactical, and that there are bigger games coming up."

Well, that last point must've been a tricky sell, though Sheringham was the only party likely to have felt genuine disappointment, that he deserved a spot even if he couldn't expect one. Nerves increasingly on top, most attempted afternoon sleeping before coming downstairs to eat, then back upstairs to change into Treble-piece suits, then gathering in the lobby far earlier than necessary to fiddle with buttonholes and generally pace, searching for elusive diversionary conversation.

The coach to the ground was unusually quiet, noisemakers and bullies Giggs and Butt keeping themselves to themselves, and even Fergie was tense. "We'd been most places, but never here before," wrote Keane. "This was not just another game." He, though, was in a different place entirely, experiencing his worst moments in football – no small accolade, given the previous year of pain and fear. Comfort came in wet matter and respect for the suffering of Scholes, left to watch as his boys lived their shared dream.

Driving through the crowds in the city served only to increase the unease, and the dressing room was less exuberant than usual. There was never any music or mood-setting – "gimmicks", as Stam called them with luscious condescension – and on Saturdays, they usually had *Grandstand* on the telly. "While other teams are limbering up to the latest thumping dance beat, we'll be sat around watching a bit of water-skiing or horse racing," he explained.

Today, though, was different, just a was a little gentle cajoling; "This is what the season has been about. Now we're 90 minutes away from it. Let's go and do it," from Stam, and "I've dreamed of this day far too long to let it slip now," from Schmeichel.

But otherwise, there was very little of anything. Blomqvist, "not the most confident of players", had been told by Fergie that he'd be playing a week earlier, so that he could get used to the idea and prepare accordingly – but still spent the night before the game writing and reading back notes to himself, messages like "You can do it, Jesper" and "You can be that player you want to be." Even Cole was anxious, usually relaxed enough to consider a few stretches in the dressing room an adequate warm-up but this time sneaking a look at the ground, with Yorke also quieter.

Fergie distributed very little in the way of advice, though he had some for those watching. "Don't hold your breath," he advised with a mischievous grin, "and get a grip of your seat and make sure you're tied down – quite tight – because it can be a roller-coaster of a match."

And it was certainly a roller-coaster getting in, the immense swarms surrounding the ground a jibber's delight. Doors off hinges, turnstiles leapt, three through at a time and plenty more, those with tickets in the wrong end discovering that they could simply make their way into a different section by walking around the concourse. Meanwhile, the police randomly cracked heads.

The stadium itself was an arresting picture, tier slapped upon tier like a glittering wedding cake; not just another club's ground, but an amphitheatre of football. United were in the European Cup final! United were in the European Cup final!

Of course, this wasn't apparent immediately, the importance of the occasion computed only when 5ive's 'Everybody Get Up' came over the tannoy. Then, onto a pitch already cluttered by oddly-shaped inflatables, came Montserrat Caballé, aboard the little buggy used for injured players in the group game. It'd be wrong to say that hearing Barcelona sung for the verymaneth time, by her, in 'Barcelona' before the European Cup final, with United in it, wasn't in some way pleasant, even if her accompaniment by Freddie Mercury, appearing on the scoreboard, was somewhat odd – but it's not hard to imagine a future in which the sideshow attracts as much fuss as the show, indulging a low-rent, high-budget concert.

As in September, Munich's announcer read out their team by fore-name, the crowd roaring the rest. Keith Fane couldn't quite match it, though would adopt the tactic for European nights the following season, with names far less favourable and far less success. But still,

Arsenal weren't dissuaded from trying the same a further decade later, announcing a goal to be kept by Manuel.

Like United, Bayern were a team on a mission, with their own redemption narrative. The previous season had gone very badly indeed, such that their manager, Giovanni Trapattoni, was inspired to express his feelings at a press conference in a shouting, table-thumping, broken-German fury.

"I'm a coach not an idiot... A coach can see what happens on the field... And these players, two, three of these players, were weak like an empty bottle. Have you seen Wednesday, what team has played Wednesday? Did Mehmet play, or did Basler play, or did Trapattoni play? These players complain more than they play. You know why no Italian team buys these players? Because they've seen them play too many times. They say, 'these do not play for the Italian champions'. Strunz! Strunz is here two years, and has played ten games, is always injured. How dare Strunz!... They must respect their other colleagues... I am tired now, the father of these players, defending these players. I always get the blame over these players. One is Mario, the other is Mehmet. I don't mention Strunz, he has only played 25% of the games."

But this was only to be expected, the team comprising a world record number of mards rivalled only by its 1970s predecessor. And when Ottmar Hitzfeld took over at the club, one of the first things he did was re-sign Stefan Effenberg, perhaps the most aggrophilic of all. He had famously volunteered to "take matters outside" after a changing room dressing-down by Jupp Heynckes, and was dropped from the national team by Berti Vogts after giving the finger to fans during the 1994 World Cup. In 2001, he would be found guilty of assaulting a woman in a nightclub, and in 2002 he would again be dropped by Germany after stating that many unemployed people were too lazy to get work.

But Hitzfeld wasn't bothered; "I want him in my team," was all the justification he felt necessary, his judgement thoroughly vindicated when the the archetypal automateuton enjoyed an exceptional season – one which prompted his manager to call him the best player in the world – and coped admirably with the stress of being only the second most majestic arsehole in the team. "He comes across as intense," wrote Amy Lawrence in the *Observer*. "In a tailored black leather sult, spiky blond hair, diamond stud in one ear, his image simultaneously demands respect and implies your respect means nothing to him anyway."

Basler, meanwhile, had caused further aggravation since being dropped for the Old Trafford game, by recording a Christmas single with a prominent porn star, which did not sit right with the gerontocracy. And the aforementioned Strunz had form too, his first spell at the club ended by Erich Ribbeck after a furious row that neither were prepared to resolve. He would eventually be relieved of his wife by his team-mate, that effen Effenberg, discovering their affair after spotting text messages on her phone. She would later be deployed in his autobiography – called, of course, *I Showed Them All* – by way of erotic photography.

But they had all gelled. "They are super, clever, perfect," Andreas Brehme told *Die Welt*. "We have never seen a team dominate to this extent in their chase for a Treble before." Frighteningly, Manfred Schwabl felt that rival clubs had no choice but to merge in order to compete, while Armin Eck compared them to the German stock market: "Whenever you feel this is it, they just keep going up, up, up. I have no idea where this one could end." "They can only beat themselves," added Ludwig Koegl, scorer of Bayern's goal in the 1987 European Cup final defeat.

Like United, Bayern had qualified for the competition as runners-up, finishing behind Kaiserslautern and generally covering themselves in vainglory. This was a sickening blow to the club's dainty ego. FCK had only just been promoted to the Bundesliga – no other side has won Germany's top two divisions in consecutive seasons – and to grind it in, they were managed by Otto Rehhagel, sacked by Bayern immediately before, following a year of failure and fallings out.

They righted the sleight in the strongest possible terms. First, they eliminated FCK from Europe in the quarter-finals – after scoring in the first leg, Effenberg motioned to his team-mates to kiss his feet – and had clinched the title two weeks earlier, with three games still to play. In total, they had played five times fewer than United, and though the Cup final was not for another three weeks, no two sides had ever met like this, with both going for a Treble.

Hitzfeld's other signings had followed the usual Bayern formula: wait for a rival side to have a good player, then buy him. So Jens

Jeremies, the only German to enhance his reputation during the World Cup, had arrived from local rivals 1860 and Thomas Linke from Schalke, and they'd both come off, too. Incredibly, even Lothar Matthäus, Chancellor Mard himself, was happy, telling the press that "we have a lot of talented players, I'm quite happy to sit and watch."

Whether the logic would have seemed quite so persuasive were it applied to final selection is doubtful, but he was picked, sweeping behind Linke and Kuffour. On his right, to combat the threat of Giggs, the game's best player in December, was Markus Babbel – owed one by United after turning down a move in the summer of 1996, unable to reach agreement over wages. At left-back was Michael Tarnat, later to star at Manchester City, with Bixente Lizarazu – owed one in advance after feigning interest in a move to United the following summer to extract higher wages – injured. Ahead of them, Basler returned for Salihamidžić and Zickler was still there, but in between, Elber was missing, injured for the season. Instead, at centre-forward could be found Carsten Jancker, a shuddering, sweating lump of flesh and flap more congruous in leather trench coat than football kit.

United had originally planned to use Giggs in the middle of midfield – he'd excelled there against Wimbledon and Leicester earlier in the season – but Beckham's performance in the FA Cup final and general passing ability persuaded Fergie to change his mind. Additionally, he felt that Giggs' pace would present Tarnat with difficulties he had not been anticipating, and that playing two proper wingers would exacerbate the paranoia that caused Bayern to successfully lobby for the Nou Camp pitch to be narrowed.

In the week leading up to the game, the newspapers were full of stories about Beckham's schoolboy prowess as a middle-distance runner and this and that, but still, the decision was a major risk. Though in those days his cup final record was excellent, everyone has a favourite Fergie selection fuck-up: dropping Hughes for Forest at home in April 1992; dropping Hughes for West Ham away in May 1995; Cantona up front alone in the Delle Alpi, 1996; preferring Yorke to Sheringham for no reason whatsoever, Bayern away, 2001; rushing back an unfit Verón for Madrid at home in 2003 to punish Beckham; rushing back an unfit van Nistelrooy for Palace and Milan in 2005; Giggs, Scholes and Neville at home to Chelsea in April 2010; everything about City away in 2012; Giggs and Scholes at home to

Spurs the following season; and removing your most likely route to goal, while compromising your most devastating player, before the biggest game of your career, had the potential to earn its place in that exulted company.

In the tunnel, the players were separated by wire mesh, but none stopped to assess the opposition; various bodily shakes, then up the steep little stairs to the pitch. The noise as they came out was quite something and there followed the Champions League anthem – with so much pomposity and circumstance, law of averages demanded that one part of it be got right. Then, the team photos, Beckham obviously crouching first and finding himself centre-front, then United were kicking off. United were in the European Cup final!

And they started reasonably enough, Babbel forced to head away a high ball with Cole prowling behind. Picking up the pieces was Giggs, whose first thought was to come inside on his left foot, curling a cross past Cole at the back post.

Already, Jeremies was scrabbling around Beckham whenever he encountered a hint of possession, and through him the ball found its way to Basler, out wide and facing touch. So he back-heeled into the path of Babbel, who swerved Butt's best best-not-get-booked tackle and then away from Beckham, finding Tarnat on the left. With Stam rushing out to greet him, he was quick to send over a cross, but it was too long for Effenberg, arriving on the far side.

Next, the first flash of Giggs, triangulating down the right with Neville and Yorke before running away from Effenberg and at Tarnat, Effenberg doing enough from behind to regain possession and Kuffour lumping into touch. Then, after Yorke was crowded out from the throw, Tarnat hooked clear and Beckham mis-controlled, the ball travelling backwards and forcing Stam into a slide-tackle with Jancker just inside the United half. Obviously, Jeremies was on hand to collect possession, clipping a reverse pass behind Zickler on the left touchline, who, facing away from the pitch, allowed it to bounce as he turned behind it and flipped a brilliant pass over his shoulder and over Johnsen for Jancker, galumphing across from the other side. With Irwin arriving to cover, Jancker nudged into the recovering Johnsen to send himself sprawling – a snideness that makes Johnsen angry even now – and Pierluigi Collina purchased the subterfuge, awarding Bayern a free-kick just outside the box and left of centre.

Schmeichel took great care in lining up his protection. "Although Basler is good in dead-ball situations," recalled Stam, "we had a solid wall and behind that was the best keeper in the world. I was convinced nothing would come of it."

But suddenly, and from Basler's angle, it appeared a man too short, then a further gap appearing when Babbel shoved Butt out of the way, compounded by Jancker's run forcing Stam to leave the scene. But even so, beating Schmeichel into the far corner looked unlikely – no way could he be thick enough to assume to know which way the ball was going and rely on the wall to deal with it if he was wrong, *again* – on the same ground, at the same end, in the same competition, in the same season, *in the fucking final*.

Except that he could, taking a little jump step to his right immediately before the ball was dispatched left before standing stupefied, ushering it in like a benevolent bouncer. "Less than unstoppable," understated Keane, while in commentary, Clive Tyldesley assumed a deflection, so ludicrous was the idiocy.

"I just couldn't see it," Schmeichel announced to the glares surrounding him, finding little sympathy. "I think that pissed off a lot of the chaps," wrote Cole in his autobiography. "If our goalkeeper, the best in the world at that, couldn't see that strike, he was left with one option. He should have adjusted the wall until he could."

Instead, and with only six minutes gone, United were behind, against a team with five men at the back and two prowling in front. And yet it was hard to be too concerned. One of the quirks of this team was the thorough inevitability of their goals, watching the vicious pressure they exerted, almost relaxing without being relaxed in the slightest.

Immediately and typically, back they came, Giggs turning to slip a low pass from Neville into Yorke's feet, and with Kuffour attached to his back he eased infield, picking a pass around the corner for Cole, who laid back to Butt. Nicking a return between Basler and Linke, Cole could then move the ball wide for Blomqvist to bend a cross around Babbel, only for Yorke to be penalised as he leapt with Kuffour, for what remaining unclear.

Then, confusion between Johnsen and Schmeichel almost let in Jeremies, before Beckham sprayed a long ball to Giggs, escaping Tarnat but his entire body straining as if magnetised left, and his cross was easily headed away by Effenberg. But United kept at it, Blomqvist wandering deep and infield before playing a great pass towards Yorke, filling his space – but six men were back defending and nothing was to be done, Bayern barely bothering to contest the midfield.

So United tried again, Collina getting in the way of a Yorke pass and allowing Matthäus to locate Basler on the right touchline. With Blomqvist just jogging alongside, he was able to aim a ball into Zickler, momentarily ahead of Stam, whose challenge harried him into a mindless punt behind.

But Bayern were now sufficiently confident for Matthäus to venture out from behind his centre-backs – "he likes to be spare", said Tyldesley, an accurate summation. When Beckham took the chance to lift a pass over him looking for Yorke, they were thwarted by Babbel's sliding block, after which United forced a throw, down by the corner flag. Hurling deep into the area, Stam arrived late and on the barrel, there before Effenberg but able only to send the ball sideways, where it hit Matthäus on the thigh and then Cole on the shin. This enabled him to bundle past Linke, but before he could contemplate a shot, Effenberg slid in from the side, deflecting the ball against his shin a second time, and behind. It had taken a quarter of an hour, but, eventually, Bayern had been forced to defend a situation of which they were not fully in control.

Next, Yorke failed to close Matthäus down, allowing him to hit a long ball for Zickler, right of centre and in front of Johnsen, nodded down for Effenberg, who controlled on his thigh. Measuring a gentle return pass over Stam and into space, it bounced just outside the box but Zickler's timing was slightly awry, arriving too early to generate any power as it stood up, his diving header going straight at Schmeichel.

The ball was rolled out to Neville, but he left it for Beckham, with Jancker – who, of course, had an hilarious rhyming nickname in the United dressing room – clodhopping across to launch into as nasty a tackle as possible and flipping him curtains over heels. But the ball ran to Giggs, forced inside and robbed by Effenberg's trailing leg, allowing Jeremies to break. Seeing United's back four high and square, with Zickler pulling off Stam, he slotted him a through-pass that also excluded Beckham and Neville, the whistle then blowing for offside, though Neville was playing him on. This prompted all-round dismay, Neville still agitated by the original tackle and wasting no time letting it be known.

Linke was doing an excellent job on Yorke, forcing him back deep into his own half in search of decent possession. Chesting a Blomqvist clearing header, he spread wide for Irwin, who lofted a pass to Cole in the centre-circle. Again it was chested down, but powerfully and right for the onrushing Beckham, who pulled away from Kuffour and rolled in Blomqvist. His first pass, a return, was poor, but Effenberg's tackle gave him another go, and spotting Butt unmarked, just outside the box and dead centre, he drilled him a pass. Eschewing the shot, he moved the ball on one more to Giggs, who stepped inside and went for goal, his effort blocked by Jeremies – but there'd at least been some consecutive passes forcing Bayern to do some running around.

Then, Beckham hit a long, diagonal ball for Cole on the left of the area, which he took down well. Though he couldn't sneak it through the two men blocking the route to Yorke, again, United were forcing the issue. And with Bayern pinned back, Kuffour kicked Yorke in the face 40 yards from goal and on the right, Linke only just stretching to head Beckham's free-kick away with Yorke waiting to score.

Next, after Butt again passed up a shooting opportunity, Jeremies robbed Beckham and allowed Matthäus to lead a break, Effenberg to his right, Zickler to his left, Jancker ahead and left. He picked Jancker, who back-heeled for Zickler but not to his feet, slowing the pace of the attack and encouraging a shot, which went low and wide of the near post.

On the half-hour, Beckham's out-swinging corner somehow evaded everyone in the box, and after Bayern cleared as far as Schmeichel, United built again after he found Giggs with a long, accurate kick. Felled by Tarnat, he was immediately up and turned, sidewinding back towards him. Opting to square for Yorke just outside the box, there existed momentary space, but a weak effort was twice deflected, barely reaching Kahn.

Though he was playing perhaps a little deep, Beckham was imposing himself now, another crossfield pass arriving at Cole, who knocked down for Yorke. Controlling on his head, he spun 180 degrees to shield the ball from Kuffour, then rolled in Beckham, somehow already outside him and ready to cross, looking for Cole. But Kuffour headed away and Matthäus broke once more, this time going for goal but welting high over the bar.

Then, with only ten minutes of the first half remaining, Jeremies again scampered after Beckham, this time in the centre circle. Forcing the ball back to Stam and maintaining his pursuit, he pounced on the ensuing mistouch, Stam, Neville and the advancing Schmeichel all required to run him out of it. "He's got an unfortunate face, you have to be honest, but he's a good player," opined Don Juatkinson.

And that was pretty much the first half; the players "crashed" into the dressing room "bitterly disappointed" by their performance, recounted Stam. They hadn't actually played that badly, though the zip wasn't quite there, but a refereeing error followed by an individual error had given Bayern the lead and the subsequent travails were an almost inevitable consequence.

"Without the control Keane brings to our game, we will have to ensure that the play is pacey," Fergie had said before the game. "I think it's one advantage we have over Bayern, that we have more pace. They may have difficulty handling it but they'll try to find a way of survival, because it's what they're good at."

But United had limited the influence of their main runner, Giggs disinclined to get down the outside and around the back of Tarnat, all narrowing the pitch even further.

And there wasn't really anywhere to run into anyway, Bayern defending so deep and in such numbers that the only remaining way to break them down was with short, imaginative passing – precisely the skills brought to the team, not just by Keane but by Scholes. His strengths might be crudely enumerated as technique and strategy – non-coincidentally, the two most significant aspects of the game – manifesting most clearly in his appreciation and use of space.

On the other hand, though Beckham was playing well enough, his longer style of provision permitted defenders to read the direction of attack, still handy on the break, but less effective given the current problematic. "He sees the furthest pass first," Glenn Hoddle once said of him, but most significant was his crossing, unparalleled regardless of variables: hooked, lobbed, whipped, chipped, driven, lifted or curled, bouncing or dead, looped or flat, and from any conceivable body position. And although this skill was, in theory, basic and predictable, it wasn't so clearly preventable; you can only wonder what the current strikers would manage with service a fraction as proficient.

But the instructions in the changing room had little to do with what was going wrong – Stam was told to be quicker into the tackle and win the ball back quicker, but that was about it, the rest of the oratory aimed at stimulating the psyche.

"You've come this far and now you're letting yourself and the club down," said Fergie. "We can play far better than this. It's not the tactics and it's not a lack of skill. You've got to go out there and work twice as hard, be twice as tough in the tackle and, most importantly, want to win twice as much as they do."

"You might never get within touching distance of this trophy again and at the moment you seem prepared to blow it without really giving it your best shot. I want you to be able to look in the mirror, even if we lose, and tell your reflection: 'I did everything in my power to try and win the game.'"

Then, the killer image: "At the end of this game, the European Cup will be only six feet away from you, and you'll not even be able to touch it if we lose. And for many of you, that will be the closest you will ever get. Don't you dare come back in here without giving your all."

Whether he simply couldn't believe he'd made a mistake, or felt that his players would eventually prevail is hard to judge, but the reticence to act was curious given his impulsive nature and gambler's mentality. *Gam zu letovah.*

Back in the ground, each stadium announcer was given the chance to play one song, Keith Fane imaginatively picking 'Sit Down'. Still going when the players re-emerged, the United end finished it off once play restarted, but this time it failed to usher in a goal.

And it was actually Bayern who attacked first, Effenberg spreading the ball left to Tarnat. With Zickler lurking behind, Stam was forced to play the cross, slicing behind him – and safely into Schmeichel's hands. Then, from the clearance, Effenberg outjumped Butt and Matthäus picked up possession, threading through for Jancker. Galooting towards goal just right of centre, Johnsen gave chase, in from behind as Schmeichel came out. But the ball stayed in play, and with the defender grounded, Jancker could focus solely on its pursuit, sliding alongside close to the byline, hoping to persuade a finish between keeper and post, the officials determining it to be out of play before Schmeichel shovelled behind.

A United break then foundered when Blomqvist's pass asked too much of Giggs, but on 50 minutes he turned with Johnsen's clearing header and pulled away from Jeremies. Seeing Cole setting off through the middle, he attempted to find him, but Kuffour was always a stride ahead, and he tidied up easily enough.

Next, Matthäus and Cole rose to meet a goalkick, Matthäus first to the ball but heading backwards, where Kuffour leapfrogged Yorke. Before anyone had time to appeal for a free-kick, Giggs was in possession, chipping and charging towards the corner, Tarnat after him. Able to turn and square him up, he crossed into the middle, where Linke and Yorke arrived together, Linke doing enough to head back towards the touchline. But showing the first sign of nerves, Jeremies, with time and space to clear properly, threw a leg at it the second it arrived, the ball bouncing just outside the box where this time the charging Linke arrived too soon, and it skidded off the top of his head to Yorke, on the edge and right of centre. Turning away from goal to see what was what, he then found the unmarked Giggs, and though he was seen behind easily enough, for the first time, Bayern had caused themselves problems.

The corner was headed clear by Jeremies at the front post, but picked up by Irwin on the edge of the centre-circle. Knocking a pass right to the retreating Beckham, it then went square to Stam and back to Irwin, Bayern still boxed. Clipping to Giggs, on the right touchline, a volleyed touch found the nearby Cole, who controlled and gave it back. Rolling his studs forwards over the ball to set for a left-footed cross, with every defender but one and every attacker but one attracted to the near post, he curled to the far, in front of Blomqvist, himself in front of Babbel and eight yards from goal. Sliding in and with the entire goal to aim at, wide though Kahn spread his arms, he couldn't control his finish, catapulting the ball over the bar. The creation of a serious goalscoring chance, for this was one, had taken 55 minutes.

Beckham then bounced a free-kick in to Yorke, wide on the right, and moved across himself to accept the return, a few yards infield and levellish with the bottom of the centre-circle. With space to rev up a pass, he flighted a long one towards the far post, betraying an exhaustion of ideas. And it appeared a matter of routine for Kahn to come and collect ahead of Giggs and Blomqvist, only for him to collide with Linke, spilling the ball as he fell – but straight to Babbel, who clanged it clear. On United's bench, Fergie and McClaren discussed changes, and the players did too.

"I remember sitting with Ole," Sheringham recalls, "and talking about it's a good result at the moment because it gives us a chance to go on. Obviously, you know, you want your team to do well, but you want to be part of it yourself, and we'd had a lot of time on the bench that season and we'd been talking about, you know, we want to have the chance to be involved for Manchester United winning the European Cup. Even though we were getting beat we were both quietly happy that if it stayed like that then we'd have the chance to do our bit ourselves."

On 64 minutes, Basler espied Schmeichel straying from his line, and just inside the United half, to the right of the centre-circle, steadied himself and aimed a lob at goal. This was not Hamilton Ricard, and turning in a panic, Schmeichel stumbled as he tried to make his ground, relieved to see the ball pass narrowly over the bar. Meanwhile, on the touchline, Fergie had seen enough; Sheringham was coming on to replace Blomqvist, who would not play for United again, a serious knee injury sustained in the summer keeping him out for two years. He did, however, appear as the eponymous hero in MUTV's *Cooking With Jesper*, before, in typical style, Fergie persuaded Walter Smith that he was just what Everton needed.

The change allowed Giggs to move to the left with Beckham shuffling right, forming a narrowish midfield three, and Yorke roaming behind Sheringham and Cole. But still, the football was a little sluggish, the next opportunity coming from a throw – which indicated, perhaps, that Bayern were tiring, mentally as well as physically. Because when Neville chucked the ball at Yorke's head, on the near side of the box, a little decoy run allowed him to pull away from Jeremies and Matthäus, a deception that would not have stood earlier in the game. This allowed him to back-head across goal for Cole, who, eight yards out, flipped into an overhead kick far easier than any of the three he'd scored by November of the following season, but he shinned this one a long way wide.

He would later explain that his performance was hampered by nervousness, though to the outsider, the poverty of the service appeared equally responsible. "Had I played another European final," he wrote, "my advice to myself would have been 'relax' – as I'd done on the way to the final when I was part of the best strike partnership In Europe. I never had another chance to relax before another European Cup final. Sometimes you just don't get a second chance."

With Fergie now on the touchline waving the team forward, Hitzfeld made his first change, replacing the physical attributes of Zickler with the clever passing of Scholl, hoping to slow down and close out the game. But Bayern were still a threat. Immediately busy in the middle of the pitch, Scholl exchanged two sets of passes with Matthäus and then found Effenberg who returned with a deft flick and accepted a back-heel, forcing Butt to fall over and Stam to backpedal. Then, zoning towards goal and left of centre, he worked the ball onto his right foot and bashed a shot from just outside the box, only just wide of the far post.

By now, Schmeichel was racing to retrieve the ball, but United's next attack abruptly aborted when Sheringham played a blind pass towards the right touchline for Beckham, who wasn't there. Tarnat, however, was, and he lifted into Matthäus to control beautifully on his chest, turning slightly and finding Scholl, back on that same right touchline but moving into the United half. Cutting inside, away from Neville, he quickly assessed his options and lifted a curl into Jancker – who let it bounce and zig across him, to zag it back over the heads of Johnsen and Irwin, into the path of Effenberg. Letting it bounce, he angled his body to cut over the ball to keep it down, at the same time as lifting it up and over Schmeichel, whose jump was quick enough to tip over the bar. Fewer than 20 minutes remained.

As Solskjær began stretching, a long Beckham ball towards Sheringham on the left allowed him to beat Basler in the air and find Irwin, just outside the box. Briefly contemplating a shot, he instead curled towards the far post, away from everyone. It was not happening.

And the players knew it, Beckham unable to avoid fouling Matthäus when the opportunity presented itself, before more United passing that couldn't quite prise an opening. Over the course of the season, on 15 occasions the team had rescued a draw or better after falling behind, such that even against Juventus, there was an air of inevitability about the comeback. But not tonight, United's slow expiration like watching someone die – occasional moments of painful, illusory hope, waiting for the breath that doesn't come.

More circulation of possession, Irwin lifting a pass into Butt at inside-left, who, forced wide, back-heeled to Irwin who returned to him. Looking square for Beckham, instead he picked out that Effen'berg, who measured back out right, to Basler. On halfway and waiting for Beckham to come to him, he hurdled his tackle and hurtled towards goal without breaking stride, throwing a right stepover to fool Johnsen before moving left, then feinting right and moving left, across the face of the box and through the D, away from Neville. Coming the other way was Scholl, who took over possession and tricked back the other way to chip Schmeichel, raised arm and all, only to see the ball strike the far post full, and rebound directly into the keeper's arms.

Then, a minute later, Matthäus departed in an absolute state, wheezing and grimacing, replaced by Fink as United tried again. To the right of the centre-circle, Beckham skidded a pass low for Sheringham, central and 40 yards out, and he took a touch before finding Butt, ahead and right. Playing immediately back inside for Yorke, who responded with a first-touch pass of his own, over Fink and back into his path, Butt, now on the burst, heading down for himself and past Kuffour. Managing to curl his foot around the ball almost from the byline, he sent it into the middle – just too high for Cole, and just too soon for Sheringham, Babbel driving behind for a corner. There were nine minutes remaining, and it wasn't happening. It'd been a great season, they'd done really well, it would happen soon.

Solskjær then came on for Cole, and Beckham's left-wing corner was headed away by Kuffour, picked up by Gary Neville along the other flank. Exchanging passes with Sheringham, he aimed towards the near post and though numbers in the box were equal, only one defender was seriously marking, the cross picking out that one combination. Solskjær contorted into a stoop to reach the ball ahead of the charging Linke, his first touch a hard glance that forced Kahn to save low to his left. "Oh, what a story that would've been!" lamented Tyldesley. *Gam zu letovah.*

With so little time remaining, Bayern were focused on retaining possession, but with United committing so many players forward, they were effectively forced to attack when not forced to defend. So Tarnat and Effenberg linked along the left to find Scholl, who moved inside, accelerated into space, and shot hard from outside the box, Schmeichel pushing around the post.

As Basler went to take the corner, he found the fans behind the goal in triumphant mood and indulged them, their cheering increasing as he addressed the ball, which went directly into Schmeichel's hands. Setting United off again, a poor pass from Neville to Sheringham allowed Effenberg to intercede, and he fed Basler along the left who waited to play it back square, Effenberg moving the ball over one more for Scholl, to win a corner off Irwin.

Again, Basler went across to parade himself. "I'm going to hit that arrogant wanker if he carries on," Stam told Johnsen. "You'll have to get in line," said someone else.

He delivered an out-swinger, Babbel rising, but able only to head the ball into the ground, and backwards – and straight to Scholl. Unmarked, he nodded over Stam, directly onto the foot of Jancker, who once failed a trial at Luton Town – and he slammed an overhead kick against the face of the bar, bouncing off the grass in time to buck a leg at the rebound but unable to make any contact, before Sheringham and Beckham half-hacked clear.

Then, with four minutes to go, Stam hit a long, straight ball that Kuffour missed, again diving over the top of Yorke, and it fell for Solskjær, in the box but facing towards the right touchline. Not in a position to shoot, he back-heeled gently for Sheringham, close to the penalty spot, and forced to drag a shot from slightly behind him, Kahn was able to gather down by the post – in the circumstances, a waste of a more than handy chance.

But on the United bench, hope was renewed. "They've gone," Keane said to Jim Ryan. "We've got them." And the law of averages told him that something was going to happen. "If you keep doing the right things," he insisted, "you'll get your break in every game."

Next, a diagonal ball from Beckham to Yorke, pulling off Kuffour, gave him the chance to head back, which he did, square and to no one, rather than angling it back to where Sheringham was arriving. But still, pressure was building.

"We know how to intensify the rhythm of a game," Keane would explain later. "Pass the ball, move, support the player on the ball: fight to win it back if you lose it, the deeper in their half the better." Or put another way, Barcelona did not invent the high press.

And Munich were nervous, playing for time. Yorke picked up possession to the right of the centre-circle and moved inside, letting Giggs take over when their paths converged. Wedging wide to Beckham, he kept the ball until Neville arrived into the box, flicking to him between Tarnat and Fink. With no one near enough to tackle or even block, the subsequent low, hard cross ran directly to the unmarked Yorke, only for him to completely miss his kick, from in front of goal. For the very first time, he did not respond by pissing himself of the intense hilarity of it all.

But still United refused to give in, pressure on Basler forcing an error and Butt collecting his pass to no one, rolling on for Giggs. Crossing before his route to the centre could be blocked, he picked out Solskjær, in space between Linke and Kuffour, but not with requisite pace for him to have a realistic prospect of scoring from 14 yards out.

As the game entered the last of its minutes, Basler was withdrawn, walking unfeasibly slowly and waving at the Bayern fans as Salihamidžić replaced him. Also around this point, George Best had seen enough and Lennart Johanssen left his seat to prepare for the presentation, Ol' Big Ears already dressed with Bayern's ribbons. Meanwhile, on the touchline, Fergie was ordering himself to be magnanimous, ever careful to retain the moral high ground, the crafty fucker. "We show our face, and keep our dignity," he thought. "We are Manchester United." But that same spirit, that same feeling of being special, forced his players to gather themselves for one last effort. "It's not too late!" shouted Gary Neville. "We've won at the death before and we can do it again!"

Yet another Bayern clearance dropped on halfway, left of centre. Butt beat Jeremies to the header, but Jeremies was then able to knock it back to Babbel, who, under pressure from Sheringham and Solskjær, played a dicey pass even further back, for Linke – who took no chances, and knocked it out.

As the ball was returned to Giggs, Gary Neville came chasing over from the other side to take it, while the fourth official displayed a board showing that there would be three additional minutes. "Italian referees seem to add more time when it's a good game," said the German commentary.

The long throw was headed away by Kuffour, but just outside the box, Beckham cut across Scholl to take the ball away from him. Running right to left, Scholl in pursuit, he feinted to go back – how that was considered feasible, it's hard to say, but Scholl bought it – and Beckham turned the corner around his outside, then moved inside towards Babbel, making space to offload back left for Neville as soon as the challenge arrived. Suddenly a left-winger, his ensuing low cross was half-blocked by Babbel and put behind by Effenberg, winning United on a corner – but Beckham was almost as shit at corners as Giggs. Schmeichel came charging forward.

"Can Manchester United score, they always score… Peter Schmeichel is forward… Beckham, in towards Schmeichel, it's come for Dwight Yorke… cleared… Giggs with the shot… Sheringhaaaaam!"

Bodies, noise, flares.

"Everyone knows that if Giggsy has a shot from the edge of the box with his right foot, it's not gonna go in," Sheringham chuckled later. "So I was alert to the situation, and it came rolling by me, and there it was… Tried to swing for it and just got a little scuff on it, I think it came off just above my boot on my sock, best sock goal I've ever scored."

Or, as Alan Green put it, "Schmeichel's inside the Munich penalty area, Beckham crosses, falls to the far post towards Yorke, half cleared, Giggs shoots, Sheringhaaaam equalises! Teddy Sheringham has equalised in stoppage time! Oh, Teddy, Teddy, went to Man United and he might win the lot yet!"

Or, as German telly put it, "Giggs… this can't be real! Teddy Sheringham… This just can't be true!"

Scarred by the Juventus home game and with Kahn's hand already up before he hit the ground, Sheringham paused to check that he was onside, then ran off with Solskjær to celebrate. "Fantastic," he told him, "we've got half an hour in this fantastic stadium and we can enjoy playing in this now."

Cut to Lothar.

"Name-on-the-trophy! Teddy Sheringham, with 30 seconds of added time played, has equalised for Manchester United, they are *still* in the European Cup!"

It had taken a while, but now, for a while at least, Sheringham was a United player. "It was a bad season for me," he recalls. "I'd lost my place for Dwight Yorke coming in, I'd had a couple of niggly little injuries. My good, fond memories would be of Sir Alex saying to me around January time look, I know you're not having a good time, I know you've had a couple of injuries, just make sure you're ready for the end of this season, I've got a funny a feeling that it's gonna be big and there's gonna be a lot of games. And he foresaw that and let me know that at a time where maybe I was itching to get back in and you try and push yourselves a little bit earlier to try and get back in, in the race for a team place. But he just calmed me down and assured me that I would be involved and I'm sure he didn't know I'd have such a big impact on the last few games, but it was a nice thing to say to me when I was having not the best of seasons."

And Sheringham had plenty to lose. He was unused to a supporting role, and not young enough to get another chance at a club of comparable stature – if he didn't make it at United, then unavoidably, his career would be defined by failure and regret. He recalls the repeating dialogue of his time in Manchester: playing in a game, then told before the next one that he was being rested, amending the terminology to dropped, and receiving confirmation that this was indeed the case, consoling himself by pretending to handle it well. "That's what being professional is all about," he tried to think.

So perhaps the impression he'd given of cocky indolence was not quite right. It was the same one taken by Schmeichel when they'd faced each another in the past, one he was keen to kibosh after getting to know him and discovering that "he's really a bit shy and quite unsure of himself at times."

Obviously, Keane disagreed, reading something quite different into the same. "Teddy is being cool. He's from London!" he jeered – and only Sheringham could name his house Camp Nou, "after the scene of one of my greatest triumphs."

"To give him his due," said that *Red Issue* piece from the previous spring, "he has weighed in with a few goals but he only ever tries in the big games, being recognisable by his anonymity for much of this season." And oddly, hilariously, wondrously, it was still largely true.

Trotting back for the restart, Stam noticed a difference in the Munich players. "As our emotions had risen, theirs had sunk in comparable amounts" – and Fergie had spotted it too: "They were gutted, they were down. They had gone."

And it was ten-storey Jaap Stam, bigger than the Nou Camp, who won the ball back for United following kick-off, after Jeremies knocked it wide for Scholl to listlessly, aimlessly waft downfield. Giggs then took possession away from Effenberg, who misread the bounce, and found Butt, behind him. In the stands, the horror of golden goal had yet to be contemplated, but on the United bench, Steve McClaren was planning. "Now let's get ourselves organised for extra time," he told Fergie. "Go back to 4–4–2." Butt spread the ball wide to Irwin. "Steve, this game isn't finished," came back the response.

Irwin clouted long into the left corner, Solskjær there well before Kuffour. Checking behind to gauge how much time he had, he paused to read the bounce, controlled, and facing the touchline, moved a yard towards his own goal then dextrously dragged back with his studs, now looking straight at Kuffour. Moving the ball from right foot to left foot and back again looking for a gap, he feinted twice, paused, stepped over with his left and went the same way, firing a cross against Kuffour's shin.

"Another corner. Somehow we're in the 93rd minute," gulped the German commentary. "Only Collina knows where the extra time has come from."

Over trots Beckham. There is bouncing behind the goal.

"You have to feel, this is their year. Is this their moment? Beckham into Sheringham… and Solskjær has *won* it! Manchester United have reached the Promised Land! Ole Solskjær! The two substitutes have scored the two goals in stoppage time, and the Treble *looms* large."

Bodies, noise and flares… haunted other bodies, frozen… Tarnat and Scholl, still against the posts, bent double. Solskjær off, then on his knees, the players in a huddle, the bench on the way, Schmeichel cartwheeling. Butt, pissing himself with manic, giggling laughter, Solskjær, eyes closed, now fully in the moment. Tarnat still on the post, Gary Neville collapsed on the ground, Kuffour beating the ground. Cut to Lothar. Scholl slumped against a post, Kahn on the ground, Collina trying to pick Kuffour up and failing, others staggering about as though hit by a lorry, Scholl suddenly inspired and racing to kick off, Effenberg still flat on his back, patted on the chest by Collina, Kuffour ranting at himself, Kuffour stomping.

In the seconds immediately following the goal, the calmest man in the ground was Solskjær, pausing to fill his cheeks and exhale before setting off apparently unflustered, arms wide, fingers pointing and mouth clenched closed – like a man agreeing with himself, and definitively so. Like a man who knew.

"I have a feeling, sometimes, when I think it's gonna be my night, I think I'm gonna score," he said afterwards, "so I called one of my friends back in Norway. And I told the reserve team coach as well, 'I think this is gonna be my night' just before the game started."

The seed had been sown by Fergie; this was "the goal that he spoke about ten days earlier", the care with which he tended him until then building the confidence that could believe it. It was only with the knee slide, a few seconds later, that the elation took over, and even then, there was sufficient calmness for cognition: "That's what the German did when he scored, so I think I wanted to overdo him." He was overdone.

And no one deserved the moment more, his dedication and enthusiasm outstanding even in exulted company – in a team full of characters befitting the cliché "he just loves playing football", he just loved playing football.

The same attitude now underpins his style of management. "We all live and breathe for football," he said of his staff. "They can see our passion and we hope it rubs off on them," he said of his players.

When Solskjær arrived back at Molde in 2011, the club boasted a grand total of no league titles in 99 years. Now, they have two in 101. Nor did he inherit a team who were ready, quite the reverse. They did have the league's top scorer, a target man – immediately done away with, to facilitate a fast, attacking, short-passing style, contrary to Norwegian tradition and in spite of Norwegian conditions. The theory, of course, is for the players to express themselves, "like the Gaffer's done with all the United teams over the years".

In a sense, all this is a long-winded way of saying that, quite simply, Solskjær is a mensch; someone you'd be proud to call a friend, rather than a public personality with an admirable trait or two. Liked by everyone, including Roy Keane, his radiant huggability is not a front; very clearly, he just gets life, ensconced in his own skin to an extent that is almost moving, an equanimity that joined him on the pitch.

He was also the only player to speak out against the Glazers – and guess what! It didn't cost him his job! Or anything else! But even before then, even before this, his was a special status. United's following is as cynical a support as exists in world sport, on first name terms with very few men: Sir Matt, Duncan, Denis, George, Eric, Ruud – and Ole. It's true that the nature of the names helps, but nowhere near as much as the nature of their owners.

And of course, despite supplying the historic Treble-winning goal in the most dramatic end to a football match that there has ever been, he retained the same serenity. He knew that the goal, though it earned him a boot deal, "never made me a better player – made me a bigger name, maybe". So his focus afterwards was the same as before: "to improve to make sure that I play more than 15 minutes next time". In the 14 years since 1999, he's watched a chunk of the game just once – the period for which he was on the pitch – when he got back to Norway, to oblige his dad, who'd not been able to make the game due to work commitments, with only a short while spare prior to setting off again. And even though, for much of his career, he was in and out of the starting 11, the only time he queried the manager's decision was when Yorke was picked ahead of him despite being effectively retired from serious football.

The same evenness manifested the following season when, after injuring Sami Hyppia with a studs-up tackle, he scored while Hyppia was off the pitch receiving treatment – then went into the Liverpool changing room at half-time to apologise. Not exactly the ethos of Hughes, Whiteside and Robson, but with a charm, if not an attraction of its own.

Now, the players who play for him are devoted to precisely that attribute. "He brightens bad days when he talks," says Magnus Wolff Eikrem, and "just has that ability to be able to inspire and to lead." But though he was meticulous in his note-taking in his time as a player, to learn from Fergie for when the time came – when he spoke to particular players, how he spoke to them – his style is far less authoritarian, the players allowed to call him Ole, or "whatever they like, really".

Yet he is no pushover. "He's professional, he's got that steely sort of temperament about him," says Giggs, who should know. "When he first took over [United reserves, in 2008] they all loved him, but in his team talks and after the game, if you'd not performed he'd tell you... he's a straight talker."

"You have to treat your players as your kids at times," explains Solskjær. "You really want the best for them, but you really want them to do the best they can, I can't do it for them, they've got to do it for themselves and if they step out of line, you sometimes – sometimes you do yell at them."

And, of course, he is still relentless. Interviewed after Molde's first title, he refused to dwell on the achievement. Instead, he talked about ex-United players who'd succeeded in their first season in management and failed subsequently, already plotting how to avoid that happening to him.

This attribute was also in evidence in his comeback from injury at the start of 2006–07, after effectively three seasons out, an abnormal devotion to the game a common factor within the squad. Giggs is still playing at 39 and Beckham retired at 38; Cole stopped at 37, Irwin 38 and Schmeichel 40; and even those who, on the face of it, might have been expected to finish early, Yorke and Sheringham, were at it until 38 and 42 respectively. And then there's Scholes, who first returned from a serious eye injury, then returned from retirement. Once asked to complete the sentence "I love football because…" he could respond only with "because I just love playing football".

In *There's Only One United*, Geoffrey Green quotes a piece from the *Manchester Guardian*, written in 1934: "Sometimes he does daredevil things that make the directors feel old before their time. But who would have him different? He laughs equally at his blunders and his triumphs, which of course is the privilege as well as the proof of a great player. He would be a certain choice for that select eleven of Footballers Who Obviously Love Football – and that is the highest praise of all." The man it's describing? Matt Busby.

Losing his father and three uncles as a young boy, during the First World War, then serving in the Second World War and losing so many of his players at Munich, Busby understood precisely the role of football as pleasure and treasure. And the Treble-winning squad understood something of this too, an unusual combination of characters, many of whom had been forced to contend with the horror of not making it.

Schmeichel and Stam both spent time in the army, Schmeichel not turning professional until he was 24, while Stam didn't play in the Eredivisie until he was 23. Irwin was given a free transfer by Leeds; Keane learnt that he was too small, writing to and rejected by every top division English club, only signing for semi-professional Cobh Ramblers at the age of 18, before suffering a career-threatening injury. Cole was released by Arsenal, rejected by Fulham, then ridiculed by the media and the England manager; Sheringham didn't play in the top division until he was 26 and Europe until he was 31. Before signing for United, Solskjær was turned down by Hamburg, Cagliari, Manchester City and Everton, while Yorke, born in a non-footballing country, sold land crabs to tourists to pay for boots, saw football as a "way out" of his overcrowded home and slept with a football in his bed until he was 25. They played like they could not believe their good fortune.

Even amongst the home-grown players, there was a mental toughness and an appreciation. The Neville brothers, dubbed the Nervous Brothers by Scholes, doubted themselves, and devoted their lives accordingly. Though Giggs and Beckham were always going to make it, both suffered formative and exceptional adversity; they were not just the most fortunate natural talents of their generation, but also the most determined.

Younger men than would usually appear in such a successful team, in strictly football terms they were adults, used to performing under pressure and practised in rebounding from thrashings and disappointments. And they experienced all these things together, developing as individuals within a collective, ticking off rites of passage: away trips with the first team, first-team debut, first-team squad, appearances on the bench, and then shared pride as each became a staple.

And they were never shy of men from whom to learn; serious, focused winners like Hughes and Robson. Robson would indoctrinate them weekly regarding what it meant to be a United player, and, most particularly, that whenever any one of them were threatened, they would all be on the scene to intervene and avenge. Also influential was Cantona, and not just because he was an exponent of the peculiar European art of practice. "A lot of the flair you see in the team today is down to him," Schmeichel observed prior to the final league game. "The young players used to look at him and say, 'I wasn't taught that in soccer school or in the FA curriculum.'"

"It's a Manchester United legacy," says Gary Neville, "that this is a club that can be the biggest football club in the world, yet can bring through young players. There's no excuse for any other club not to follow this. The best teams that have ever been produced, produce their own players more often than not, because they have that ingrained loyalty and desire to play for that club, to do everything that matters, no matter what it takes, and that is Manchester United's legacy, it's not the class of '92's legacy, it's the manager, it's Sir Alex Ferguson, it's Sir Matt Busby, we're just players that have come through it because they have had the courage to actually implement that system."

In October of the previous season, United beat Barnsley 7–0. But what gave Neville the most pleasure was the composition of the team: a back four including him, his brother and John Curtis, and a midfield of Beckham, Butt, Scholes and Giggs, with Ronnie Wallwork on the subs' bench.

"Everything we did, we were together," recalls Butt. "We trained together, we got changed together, we ate together. Obviously Eric and the coaches there made us know that we're all in it together, it's not an individual thing, because we'd never have got anywhere without our team-mates."

And this transmitted to the terraces, supporters watching them grow, investing in their potential then harvesting the kinetic. The buzz of their buzz was special enough, but it was more personal than that, their experiences so easily relatable. Playing in a team of mates as opposed to a team of other people is a decision that bothers most Saturday and Sunday league types at one time or another, and here they were, having their red velvet cake and guzzling it. But more generally, the empathy, connection and experience shared with them by virtue of loving United, of United being an intrinsic part of life and memory, something inculcated from an early age and always there, is a special thing. And more generally still, the empathy, connection and experience shared with them, in simply the being of friends.

Just after Scholes announced his second retirement, he was interviewed by Neville, who asked what motivated his comeback. "I decided," he said. "Well, I spoke to you and your Phil."

And the connection is evident whenever they appear together. Giggs is meant to have a dry sense of humour, but in hundreds of "just use my experience" interviews, it has emerged only once – when talking to Neville following the 2013 title. His ability to reveal them and get them to reveal themselves is far removed from the top man, great friend of the show knee-slapping, phony couch-cliché, rather the warmth that comes with being part of something real.

"They form the core of the team, on and off the field," wrote Keane in his autobiography, before adding with typical morbidity, "and are bonded in a way that excludes the rest of us." But crucially, he knew this was to the benefit of everyone. "At the heart of our club there is something solid, something real, something identifiably Mancunian, an attitude created by the Six Amigos, that is fundamental to the team and its success. When players join United, however much they cost, wherever they come from, it is this attitude they must plug into."

Stam, though, felt slightly differently, categorising his team-mates not as friends, but "good colleagues". He struggled to get their jokes as quickly as they made them, and though everyone was friendly, found being on the periphery less to his taste than being part of the main group, as he was when playing for Holland. "Sometimes you just miss the amateurism of football. Sitting in the canteen, drinking a beer, talking about this and that," he said. "But that's not here."

Off the pitch, perhaps not – but the magical on-pitch camaraderie that swept them across Europe was exactly here, and included the entire squad. "The atmosphere and the team spirit is fantastic, and without that we could never have come to this point," Schmeichel told MUTV, interviewed by the pool in Sitges. "If you have knackling and all this in the dressing room, I don't think you'll ever get results. Our atmosphere and team spirit is fantastic, and *that's why* we get results."

The feeling and philosophy was of a family; if someone needed telling, then they were told, not gratuitously, but because it was important. And though, inevitably, not everyone liked everyone else, they all recognised that they were bound to and reliant upon one another, all working together for the greater good. Easy to say.

Making it happen was, of course, the genius of the manager, constantly on to his players about what it meant to be a team. "It was the upbringing he had in Glasgow," wrote Neville, "that sense that you all work bloody hard together but that you stick together through that."

So it was that when individual players found themselves in trouble, anger was directed more towards those who had allowed it to happen than the character in question; when Keane was arrested in Cup final week, it was the squad who got the going over. "Why didn't you ring me?" asked Fergie. "Why didn't you tell me this was happening? You've all gone home and got into your beds and left one of your team-mates on his own! Why didn't any of you think to tell me?"

Similarly, when Fergie announced his retirement, the media was naturally eager to know how he'd communicated the message to the players – but in the first instance, found nobody prepared to enlighten them, the detail that did emerge later an abridged version. "It's obviously a personal moment between us and the squad and the manager," said Rio Ferdinand. Obviously.

And though plenty of things leaked because they always do, plenty didn't. David James recalls his experience of the culture through time spent away with England, and how the United players would police themselves, supporting one another to the fullest extent. "All those hours of sitting around… and not once did any United player ever reveal anything to me about their team-mates, their dressing room or their manager. In an industry renowned for its gossip I find that extraordinary… Even when the media reported chaos in the United dressing room… there were no comments from the United boys. There were plenty of questions, of course. But their answers were only ever vague, or meaningless. It all contributed to that sense of separation: there were United players, and then there was the rest of us."

And this, all of this, manifested on the pitch: outrageous perseverance, individual brilliance, collective brilliance, improbable comebacks, late goals, and intimidating unity. That's how the Treble happened.

*

Munich kicked off, the ball given to Effenberg, who wellied long towards Babbel. Stam was first to the header, Butt cracked it away, and the final whistle went.

"History is made… Manchester United are the champions of Europe again. And nobody will *ever* win a European Cup final more dramatically than this. Champions of Europe, champions of England, winners of the FA Cup, everything their hearts desired… Down and out, not a bit of it, they are *never* out. Memories are made of this forever and a day."

Or as Alan Green put it: "And Manchester United rule Europe! I don't believe it, but it's happened!"

Suddenly, all the disappointments – Galatasaray, Barcelona, Gothenburg, Dortmund, Monaco – all of them all leading up to these moments, all *gam zu letovah*.

"I can't believe it," said Lennart Johanssen, arriving at pitch level. "The winners are crying and the losers are dancing."

Meanwhile, Fergie was interviewed by Gary Newbon, even under the stress of realising his life's work, able to produce a line of genuine brilliance. Then, after "Football, bloody hell", the eyes narrow and the head jolts. "But they never give in," he barks, "– and that's what won it."

While United celebrated, the Germans went up to collect their losers' medals, walking past the trophy. "Have a good look but don't touch," thought Stam, "it doesn't belong to you."

And really, they couldn't miss it, placed precisely in their way and exactly in their phizogs, each responding to its presence; Kahn a filthy look up and down, Effenberg a rueful, knowing, down and up, Jeremies trying so hard not to look at it he almost walked into it, unable to look but unable to help it, Scholl's head pulled towards it, barely suppressing a spit, Tarnat and Zickler avoiding its stare, Fink averting his eyes, Babbel out of the corner of his eye, Daei not looking, Salihamidžić a long, lingering glance, Jancker, in a terrible state, just couldn't.

"For a long time, every night when I went to bed I thought about the bicycle kick," he said later. "Others were able to move on easily, but not me. For example, that night, after we lost, I drank a couple of beers, then I walked across the room and turned on the television. At the sight of the result I felt so awful that I threw up. It took a very long time for the result to sink in, and even longer to deal with it."

Linke, eyes almost shut, Strunz sidling by, then Kuffour, bent over, holding hands with, supported by Helmer – and Matthäus, snivelling at the rear, his medal immediately removed. Captain of Bayern in the 1987 final, they led Porto with 12 minutes to go and lost, the European Cup the only honour to elude him. He was not grateful for what he had.

"Tonight it was not the best team that won but the luckiest," he rationalised. "It's bitter, sad and unbelievable. We're all disappointed. You can't blame the team. We had the match in control for 90 minutes. We had bad luck, hitting the post and the crossbar. What happened afterwards is simply inexplicable."

Later, Fergie would observe his departure as a crucial moment – "it opened up the game for us, we were pleased and started creating chances" – and the move did not find favour in the eyes of Effenberg.

"He's a real quitter," he wrote. "I still don't understand today why he left his place to Thorsten Fink in the 80th minute. We were leading 1–0 and we had to hold on to that lead. How can you let yourself be substituted when you're the libero? I would have rather broken my leg."

Bayern went on to lose the DFB Cup final to Werder Bremen, on penalties.

And then it was the turn of the United players to ascend the podium, Schmeichel leading them up. Phil Neville opened the flood-gates by stroking the trophy, Phil and May pointing at it, Beckham kissing it tenderly and Gary following. Back came Sheringham for a kiss, Stam a stroke and a drum, Cole deliberately at the back, trying to take everything in. Jonathan Greening was there. The United end were singing "Champions of Europe", then Schmeichel and Fergie came in for the lift, no organisation, not taking a handle each, Fergie grabbing the base, trophy lopsided, a complete mess. United were champions of Europe!

And then the lap of honour, the celebrations in the ground extending beyond all others. Bobby Charlton, clapping and singing, the players in a line, bouncing in front of the United end, Fergie on the shoulders of Brown and van der Gouw. "I was desperate to cram my head with every sight possible, so I could replay it in my mind whenever I felt like it," said Stam, by now wearing a red, white and black wig.

Schmeichel alone, lifting the trophy repeatedly, each one cheered. Then David May, without the resources to tell a joke, somehow shushing and silencing the entire end, Sheringham crouching to raise and spin the trophy around his arm, conducting the debut performance of his song, joining in, his catharsis complete, a Red. Next, more shushing and silencing, each member of the team taking a turn to approach the cup, set it down on the grass, and lift it to cheers: Beckham understated, Butt with a little leg wiggle and Elvis hip, Giggs dead straight, then Irwin the same, Johnsen from his tippy toes through his entire body, eyes closed, Yorke after a calypso sashay, hip swing and a turn, Solskjær from between his legs, Cole only after line dancing alone to his song.

And finally, after persuasion, a players' guard of honour for Scholes and Keane, taking the trophy from the men at the end. Scholes would wait nine years for redemption, but for Keane it would never arrive, let down by his team-mates against Leverkusen in 2002, first in his absence and then in his presence.

Back in the dressing room, in the first instance the atmosphere was surprisingly restrained, Fergie and Bobby Charlton exchanging hugs and seeking champagne. After lifting the European Cup in 1968, all the United players went to celebrate – all apart from Charlton, still too overcome with loss. But Matt Busby was there, and with dignity, bravery and feeling, sung 'What a Wonderful World'. And now, on the day that he would have been 90, a day on which all of Wembley once sang him 'Happy Birthday', a United team in his image, deliberately constructed according to his image, had beaten a team from Munich, to achieve a dream that he invented. "Well, happy birthday, you know," said Fergie.

The Nevilles covered their clothes, Gary already thinking about doing it again, Yorke less so. Keane threw booze around, Albert Morgan was chucked in the bath, and the serious drinking began. Fergie looked at the names on the trophy, the detail he found most rewarding, personal pleasure in the company of which he now resided. But even then, he was numb for an hour, the achievement grounded by the sight of his family.

"I wish we'd have played better," Cole said later, "but we went to every ground in Europe playing football, playing the Man United way." And ultimately, the trophy was won by scoring more goals than the opposition, without even the need for extra time, let alone penalties. Bayern might have missed chances, but had they been better at the crucial moments, they wouldn't have lost – and part of being the best team is riding out the dodgy moments, and finding a way.

Which isn't to say that way wasn't peculiar – it was. "Something just happened," said Gary Neville. "We scored just two goals… why, a German team, who *never* concede two goals from set pieces conceded two goals from set pieces in the last two minutes of a European Cup final I'll never know." But then, no German team had ever met this Manchester United team.

Then, already well on the way, the players left for a party. "The drinking that went on that night was awesome," said Stam.

Back in Manchester outlandish numbers come out to greet the players, all the way from Sale to town, people sitting on traffic lights, road signs and *that* scaffolding. "Look what they've done to

Manchester," a celebrant told MUTV. "Everyone's in a superb mood and everything," the surfeit of backwards cap wearing on the bus overlooked just this once.

"You've seen grown men, just *screaming*, the veins popping out of their 'eads," said Gary Neville. "And to see people like that, and these are normal people, these aren't idiots... the emotion that was inside them was unbelievable. Teddy and Ole probably still don't know what they've done now; it'll probably sink in about another 15 years' time."

Well, 15 years' time, here we are. Anyone experiencing any sinking? Any in? Any sinking in? No? Good.

****

EPILOGUE

Not just the most dramatic end to a football match that we'll ever see, or even the most dramatic end to a football match that anyone will ever see, but the single most dramatic, consuming event that most of us will ever see in the course of our lives. United: the vaguely acceptable face of mania, obsession and ecstasy.

There've been last-minute goals before; there've even been two last minute goals before. But never in the last minute of the European Cup final, for a team trailing by one, needing a win to secure an unprecedented Treble.

And yet it's not the success that's truly special, but the glory. 1998–99 featured every single aspect that could possibly be desired of any season, and there's never been another remotely like it. Astounding, varied games, featuring kickings, robberies, comebacks and thrillers, amazing goals, exceptional competition, absurd characters, elephantine testicles and staggering plot twists. Or, put another way, it encompassed so much of what makes United, sport and life so compelling.

The team itself was a classic United composition, featuring a core of local kids mixed with expensive signings and previously unknowns, melding icons, greats and at least a couple of all-time greats. More than half played the season of their lives.

And amongst them were few you had to like despite yourself. There was no constant justification that the players were just passing through, and they played with a definitive love and fight.

Then, of course, there's Fergie – "this man on the touchline, he's not on the pitch but he's running everything, his whole heart was in it," said Bobby Charlton after watching him at Aberdeen.

Writing in the summer of 2013, the feeling that a significant aspect of our lives is being attended to by him has yet to dissipate entirely, that joyous security of knowing that something over which you have no control is under control. If another team improved, well, he would make sure that United did the same, and if not, compensate for any shortfall in talent by making the difference himself – only he could mitigate his own appalling errors with his own appalling brilliance. He's made our lives better, and it's embarrassingly hard to conceive of how they'd have been without him. It is only football, but it makes us very euphoric; it is only reflected glory, but never has there been such a powerful mirror. Would we be different people without 23 years of immense, intense pleasure?

Crucially, Fergie understood that football is simple and humans are complex, and had an instinctive, considered and profound feel for both. It's because of him that life is something that happens while United are winning things, mainly in inspiring style, and his addiction to the buzz of existing is a strong lesson. For all his faults, the world is a better place for his presence, and that's a mightily rare accolade.

You have to wonder how it's possible to sustain an argument his Treble team wasn't the most brilliant that England has ever seen; in 52 years of trying, United are the only team to win all three major trophies in the same season, achieved with the highest possible tariff of difficulty and close to the highest possible standard of execution. But given that we're here for our gratification, let's gratify ourselves and spell it out.

United won arguably the best league in British football history. They finished above an excellent Chelsea side, holders of European and domestic trophies, and which lost only three games all season. They finished above an exceptionally tough and balanced Arsenal side, defending double champions, boasting one of the tightest defences ever assembled and abetted by an easy Cup run and early European elimination.

United, on the other hand, reached Wembley after playing a Premier League side in every round but one, including Liverpool, Chelsea and Arsenal. To win the European Cup, they escaped a group containing Barcelona and Bayern Munich, then despatched both Italian sides in the competition, without resorting to away goals or extra-time – and then Bayern Munich, without resorting to extra time or penalties. That there were moments when it all might have slipped away serves only to accentuate the quality of opposition and illuminate United's durability and brilliance under pressure.

And through it all, they attempted fast, exciting, original football, regardless of the opposition, and proved that they could perform in any circumstance. Famous for late goals, they were just as devastating early, and required little in the way of tactics: defend properly, attack whenever possible.

Late seventies' Liverpool may have won more European Cups, but they didn't play 13 times to get them, the games, all knockout, generally easy until the last eight, and even afterwards, the clubs they beat were not comparable in quality to those faced by United. Similarly, those finishing second and third domestically were not remotely the equal of their 1998–99 counterparts.

Another comparator is, apparently, the Arsenal of 2003–04. But again, as with Chelsea in 2004–06, the standard of challengers was miserable, and both failed in Europe, where the same was roughly so. You can only beat who's there, but every protagonist is defined by his antagonists, and quite simply, there weren't any.

It's true that Arsenal remained unbeaten in one competition all season, but also lost as many times in the Champions League as United did overall, their longest such sequence 31 games, United's 33. But in any event, avoiding defeat has never been the point.

Every year, the Arsenal players from that period – they call themselves "the Invincibles" – meet up to celebrate themselves. They never won another title. Every year, the United players from their season – they do not call themselves "the Treblincibles" – do not meet up to celebrate themselves. They won the next two titles.

And then there are the great United sides. The Busby Babes would have become the best, but could not, and 1965–68 iteration had the best individuals, but nothing like the quality or consistency. And of Fergie's finest, though the 1994 lot were hamstrung in Europe, it's nonetheless hard to argue for the ability of its defence to cope with the leading attackers of the day, while the 2007–2008 team was more solid than that which won the Treble, but neither as complete nor destructive further forward, excellent but not eternal.

So, with the order of things established, the difficulty is what happens next. Should any team repeat the achievement – well, it's been done already, in circumstances we can be sure are superior, which is a very nice feeling; United have won football. But, paradoxically, they have also beaten every future United, which brings with it a strangeness of its own: each time one threatens the Treble, there brews a guilt, of being sure that it's not good enough, almost hoping that it doesn't cheapen the achievement by turning out to be good enough, followed by relief when it isn't good enough.

But let's not finish with existential crisis. Fergie later observed that the celebrations begun by Solskjær's goal will never really stop. "Just thinking about it can put me in party mood," he said. And he's right; part of us shall forever remain in the Promised Land, and part of the Promised Land shall forever remain part of us. Savour it, every day of your life.

BIBLIOGRAPHY

For Club and Country – Gary & Phil Neville, with Sam Pilger and Justyn Barnes, Manchester United Books, an imprint of VCI Ltd, 1999

Head to Head – Jaap Stam with Jeremy Butler, Collins Willow, 2001

Keane: The Autobiography – Roy Keane with Eamon Dunphy, Penguin Michael Joseph, 2002

Managing My Life – Alex Ferguson with Hugh McIlvanney, Hodder and Stoughton, 1999

Manchester United: The Untold Story – Ned Kelly with Eric Rowan, Michael O'Mara Books Limited, 2003

Not For Sale: Manchester United, Murdoch and the Defeat of BSkyB – Adam Brown and Andy Walsh, Mainstream Publishing, 1999

Red Issue fanzine

Red: My Autobiography – Gary Neville, Bantam Press, 2011

Schmeichel: The Autobiography – Peter Schmeichel with Egon Balsby, Virgin, 1999

Scholes: My Story – Paul Scholes with Ivan Ponting, Simon & Schuster, 2011

Andy Cole: The Autobiography – Andy Cole with Peter Fitton, Manchester United Publishing, an imprint of André Deutsch Ltd, 1999

The Day A Team Died – Frank Taylor OBE, Souvenir Press, 1983

There's Only One United – Geoffrey Green, Hodder and Stoughton, 1978

The Unique Treble – Sir Alex Ferguson with David Meek, Hodder and Stoughton, 2000

www.red11.org